Ref. HF 5604 .K34 1993

Kahle, John J.

American accountants and
their contributions to

DATE DUE

WITHDRAWN

D1416947

NEW WORKS
INACCOUNTING
HISTORY

Richard P. Brief, *Series Editor*

Leonard N. Stern School of Business
New York University

A Garland Series

AMERICAN ACCOUNTANTS AND THEIR CONTRIBUTIONS TO ACCOUNTING THOUGHT, 1900–1930

John J. Kahle

Garland Publishing, Inc.
New York and London 1993

Library of Congress Cataloging-in-Publication Data

Kahle, John J.
   American accountants and their contributions to accounting thought,
   1900–1930 / John J. Kahle.
   p. cm.—(New works in accounting history)
   Originally presented as the author's thesis (M.A.)—Catholic University of
   America, 1968.
   Includes bibliographical references.
   ISBN 0-8153–1216–4
   1. Accountants—United States—Biography. 2. Accounting—United
   States—History. 3. Accounting—Bibliography. I. Title. II. Series.
HF56C4.K34   1993   93–9761
657'.0973—dc20

All volumes printed on acid-free, 250-year-life paper.
Manufactured in the United States of America.

Design by Marisel Tavarez

CONTENTS

298968

Chapter III

Foreword to the Garland Edition

Today, nearly two decades after I completed my doctoral studies at the University of Florida, I was pleased to learn that Professor Brief has chosen to reprint the thesis of John J. Kahle, *American Accountants and Their Contributions to Accounting Thought*, completed in 1956.

This study, which profiles 26 individuals, is a useful, albeit limited, early example of biographical description (yes, D.R. Scott *should* read DR Scott).

The important value of Kahle's thesis today is its ready reference quality. It provides a biographical sketch and bibliography of those individuals who have been, as yet, not fully studied — persons such as Bliss, Eggleston, Klein, Saliers, among others. The appendices also provide an example of awards, events and dates considered important at the time the study was undertaken.

We are fortunate to be able to add this item to the working inventory of biographical literature. It restores the availability of a set of useful profiles — and reacquaints us with the personalities of a generation which is in peril of becoming extinct — at least from the living memories of those whose ranks are swiftly being depleted by the passage of time.

Thanks again to Professor Brief and Garland for assisting in preserving this valuable study.

Gary John Previts
Weatherhead School of Management
Case Western Reserve University
Cleveland, Ohio
June 5, 1992

PREFACE

The growth of any field of human knowledge goes hand in hand with the growth of those ideas, both theoretic and practical, which are allied with that field. Thus, accounting carries with its history a vast number of ideas which have slowly but surely developed along with it. According to Professor Sanders[1] the characteristic evolution of new thought in accounting is quite similar to that which takes place in law. First come the practical adaptations and new devices designed by accountants and financial men to deal with the exigencies of a constantly changing world. Secondly, those who are sufficiently versed in the theory of accounting evaluate the new concepts of accountants and report their findings in appropriate periodicals and occasional papers. Finally, formal treatises are written which absorb and systematize the reports of the occasional papers.

The present dissertation is in the main an attempt to relate the story of this three-fold evolution as it took place during the first three decades of the present century in the United States. In particular it will deal with those individuals who were for the most part responsible for it. In other words, primary emphasis will be on men whose pioneering efforts actually brought into being the fruits of the three steps outlined above.[2] It was they who, with perseverance and zeal, recorded their observations of the actual workings of the myriad adaptations and new devices which had slowly eased their way into accounting theory and practice in the States during the first thirty years of this century.

Before setting down a general outline, it would be well to point out that it has not been an easy task to determine the twenty or twenty-five leading American pioneers most worthy of discussion. The names were determined after a most thorough examination and review of accounting literature from 1900 to 1930.[3] Indeed, after the turn of the century and particularly in the late teens and early twenties there came a great influx of accounting literature. There were numerous contributors, but obviously all were not of the same calibre.

Lawton, in his review of the fifth edition of Charles Ezra Sprague's *The Philosophy of Accounts*, has set forth a suitable definition of an accounting pioneer. He described him as

> one who has blazed a trail of broad principles, marking the path that must be followed by future generations, trails that humbler workers may smooth and broaden, as woodland and prairie trails have been transformed into smooth pikes and shining rails, but whose direction cannot be changed.[4]

It is to this group that the present work is devoted. These were the men whose articles and treatises were lauded both by their contemporaries and those who were to follow. Some, in fact quite a number, of the individuals treated were most prolific writers, but this fact was not the primary criterion for their being selected. Of paramount importance is the quality of their writings.

It should be noted further that the present writer does not attempt to settle definitively who were *the* ten, twenty, etc., "best" or foremost contributors to accounting literature during the period under observation, but rather merely to point out those men who by their writings seem to have led the way for others. As far as the writer has been able to ascertain there has been to date no particular author who has boldly stated that a certain number must or should be included in such a list. In a matter as relative as this there are always bound to be differing opinions. Present-day authors will inevitably differ in their appraisal of those who have written more than a quarter of a century ago.

Thus, although the present writer has attempted to single out for recognition those men most worthy of it, he by no means wishes to give the reader the impression that the list of men selected for use in this dissertation forms the last word on the subject nor that it admits of no exceptions.

Now for an over-all conspectus of the study itself. The work has been divided into three principal parts. In the Introduction the writer has attempted to trace the development of thought and the general tendencies which prevailed in accounting literature for the brief period prior to and the period during the first three decades of the twentieth century.

Chapters I, II, and III embody the major portion of the study. In these chapters the writer has treated the authors in alphabetical order, and has given a brief biographical sketch of each. These sketches include information concerning each man's origin, his educational background, his teaching experiences, his experiences as an accounting practitioner (if any), and other relevant details.[5] After this brief description of the principal points of each writer's life follows a discussion, based upon the comments of either contemporary or subsequent reviewers, of each one's principal contributions to accounting literature.[6] The present writer concludes this work by setting down his own impressions of the over-all picture, drawing conclusions from and basing his remarks on the combined contents of the Introduction and the three chapters which follow.

Several final remarks need be made before turning to the Introduction. In the first place it must be pointed out, lest the reader be confused, that the general bibliography consists of references directly employed in the writing of this dissertation, while, on the other hand, Appendix F contains a listing of the titles of books and periodical articles by authors in order to quickly ascertain the extent of each pioneer's contributions. Secondly and lastly, although the principal emphasis of this work is centered on the years 1900 to 1930, in several instances, viz., in the case of Scott, Littleton, Gilman, and Guthman, it was found helpful to extend the discussion of a particular author's foremost contributions to accounting literature beyond 1930. These remarks will obviate any questions the reader might otherwise have upon noticing that in the body of this work treatises written later than 1930 are discussed.

NOTES

[1]Thomas H. Sanders, "Significant Recent Accounting Literature," Harvard Business Review, XV, No. 3 (Spring 1937), 366.

[2]In order to serve somewhat as a source book for anyone who would desire particularly to explore more fully the thinking of these pioneers the present writer has compiled a bibliography of books and periodical articles which these American accountants contributed to accounting literature in the States from 1900 to 1930. This enumeration comprises Appendix F of this work.

[3]The fact that the present work is limited to the terminal years 1900 and 1930 does not mean that there were no contributions made prior to 1900. Because there

appears to be very few *important* contributions made to accounting thought before 1900 it was deemed advisable to limit the present study to the first thirty years of the present century. Anyone interested in determining American contributions to accounting though before the period designated will find them enumerated in the first volume of H.C. Bentley's two-volume work, *Bibliography of Works on Accounting by American Authors.*

[4]W.H. Lawton, Review of *The Philosophy of Accounts,* 5th ed. by Charles Ezra Sprague, *The Journal of Accountancy,* XXXV, No. 1 (January, 1923), 67–8.

[5]The enumeration of the various organizations and societies of which each of the individuals was a member is not meant to be all-inclusive. Only those which were found in the biographical sources have been listed. Since such sources are of a highly synthesized nature it is quite probable that a particular individual participated in other organizations which, in order to conserve valuable space, have been omitted.

[6]Contributions have been evaluated primarily from the standpoint of books, which were more accessible and which were generally reviewed by competent authorities.

American Accountants and Their Contributions to

Accounting Thought--1900-1930

Introduction

According to Littleton,

> Whether in the incubation period between the years 1200 and 1500, or
> in the four hundred years of adolescence between 1500 and 1900, or in the
> period of young manhood since 1900, the explanation of accounting is always
> to be found in the financial requirements of the time. Accounting and the
> literature of accounting have grown only as commerce and industry have
> grown; never far ahead, yet never lagging. Never far ahead of the needs of
> commerce, yet always offering more than most enterprises of the time were
> ready to use; never far behind the needs of industry, yet always developing
> when the need became urgent. It has always been so in the twentieth century
> as well as in the Middle Ages.[1]

Further on in the article just quoted the author remarks that the new

developments of the period of accounting literature's youth, i.e., the period

since 1900, were largely mothered by the factory system. It was with the works

of such English pioneers as Pixley, Dicksee, Garcke, Fells, and others that the

period of the young manhood of accounting literature actually began and that of

adolescence terminated.[2]

From that time on writers began to emancipate themselves from the purely

---

[1]A. C. Littleton, "The Development of Account Literature," The American
Association of University Instructors in Accounting, Publications, IX, No. 2
(December, 1925), 7.

[2]Littleton notes that while the year 1900 has no special significance in
its serving as the commencement year of the young manhood in the continuous
development of accounting literature, it nevertheless is a date convenient to
remember as the beginning of the present period and one which is closely allied
with the transition from small to large enterprises. cf. Littleton, op. cit.,
p. 11.

recording aspect of accounting. Not content merely to imitate the works of their predecessors, they struck out into new paths. Writers of the several decades prior to 1900, e.g., Pixley in his Duties of Auditors (1881), and Dicksee in his Auditing (1892), show this fact unmistakably. These men were first to recognize the new educational needs, and who accordingly wrote not merely of bookkeeping practice but rather of accounting science. Hatfield, in comparing this new generation with its forerunner, remarked in a similar vein:

> But the present generation starts a new line of texts. Accounting treatises, beginning with Pixley and Dicksee, taught accounting. They dealt with its theory and really wrestled with the unsettled problems of valuation, of the apportionment of depreciation, of how to tell an asset from an expense and, ever and above all, the determination of profits. If fewer of the books were called "science of accounts," they were, as never before, rigidly and boldly scientific, at least in the sense that they attempted the formulation of a definite body of knowledge dealing with a specific limited sphere.[1]

Once these germs had matured and spread throughout England it was only a relatively short time before they penetrated the United States. Hence, the decade from 1900 to 1910 witnessed a healthy growth in accounting works which, for the most part, were along the lines marked out by the English pioneers just referred to. One of the more patent examples of this development took place in 1905, when Montgomery was induced to edit an American edition of Dicksee's Auditing because of the rapidly increasing divergencies in practice here and abroad. Only several years later, however, the appearance of Sprague's The Philosophy of Accounts (1907), Hatfield's Modern Accounting (1909), and Nicholson's Factory Organization and Costs (1909), may be said to mark the real beginning of American contributions.[2]

Before continuing this article on the development of accounting literature,

---

[1] Henry Rand Hatfield, Review of Managerial Accounting, by James Oscar McKinsey, The Journal of Accountancy, XXXIX, No. 5(May, 1925), 432.

[2] A. C. Littleton, op. cit., p. 12.

Littleton most deftly pauses to pay the following fine tribute to the gentlemen just mentioned:

> It is difficult to express our indebtedness to these and other writers of this period, for they widened the horizon of accounting greatly by the breadth of their vision. We may be sure they realized that the growing profession had urgent need of the written word--of digested practical experience and systematic thinking formulated into principles. They saw that education by precept and example alone was too slow and inefficient to be an effective means of passing on the wealth of knowledge already available and so much needed for continued progress. They saw the need, and the responses, forming as they do the foundations for subsequent publications, have left their indelible imprint upon the profession.[1]

During the first thirty years of the present century there were certain factors which stimulated writing in the field of accounting. They were years marked by gigantic combinations of capital, by far-reaching banking reform, by a great war, and for the most part by conditions of general prosperity. Also influential were the augmentation of governmental regulation of public utilities, cost-plus contracts, and Federal and State income tax laws. These conditions produced three momentous reactions from accounting. First, there was an increased interest in accounting generally. In the second place, there was a most speedy growth of collegiate instruction in accounting. Finally, in comparison with years gone by, there was a tremendous output of books on accounting.

The aforementioned responses followed each other quite logically. Yet, there seemed to be a fourth reaction. As the years passed increasing numbers of books on accounting were being written by educators rather than professional practitioners. As Lawton[2] noted, such a response was only natural in view of the growing number of accounting courses which were then being installed in colleges and universities throughout the United States. Those intending to make accountancy their profession were not alone in realizing that knowledge of the

---

[1] Ibid.

[2] W. H. Lawton, Review of Accounts in Theory and Practice, by Earl A. Saliers, The Journal of Accountancy, XXX, No. 6 (December, 1920), 471.

principles of accounting was a very necessary part of the equipment for any business or profession. Thus, it was only a natural consequence that books began to be written by teachers of accounting in great number. True, such books were text-books pure and simple, but it would have been a mistake to pronounce them superfluous merely because they taught what had been advanced as a standard by professionals. These writers were practically pioneers blazing the pedagogical ways of accounting; and just as active practitioners had after long years attained some degree of success in standardizing theory and practice, so did educators, to some extent at least, gradually standardize the methods of teaching them.

In the various writings which flowed from the pens of educators and practitioners alike during these early manhood years there can be detected several outstanding tendencies. By following Littleton[1] and Paton[2] one can get a fairly comprehensive picture of the more important tendencies in accounting literature during the period under review.

The apparent tendency to give separate consideration to the theory and the practice of accounting was perhaps the most important general characteristic visible in the writings which appeared during these years, especially the years from 1915 on. Under this more general tendency were several particularly evident tendencies within each of the two camps of theoretical and practical writers.

Concentrating first on the theoretical aspect, accounting literature developed in the direction of wider and more reasonable points of view, i.e.,

---

[1]A. C. Littleton, op. cit., pp. 13-4.

[2]William A. Paton, "Tendencies in Accounting Literature," The American Association of University Instructors in Accounting, Papers and Proceedings of the Ninth Annual Meeting (Chicago, Ill., 1924), IX, No. 1(February, 1925), 64-9.

the willingness of those especially devoted to principles to recognize and empha-

size the underlying aims and purposes of accounting. This tendency was aptly

exemplified by those publications which leaned toward a philosophical exposition

of accounting; such works built up accounting principles on a strictly logical

basis.

Another feature of writings which treated principles was that which tended

to avoid the strictly mercantile point of view. A most satisfactory reason for

the existence of this tendency was expressed by Paton:

> In this connection it may be pointed out that the tendency in litera-
> ture which I am trying to indicate may be viewed as merely a reflection,
> occurring somewhat belatedly, of industrial developments. Undoubtedly
> literature tends to lag behind practice in some respects, and the trends in
> literature in some measure represent the recognition of business changes
> and accompanying and consequent developments in the art of accounting.[1]

This quotation, taken from a paper which Paton delivered at the Ninth

Annual Meeting of the American Association of University Instructors in Account-

ing in Chicago, 1924, later furnished a topic of discussion by several other

members of the Association. One of them, Professor Kester, backed up Professor

Paton's words by making the remark that he thought that Paton had summed up the

true situation of the tendencies in accounting literature by his statement

> that literature must almost from necessity lag behind practice in a given
> field. Until principles, particularly new principles, have been submitted
> to the test of practice they do not usually find their way into the litera-
> ture of the subject which is supposed to deal with established and accepted
> principles and methods of doing things. . . .[2]

A third tendency found in the literature on accounting principles consists

in laying more emphasis upon income accounting, i.e., in stressing the point of

view of income reports rather than that of the balance sheet. The balance sheet

---

[1]William A. Paton, op. cit., p. 67.

[2]Roy B. Kester. "Discussion," The American Association of University
Instructors in Accounting, Papers and Proceedings of the Ninth Annual Meeting
(Chicago, Ill., 1924), IX, No. 1(February, 1925), 86.

was no longer recognized as the only accounting statement, for accountants began
to realize that the operating and income report were of equal practical value.
Hence, deserved attention was given to the problem of the nature and form of the
operating and income report.

The more general tendency to treat separately the aspect of practice in
accounting also had several important corollaries. Many authors, having in
mind the various viewpoints of the private accountant and business executive,
began to investigate the many special phases of accounting in which he was or
would be soon involved. There began to develop a literature of managerial
accounting, one which was keyed toward the solution of the many managerial
problems encountered by the executive and his assistants. This literature
represented a definite step forward in the formulation of the specific needs of
management and the working out of the accounting and statistical methods and
various other procedures necessary to meet these demands.

Nor did the literature in the field of public accounting lie dormant.
The setting to writing of the various aspects of current practice led to a
marked appreciation for the widening scope of the professional accountant's
function. This was especially true with regard to auditing.

The tendency toward a development of special applications of accounting
seems to have flowed also from the general tendency to treat separately the
practical side of accounting. Consequently, there arose a great number of
lengthy treatises which dealt with the accounting set-up for special classes
of business, as, for example, general contractor accounting, meat-packing
accounting, coal mine accounting, brokerage accounting, municipal accounting,
and so forth.

Another tendency, and one already hinted at in the previous discussion of
the increase in the number of writers among accounting teachers, was an

ever-growing number of textbooks. Classroom experience, stemming from accounting classes in universities, brought to light the fact that business required trained thinkers as well as trained bookkeepers and clerks. In response to those needs there appeared an accounting literature of textbooks and special treatises which steadily grew in volume and refinement of analysis.

Having investigated some of the most perceptible turns in accounting literature for the first third of the present century, it is now fitting that the discussion focus itself on the men who were in many instances responsible for the actual existence of these tendencies. The tendencies themselves were certainly effects, and as such demanded either remote or proximate influences. While, as has been seen, the remote causes were more than likely to be found among English writers in accountancy, the proximate causes were here in the United States. Hence, it is to the leading pioneer contributors to accounting thought and literature that the investigation now turns. For it was precisely because of the keen foresight and daring efforts of these men that both accounting theory and accounting practice made and presently continue to make great strides forward. It should be noted that the writers spoken of in the subsequent chapters have for convenience sake been arranged alphabetically.

CHAPTER I

Spurgeon Bell

A. Biographical Sketch[1]

Spurgeon Bell, the son of M. H. and Virginia (Cochran) Bell, was born on
June 28, 1880, in Blanco, Texas. In 1903 he received his Bachelor of Science
Degree from the University of Texas. He attended the University of Chicago
from 1905 until 1907, but it was not until 1915 that he received an M.B.A.
Degree from the Harvard Graduate School of Business Administration.

After graduation from the University of Texas in 1903, Bell became a
professor of mathematics at John Tarleton College, Stephenville, Texas. Later,
while in Chicago, he served as assistant editor of The Economist, a periodical
published by the University of Chicago, from 1907 until 1909. During the years
1909 and 1910 he held the position of secretary for the Chicago Commission on
City Expenditures.

Bell apparently had had his mind set upon the teaching profession, for he

[1]American Accounting Association, 1955 Membership Roster. (Inside back
cover.)

Rita Perine (ed.), The Accountants' Directory and Who's Who--1920(New
York: The Forty-Fifth Street Press, 1920), p. 323.

"University Notes," The Accounting Review, I, No. 4(December, 1926),
p. 103.

Who's Who in America. Vol. XXVI, 1950-51(Chicago: A. N. Marquis &
Company, 1950), p. 191.

Who's Who in America. Vol. XXVIII, 1954-55(Chicago: A. N. Marquis &
Company, 1954), p. 190.

took it up once more in 1910, this time at the University of Missouri. It was
there that he served in the role of both a professor of business administration
and an assistant professor of economics until 1912. He then returned to his
alma mater, the University of Texas, where until 1925 he held the position of
professor of business administration. Bell spent the final three years of this
time in the capacity of dean of the School of Business Administration. In 1925,
however, Bell moved once again, now to Ohio State University, where until 1934
he acted as a professor of business research and also as the Director of the
Bureau of Business Research, which at that time was engaged in the study of
Ohio business problems. In this latter capacity Bell directed studies made of
the furniture trade in Ohio, of operating costs of wholesale grocers, sales
force compensation in furniture stores,. the effect of weather on the construction business, installment selling of clothing, and various other subjects.

The year 1934 seems to mark the end of Bell's teaching career in colleges
and universities, for in that year he was appointed as the Director of the
Bureau of Research and Statistics of the Federal Home Loan Bank Board. He held
this position until 1936. From 1937 until 1940 he served as a research economist for the Brookings Institution. He worked as principal economist for the
National Resources Planning Board from 1940 to 1941, and served this same Board
as head economist from 1941 until 1943. Bell spent the remaining war years and
several of the post-war years as head economist of the Interstate Commerce
Commission. Since 1951 he has acted as a consulting economist on this same
Commission.

In 1910 Bell served as a member of the Board of Economists for the census
taken that year. During World War I he held the rank of major in the Statistics
Branch, General Staff, of the United States Army. Since 1926 he had held the
rank of lieutenant-colonel in the Specialist Reserve. A former member of the

American Association of University Instructors in Accounting, he served as vice-president in 1923. He presently maintains membership in both the American Economic Association and the American Statistical Association.

B. Principal Contributions

Although Bell was not a prolific writer, an examination of his writings, especially his books, reveals one characteristic aspect; namely, his concern for the practical side of accounting. In his treatment of the practical aspects of accounting he has in mind particularly the manager. In his first work, Accounting Principles, Their Use in Business Management, which appeared in 1921, he attempts to show the function of accounting principles in business management. From several contemporary reviewers,[1] one learns that while the work itself was practically a comprehensive manual of bookkeeping and accounting with little to distinguish it from other texts of its kind, nevertheless, in Chapter XIV, its author briefly explained methods of analyzing the balance sheet and revenue statement. According to Lawton, this analysis was a valuable feature that should have received better treatment in all textbooks on accounting. This same reviewer went on to say that it was not difficult for an accounting student with ordinary intelligence to learn how to keep books, but that few really understood how to read the story told by the resulting financial statements. As his concluding remark Lawton noted that Bell's work was "altogether an excellent working manual for the student."[2]

Bell's second contribution to the literature of the field, a two-volume

---

[1]J. Hugh Jackson, Review of Accounting Principles, Their Use in Business Management, by Spurgeon Bell, The American Economic Review, XII, No. 2(June, 1922), 296-7.

W. H. Lawton, Review of Accounting Principles, by Spurgeon Bell, The Journal of Accountancy, XXXV, No. 1(January, 1923), 66.

[2]Ibid.

work entitled <u>Theory and Practice of Accounting: Use in Managerial Control</u>, which appeared around 1922, seems also to have been a rather important contribution, for in 1932 the first volume, which in 1927 had been reprinted under the title <u>Practical Accounting: Its Use in Managerial Control</u>, was a third time reprinted as volume seven of the encyclopedia <u>Practical Business Administration</u>; the second volume, <u>Managerial Accounting</u>, likewise went through several reprintings, and in 1932 was inserted as volume eight into the encyclopedia just mentioned.

A detailed listing of Bell's contributions to the field of accounting literature has been included in Appendix F along with the works of the other authors which are to be discussed subsequently.

James H. Bliss

A. Biographical Sketch[1]

James Harris Bliss, the son of J. Harris and Grace (Carter) Bliss, was born on October 13, 1889, in Kane County, Illinois. He received his high school education at the Aurora, Illinois, High School. From 1911 until 1913 he attended night school at the Northwestern University School of Commerce. In 1916 he became a certified public accountant in the state of Illinois.

Although Bliss was what may be considered a full-time practitioner in accounting work, he nevertheless spent some time at teaching. Thus, after lecturing for a relatively short while at the Northwestern University School of Commerce, he was in 1927 promoted to the rank of professor in accounting. From 1916 until 1918 Bliss served as secretary-treasurer of the Siegel-Cooper Company of Chicago. He next worked as an accountant for Swift & Company from 1918 until 1922. Then, for more than a decade, from 1922 to 1935, he served as comptroller of Libby, McNeill and Libby. Having returned to Swift & Company, he served as assistant treasurer from 1935 until 1945. From 1945 to 1950 he served as vice-president, treasurer, and director respectively for the Swift International

---

[1]Rita Perine (ed.), The Accountants' Directory and Who's Who--1920(New York: The Forty-Fifth Street Press, 1920), p. 330.

Rita Perine Merritt (ed.), The Accountants' Directory and Who's Who--1925 (New York: Prentice-Hall, Inc., 1925), p. 387.

"University Notes," The Accounting Review, II, No. 2(June, 1927), p. 209.

Who's Who in America. XXVIII, 1954-55(Chicago: A. N. Marquis & Company, 1954), p. 248.

Company, Ltd. He has been associated with International Packers, Ltd., since 1915.

Bliss is a member of the American Institute of Accountants, the Illinois Society of Certified Public Accountants, and was a past member and former president of the Illinois Manufacturer's Cost Association.

B. Principal Contributions

As was the case with Bell, Bliss is a man who does not write very extensively. However, as will be seen shortly, he wrote well. In his portion of the general discussion concerning a paper given by Professor Paton[1] at the Ninth Annual Meeting of the American Association of University Instructors in Accounting, Greer of Ohio State University sums up well the general consensus of opinion with regard to the writings of men like Bliss, when he says:

> Most of us in this profession have so far done little more than look around us, see what is going on, gather together in writings, in lectures, and in practice what we have thought to be the best of the practice with which we have come in contact. A very few have forged ahead of the current and struck out in new directions, developing something definitely new and scientifically sound to which accountancy could lay claim. Mr. Paton, Mr. McKinsey, and Mr. Bliss have made notable contributions in this direction.[2]

According to Sister Isadore Brown, O.S.U., "as Alexander Wall is considered the pioneer in credit barometrics, so James Harris Bliss is considered the pioneer in the declaration of principles for the use of ratios in management."[3]

The "notable contribution" which has given Bliss title to being among the

[1]William A. Paton, "Tendencies in Accounting Literature," The American Association of University Instructors in Accounting. Papers and Proceedings. IX, No. 1(February, 1925), 64-9.

[2]Howard C. Greer, "Discussion," The American Association of University Instructors in Accounting. Papers and Proceedings. IX, No. 1(February, 1925), 89-90.

[3]Sister Isadore Brown, O.S.U., M.A., The Historical Development of the Use of Ratios in Financial Statement Analysis to 1933. Ph. D. Dissertation, The Catholic University of America. 1955. pp. 100-101.

first in this field was his <u>Financial and Operating Ratios in Management</u>, which
was first published by the Ronald Press in 1923. From a brief look at various
reports on this work it can easily be seen that Bliss fits quite well in that
category of authors who stress the practical aspects of accounting. One
reviewer[1] notes that although Bliss writes with the knowledge of a trained
accountant, he nevertheless writes also as an experienced manager and relates
what he, as such a manager, requires and what he learns from the facts submitted.
Mucklow attributes the high value of the work to several factors, namely, the
prime importance of the matters treated and the clear and logical manner in
which these matters are set down. Other important remarks of this same reviewer
are:

> While it might be too much to say that the author has taken a new line,
> it is well within the mark to say that he describes a field to which too
> little attention has often been paid in the past. . . . It is without doubt
> the most comprehensive study of "turnovers" and "ratios" which has appeared.[2]

Armstrong, in his review of the same treatise, remarked quite fittingly:

> This volume is not notable for any transcendent presentation of the
> subject, nor great originality in detail or principle, but in the clear
> enunciation of the subject and invaluable reference tables which are con-
> tained the volume is a real pioneer, and as such deserves to be recognized
> along with the previous efforts of Alexander Wall.[3]

<u>Management Through Accounts</u> was Bliss's second outstanding contribution
to accounting literature during this period. The work first appeared in 1924.

---

[1]Walter Mucklow, Review of <u>Financial and Operating Ratios in Management</u>,
by James H. Bliss, <u>The Journal of Accountancy</u>, XXXVII, No. 2(February, 1924),
152-4.

[2]<u>Ibid</u>. p. 154.

[3]George S. Armstrong, "Increasing Use and Values of Ratios," <u>Management
and Administration</u>, VI(September, 1923), 375; as quoted in Brown, <u>op</u>. <u>cit</u>.,
p. 101.

From several discussions[1] concerning the book in question it is readily understood that it is an extensive treatise on accounting from the standpoint of the
manager. Moreover, the work is a sequel to the author's earlier treatise on
Financial and Operating Ratios in Management, as is evidenced by the special
stress which it lays on the use of financial and operating ratios. The author's
wide experience in practical matters and his frequent contacts with operating
men and executives is quite vividly noticed throughout the entire book.

Of the many merits of this work, only several need be mentioned here.
Most praiseworthy is the author's ability to refrain, for the most part, from a
dogmatic attitude toward controversial questions. Moreover, that special
section of the book which treats of opportunity costs at the time was a distinct
contribution to the field of cost accounting. According to Stevenson, Bliss's
particular treatment of this phase of cost accounting "is probably the most
logical analysis of this question that has yet appeared."[2] Another matter which
merits praise is the author's fine treatment of the undoubtably difficult topics
of joint products and by-products. Adams[3] mentions the special importance which
Bliss gives to the functions of the accountant in the management of business
enterprises, an importance which prior to that time was larger in scope.

---

[1]"Book Notices," Review of Management Through Accounts, by James H. Bliss,
Harvard Business Review, III(January, 1925), 252.

R. A. Stevenson, Review of Management Through Accounts, by James H. Bliss,
The American Association of University Instructors in Accounting. Papers and
Proceedings. IX, No. 2(December, 1925), 161-2.

W. H. Lawton, Review of Management Through Accounts, by James H. Bliss,
The Journal of Accountancy, XXXVIII, No. 6(December, 1924), 474-5.

James P. Adams, Review of Management Through Accounts, by James H. Bliss,
The American Economic Review, XVI(June, 1926), 309-11.

[2]Stevenson, loc. cit., p. 161.

[3]Adams, loc. cit., p. 311.

According to Bliss the accountant no longer was to serve merely in the analysis of business facts, but he was henceforward responsible for interpreting these facts and presenting them in such condition as to be readily usable for purposes of administrative control.

Lawton remarks, that having taken into consideration the contents of the entire book, ". . . one has a remarkably complete and compact guide whether for training students for a C.P.A. examination or for general business."[1]

Adams seems to have summed up the relative merits of this treatise in his review of it. He noted that

> while written ostensible from the standpoint of management, the work constitutes a valuable contribution to the literature of accounting, . . . The reviewer knows of no book in this field, except the companion volume Financial and Operating Ratios, in which the author has recognized and so ably stated the basic economic character of the problems of management. Mr. Bliss has performed a real service in pointing out the relationship between general economic facts and business administration. Emphasis has been given where emphasis is needed.[2]

---

[1]Lawton, loc. cit.

[2]Adams, loc. cit.

William Morse Cole

A. Biographical Sketch[1]

William Morse Cole, the son of Albert Birney and Mary Elizabeth (Morse) Cole, was born on February 10, 1866, in Boston,Massachusettes. Some time later the family apparently moved to Portland, Maine, for it was there that William received his high school education and later attended the Portland Business College. He received both his A.B. and A.M. degrees from Harvard University, the former in 1890, the latter in 1895(6). Cole's pre-teaching experience included the task of bookkeeper for several wholesale houses and also that of auditor for two corporations.

Cole began his teaching career as an instructor in political economy at Harvard in 1890, and held this position until 1893. From 1899(1900) until 1908 he served as an instructor in the principles of accounting at this same university. In 1908 he was promoted to assistant professor, in 1913 to associate professor, and in 1916 to a full professorship. Since 1933 he has held the rank of Professor Emeritus of Economics and Social Philosophy at Harvard. However, not all of Cole's vast teaching experience was confined to the field of accounting, for he also taught English literature and composition

[1]Jaques Cattell (ed.), Directory of American Scholars, 2d ed.(Lancaster, Pa.: The Science Press, 1951), p. 173.

Albert Nelson Marquis (ed.) Who's Who in America. Vol. XIII, 1924-25 (Chicago: A. N. Marquis & Company, 1924), pp. 767-8.

Rita Perine (ed.), The Accountants' Directory and Who's Who--1920(New York: The Forty-Fifth Street Press, 1920, p. 357.

both at the Fall River, Massachusettes, High School from 1898-1901, and at
South High School, Worcester, from 1901 to 1908.

During the years 1894 and 1895 Cole served as secretary for the Massachusettes Commission on Unemployed. From 1895 to 1898 he lectured at the Harvard
University Extension. During World War I he served as a captain in the Quarter-
master Corps from May 15, 1917 until January 17, 1919. He was a member of the
Delta Kappa Epsilon Fraternity and also of various literary, musical and outing
associations. Although the greater part of his writings were in the field of
accounting, he nevertheless found time to write several other works, namely,
An Old Man's Romance, written under the pseudonym of "Christopher Craigie,"
and The American Hope.

B. Principal Contribution

Of Cole's various accounting works, one in particular deserves special
mention here, namely, his Accounts, Their Construction and Interpretation. In
In the July, 1954, issue of The Accounting Review, there appears an article
entitled "Historical Dates in Accounting," which is a chronological listing
of dates which are significant in the development of accounting as it is
known today. This article notes that the publication of Cole's work was one
of the two outstanding events that occurred in the year 1908. It was in this
work that Cole introduced the "Where Got-Where Gone" statement. He advocated
setting up sales and purchases net, and showing discounts lost and gained.

From various reviews of both the 1908 and 1915 editions of this volume
one obtains further insight into Cole's outstanding contribution to accounting
literature. Cole's purpose was not to present short-cuts and bookkeeping

---

[1]H. G. Phillips, Review of Accounts, Their Construction and Interpretation,
1908 ed., by William Morse Cole, The Journal of Accountancy, VII, No. 1(January,
1909), 244-5.

made easy, but rather to set forth a thorough discussion of principles, so that
the student using the book would be master of something more than mere rules of
thumb, and would be able to judge for himself what short-cuts would serve his
purpose. For the convenience of those already familiar with both bookkeeping
practice and the philosophical basis upon which it rests, routine matters are
treated by themselves in part one; on the other hand, part two, "The Principles
of Accounting," is devoted to the analytical side of accounting, with a view to
making general principles more concrete by applying them to the problems of
different lines of business in which they can best be illustrated.

According to Steele,[1] Cole's treatment of the general principles of factory
accounting is the most interesting part of his book. In that section the subject of machine rates is enlighteningly discussed. It is interesting to note
in this same connection that Cole regarded "idle time" as a cost of the manufactured product. Moreover, he also suggested that such elements of manufacturing burden as freight, cartage, storehouse space, storehouse wages, etc., should
be distributed in the cost accounts as a percentage upon the value of materials
used.

Cole's work embodies several other matters worthy of note. In the first
place, he believed that the railroad accounts of the country were better than
any other accounts, and he devotes considerable space to their consideration.
His suggestion that the word "allowance" be used where there is question of an

---

F. R. Carnegie Steele, Review of Accounts, Their Construction and Interpretation, 1915 ed., by William Morse Cole, The Journal of Accountancy, XX, No. 9
(September, 1915), 242-3

R. H. Montgomery, Review of Accounts, Their Construction in Interpretation,
1915 ed., by William Morse Cole, The American Economic Review, V, No. 3(September,
1915), 606-8.

[1]Steele, loc. cit.

item to be deducted from an asset account and the word "reserve" only where such an account is created out of net profits, is also most interesting. Finally, as Montgomery[1] remarks, Cole deserved great credit for his advanced stand in suggesting that contracts for future contracts be reflected in the balance sheet. While this suggestion was in agreement with then current theories of professional auditors, it was seldom seen in practice.

As Phillips expressed it, Professor Cole's work, ". . . as a whole, is excellent . . . , as more care has been shown in its preparation than is the case in a number of works on accounting recently published in this country."[2] Several others remarked:

> Professor Cole's work is unquestionably a valuable addition to modern accounting literature. . . . Cole's arguments are sound and logical, and his book, . . . is remarkable for its clarity of expression and originality of treatment of a wide range of accounting topics.[3]

> Professor Cole is an unquestioned authority on accounts, and the recent edition of his book furnishes additional evidence of his mastery of a science that is more difficult than any other to reduce to writing.[4]

Thus, this contribution, which in the words of Arnett[5] was "the exception" to accounting books which were generally "dry and dull," filled a long-felt need on the part of business men and students of affairs, for whom the work had primarily been written.

---

[1]Montgomery, loc. cit.

[2]Phillips, loc. cit.

[3]Steele, loc. cit.

[4]Montgomery, loc. cit.

[5]Trevor Arnett, Review of Accounts, Their Construction and Interpretation, by William Morse Cole, A.M., The Journal of Political Economy, XVII, No. 2 (February, 1909), 166.

Sir Arthur Lowes Dickinson

A. Biographical Sketch[1]

Sir Arthur Lowes Dickinson was born in London, England, August 8, 1859.
He received his education from the Charterhouse School (Scholar) and King's
College (Scholar), Cambridge University, England. He graduated as a Wrangler
in Mathematical Tripos in 1884 and received his M.A. in 1888. He practiced in
London as a chartered accountant from 1888 to 1901, at which time he left
England and came to the United States. Soon after he landed on American shores
he became senior partner of Price, Waterhouse and Company, with which branch of
this company he remained until 1913.

---

[1]"Accounting Hall of Fame," Canadian Chartered Accountant, LXV, No. 10 (October, 1954), 182-3.

American Institute of Accountants Fiftieth Anniversary Celebration, 1937 (Concord, New Hampshire: The Rumford Press, 1938), p. 24.

E. Burl Austin, "Association Notes," The Accounting Review, XXVI, No. 3 (July, 1951), 431-2.

C. W. DeMond, Price, Waterhouse & Co. In America (New York: The Comet Press, Inc., 1951).

"Dickinson, Hatfield Chosen for 1951 Awards at Ohio State's Hall of Fame," The Journal of Accountancy, XCII, No. 2 (August, 1951), 135.

Edward E. Gore, (Editorial) The Journal of Accountancy, XXXVIII, No. 3 (September, 1924), 207.

J. Brooks Heckert, "Accounting Hall of Fame," The Accounting Review, XXV, No. 3 (July, 1950), 260-1.

W. Mayors, "Four-Year Struggle Made Accounting Law Possible in Missouri," The American Accountant, XII, No. 6 (July, 1927), 26-30.

While in this country Dickinson assumed an active part in organizing and expanding the American accounting profession along lines similar to those followed by public accountancy in England. Thus, in 1903 he served as president of the Federation of Societies of Public Accountants in the United States of America. Along with George Wilkinson, Federation Secretary, Dickinson made strenuous efforts to encourage the formation of state societies which could eventually be grouped into a national or federal organization. In September, 1904, at the International Accounting Congress held in St. Louis, Dickinson spoke on the Federation plan, citing its advantages and pointing out the future path to be followed by the society. At this same Congress Dickinson delivered a paper entitled "The Profits of a Corporation," in which, though written more than forty years ago, there are contained principles which are applicable, for the most part, to practice at the present time. His well-chosen, thought out comments on consolidated financial statements, based upon his wide experience with some of the large mergers in this country, opened an entirely

Rita Perine Merritt (ed.), The Accountants' Directory and Who's Who--1925 (New York: Prentice-Hall, Inc., 1925), p. 442.

Mary E. Murphy, "Arthur Lowes Dickinson: Pioneer in American Professional Accountancy," Bulletin of the Business Historical Society, XXI, No. 2(April, 1947), 27-38.

Rita Perine (ed.), The Accountants' Directory and Who's Who--1920(New York: The Forty-Fifth Street Press, 1920), p. 374.

A. P. Richardson (ed.), "An International Accountant Passes," The Journal of Accountancy, LIX, No. 4(April, 1935), 248-9.

_____,"Sir Arthur Lowes Dickinson," The Journal of Accountancy, XXXVI, No. 3(September, 1923), 202.

Nicholas A. H. Stacy, "Accounting Hall of Fame; Americans Pay Homage to Leaders of Profession," Accountant, CXXXI(July 31, 1954), 108.

Who's Who--1923(London: A&C Black, Limited, 1923), p. 758.

Who's Who--1935(London: A&C Black, Limited, 1935), p. 900.

new field of accounting and auditing practice.

Dickinson's vital and constant interest in accounting enabled him not only to carry out the many important engagements of Price, Waterhouse and Company in all parts of the country, but also to attend meetings of accountants in remote areas. In October, 1905, he was elected secretary of the American Association of Public Accountants. Moreover, he had received honorary certified public accountant certificates from many states, and in 1906 became an American citizen. He spent a great amount of his time in stamping out various illegitimate professional groups which appeared from time to time.

Dickinson, knowing full well the need for professional fitness, pointed out that the qualifications of the accountant included

> A sound knowledge of accounting principles gained from theory and from practice under the supervision of his supervisors; familiarity with figures coupled with the faculty of quickly grasping the meaning and purpose of accounts and statements, and the legal and commercial principles upon which they were based; a legal and judicial mind accustomed to weighing facts, reaching the core of the case without delay, and forming a conclusion as to the equities involved; ability to argue and discuss a point either as an advocate, for the purpose of obtaining the other side of the question, or as a judge of all sides of the issue in their proper relation to each other; sound knowledge of business and financial methods and the economic and legal principles which govern them; and above all, absolute integrity combined with a superabundance of tact and good temper.[1]

Indeed, Dickinson was definitely a leader in stressing for his fellow practitioners that moral standards as well as legal tenets must serve as the bed-rock of all accounting practice.

Shortly before World War I Dickinson returned to his native England and resumed practice there. Thus, in 1913 he rejoined the London branch of Price, Waterhouse & Company, where he remained as a partner for little longer than a decade. Those years which followed his departure from the United States were quite eventful ones. He traveled extensively with his family in Continental

---

[1] Murphy, op. cit., pp. 36-7.

Europe and other parts of the world. He received knighthood from King George
for services rendered during the war. After that first great conflict Dickinson stood among the foremost accountants in the British profession and took an
active role in the work of the council of the Institute of Chartered Accountants
of England and Wales.

The first quarter of the twentieth century had nearly drawn to a close
when Dickinson retired from Price, Waterhouse & Company of London and gave up
active participation in the practice of the profession. After his retirement
he was appointed by the government to undertake various investigations, notably
an examination and a comprehensive report on the condition of railways in India.

In addition to the many duties mentioned above, Dickinson found time for
several return visits to the United States. His final public appearance in
this country was at the annual meeting of the American Institute of Accountants
in Philadelphia in 1931. In 1933 he was present at the international conference
in London, and up to the day of his death, February 28, 1935, he was in constant
touch with the growth of the profession. Upon the occasion of Dickinson's death,
A. P. Richardson, editor of The Journal of Accountancy, wrote the following
words of encomium:

> . . . his entire mature life was devoted with great unselfishness and re-
> markably wide vision to the building up of accounting in his native land,
> and in the land which was for many years his adopted country. He played so
> many parts in the development of this new accountancy of ours that it is
> difficult to select anyone as the most important. . . . Probably his most
> valuable service to humanity was the great assistance which he rendered to
> the establishment of friendly and cooperative understanding between the
> accountants in the two great branches of the Anglo-Saxon race.[1]

As has been pointed out, Dickinson was both a chartered accountant and a
certified public accountant. He was a member of the American Institute of

---

[1]A. P. Richardson (ed.), "An International Accountant Passes," The Journal
of Accountancy, LXIX, No. 4(April, 1935), 248-9.

Accountants, the Ontario Institute of Chartered Accountants, a fellow in the Institute of Chartered Accountants of England and Wales and a member of the council, a fellow in the Institute of Chartered Accountants of British Columbia, an honorary member of the New York State Society of Certified Public Accountants, one of the twenty-three charter members of the Missouri Society of Certified Public Accountants, and a member of the Institute of Actuaries.

B. Principal Contributions

Although Dickinson was primarily an accounting practitioner he nevertheless spent a considerable amount of time in writing. He was very well-known as an author of valuable accounting texts, the chief of which was his Accounting Practice and Procedure which, according to DeMond,[1] constituted an incorporation of Dickinson's professional experience in America. One contemporary reviewer[2] seems to speak more precisely when he noted that this notable contribution to the literature of accounting reflected the mature views and wide experience of an accountant whose qualification as a leading authority had grown out of extensive practice both in England and in the United States. At any rate, this volume, which appeared around 1913(14), quickly became a recognized source and achieved such popularity that a number of printings were made. In this work the author stressed that every balance sheet must be largely a matter of opinion, and emphasized that the phrase "in my opinion" should be considered as strengthening the auditor's certificate, in that the words implied that the signer had given his certificate not with foolhardy assurance but with a realization of the inherent possibility of saying, absolutely, that one balance sheet was correct

[1]DeMond, op. cit., p. 113.

[2]W. R. Gray, Review of Accounting Practice and Procedure, by Arthur Lowes Dickinson, The American Economic Review, IV, No. 4(December, 1914), 909-11.

and another incorrect. In his review of this book Hatfield[1] noted that it was one wherein the subject had been handled with a breadth which in too many instances had been lacking in other accounting works. Hatfield also lauded the author for his searching analysis, his richness of material, and his cleverness of exposition. Speaking some ten years after the initial appearance of Accounting Practice and Procedure, Gore, president of the American Institute of Accountants, deemed it "a classic in the literature of the profession."[2]

In addition to his contributions of various textbooks Dickinson also wrote many serious and learned articles which served to strengthen the periodical literature of his day. One author remarked as follows concerning one of Dickinson's more outstanding articles:

> From his intimate knowledge of the accounts covering the formative years of operation, Dickinson formulated and summarized the theories and techniques of consolidated statements in "Notes on Some Problems Relating to the Accounts of Holding Companies," printed in the Journal of Accountancy for April, 1906. Modern writers on holding company accounts often cite Dickinson's contribution not only to the design of basic principles but also to the literature in this specialized field.[3]

Of another of Dickinson's articles, "The Construction, Use, and Abuse of Cost Accounts," Kapp noted that a ". . . master craftsman can be distinguished by his product. Even though the difficulty of summarizing the major problems of the entire field of cost accounting in a space of twenty pages would seem insurmountable, this article would prove that it is not."[4]

---

[1]Henry Rand Hatfield, Review of Accounting Practice and Procedure, by Arthur Lowes Dickinson, The Journal of Accountancy, XVIII, No. 6(December, 1914), 480-2.

[2]Gore, loc. cit.

[3]DeMond, op. cit., p. 62.

[4]Edgar B. Kapp, (ed.), Review of "The Construction, Use, and Abuse of Cost Accounts," by Sir Arthur Lowes Dickinson, The American Accountant, XIII, No. 12 (December, 1928), 40.

Dickinson was certainly an accountant of international acclaim, a fact substantiated by several outstanding events that occurred in American Accountancy the past three or four decades. The first was the establishment in the autumn of 1924 of the Arthur Lowes Dickinson Fund at the Harvard Graduate School of Business Administration by the firm of Price, Waterhouse & Company "in recognition of the debt due by the accounting profession in general, and particularly by this firm, to a former partner, Sir Arthur Lowes Dickinson."[1] A second great honor was accorded Dickinson in 1951 when, together with the late Professor Henry Rand Hatfield, he was selected for a position in the Accounting Hall of Fame at Ohio State University, Columbus, Ohio. Truly, such distinction was well-deserved.

Murphy has quite fittingly expressed American accountancy's sentiments concerning the late Sir Arthur Lowes Dickinson:

> The charge of Francis Bacon to professional persons: "I hold everyone a debtor to his profession from which, as men do seek to receive countenance and profit, so ought they of duty to endeavor themselves by way of amends to be a help and an ornament thereto" was fully accepted by Dickinson as the motivating force in his life. In retrospect, his professional endeavors in the United States are seen to have advanced public accountancy far beyond the limits originally conceived for it by both the profession and the general public. Dickinson, therefore, remains one of the pioneers in the field, occupying a position which time and circumstance can never alter.[2]

---

[1] William A. Paton, "Recent and Prospective Developments in Accounting Theory," (Boston, Mass.: Harvard University Press, 1940), p. iii. The above quotation continues: "The income from this Fund was for a number of years used exclusively for the purpose of conducting research in the field of accounting. In 1936, the provisions of the Fund were modified to provide that 'in addition there may from time to time be appointed, for one year, a man outstanding in Accounting who shall deliver at the Graduate School of Business Administration one or more lectures, and shall be designated as Dickinson Lecturer.'"

[2] Murphy, op. cit., p. 38.

DeWitt Carl Eggleston

A. Biographical Sketch[1]

DeWitt Carl Eggleston, who, interestingly enough descended on his mother's side from Alexander Hamilton, was born at Chagrin Falls, Ohio, on May 5, 1881, the son of Dewitt Clinton and Mary K. Eggleston. He later graduated from Brown University with LL.B. and M.E. degrees. He was a licensed mechanical engineer in New York State. He held a certified public accountant certificate in two states; Connecticut(1908), and New York(1923). Shortly after World War I he began work as a special partner for the firm, Klein, Hinds & Finke. At the same time Eggleston was also an assistant professor of cost accounting at the College of the City of New York, where in addition to cost accounting he also taught brokerage, bank accounting, and business systems.[2] Prior to his association with Klein, Hinds & Finke he had been with the Department of Finance of the City of New York.

Eggleston was a member of the New York State Society of Certified Public Accountants and also of the American Institute of Accountants.

---

[1]Rita Perine Merritt (ed.), The Accountants' Directory and Who's Who--1925 (New York: Prentice-Hall, Inc., 1925), p. 451.

Rita Perine (ed.), The Accountants' Directory and Who's Who--1920(New York: The Forty-Fifth Street Press, 1920), p. 382.

[2]By August, 1930, Eggleston had spent nearly twenty years as a lecturer on accounting at the College of the City of New York. This fact, noted by Kapp in his review of Eggleston's Modern Accounting Theory and Practice in the August, 1930, issue of The American Accountant, is unfortunately the latest biographical information that the present writer has been able to find.

28

B. Principal Contributions

As can easily be surmised from the foregoing comments, Eggleston, by reason of his proximity to business and businessmen, was primarily a writer of the practical order. This remains true despite the fact that the titles of several of his works might lead one to think otherwise.

Three of Eggleston's works will be discussed here, namely, Auditors' Reports and Working Papers, Modern Accounting Theory and Practice, and Wall Street Procedure. The first and third of these works appeared in 1929, while the second appeared in 1930. In noting the more significant accounting events for the year ending May, 1929, Tucker, writing in the May, 1929, issue of The American Accountant, listed Eggleston's first-mentioned work among some thirty-five others he had singled out as noteworthy. Like the other works, this also was the product of a man who had divided his time between teaching and practice. Thus the book itself was designed primarily for instructional use, being based on the theory that the best pedagogical method is to show how a thing is done by doing it. This work was designed to supplement the author's previous work Auditing Theory and Practice. Thus, the combination of the two works, by reason of the special stress laid on the procedural aspects of accounting, provided an excellent tool for instruction in accounting.

The second and third works listed above were two of sixteen works selected to form a list sent out for popular vote by a special committee of the Grand Council of Beta Alpha Psi, national fraternity of students of accounting. It is interesting to note that after the final tally of the popular vote, Eggleston's Wall Street Procedure placed among the first seven. This work was also the expansion in textbook form of subject matter contained in the author's lectures to his students at the College of the City of New York. Among other things, the highly specialized organization of the stockbroker's office and the procedure followed in the preparation of the answers to the New York stock-exchange ques-

tionnaire are thoroughly treated. According to one reviewer, the book was "a

highly practical, timely and valuable text, . . . both to the student and

professional accountant alike."[1]

Modern Accounting Theory and Practice, a two-volume treatise, served not

only as an excellent manual for the accounting teacher, but was also of very

real worth to the practising accountant who needed to be brought up to date on

the latest procedure in a wide number of fields. Various reviewers[2] were unani-

mous in noting that the author of this work, by reason of his many years both

as a lecturer on accounting and as a busy practising accountant with one of the

leading firms of New York, was indeed in a good position to present a text on

accounting which combined both the theories of accounting and the practical

applications of those theories.

Neither of the two volumes comprising this work was intended as a primer,

for both assumed a basic knowledge of bookkeeping and the principles of account-

ing. Both volumes occupied themselves with the procedural aspects of accounting

practise. The first was devoted to the more common problems of accounting,

particularly to the content of real accounts, while the second treated a series

of accounting subjects which were, according to the author, governed to a certain

---

[1] Elmer O. Stevens, Review of Wall Street Procedure, by DeWitt Carl Eggleston, The Journal of Accountancy, L, No. 1(July, 1930), 67.

[2] Wayne F. Gibbs, Review of Modern Accounting Theory and Practice, by DeWitt
Carl Eggleston, The Accounting Review, V, No. 4(December, 1930), 325-6

Edgar B. Kapp (ed.), Review of Modern Accounting Theory and Practice, by
DeWitt Carl Eggleston, The American Accountant, XV, No. 8(August, 1930), 376-7.

F. W. Thornton, Review of Modern Accounting Theory and Practice, by DeWitt
Carl Eggleston, The Journal of Accountancy, XLIX, No. 5(May, 1930), 384-5.

extent by the laws of the country; these subjects included corporate accounting, mergers, reorganizations, and income tax problems.

The two volumes were not, therefore, prolific reference sources on moot points. Rather they describe how accounting is done with a brief explanation of the reasons.

Paul-Joseph Esquerre

A. Biographical Sketch[1]

Paul-Joseph Esquerre was born at Gers, France, on May 16, 1872. He
studied at the Lyceum of Auch, the Academy of Toulouse and the University of
France, and held a B. es L. Degree. Prior to his entrance into the accounting
profession, Esquerre was a biologist and a bacteriologist. However, in 1911 he
became a licensed certified public accountant in the state of New York. Simul-
taneously he practiced accounting individually and served as head of the Post-
Graduate School of Accountancy in New York City. He was a member of the American
Institute of Accountants, the New York Society of Certified Public Accountants
and the American Society of Certified Public Accountants. Prior to his departure
from France he served in the French Army for three years as a member of the
Second Regiment of Zouaves. The late Homer S. Pace, for many years the editor
of the now non-existent The American Accountant and its predecessor The Pace
Student, has pointed out quite well the prominence which Esquerre held in the

---

[1]"Accountant Criticises Alternative Plan for Railroad Depreciation Accounting," The American Accountant, XIII, No. 10(October, 1928), 18.

"Advertisement," The American Accountant, XII, No. 5(June, 1927), 49.

Rita Perine Merritt (ed.), The Accountants' Directory and Who's Who--1925
(New York: Prentice-Hall, Inc., 1925), p. 456.

Rita Perine (ed.), The Accountants' Directory and Who's Who--1920(New
York: The Forty-Fifth Street Press, 1920), p. 385.

"Philosopher-Accountant Takes Inventory of Soul of Profession," The American Accountant, XIII, No. 7(July, 1928), 19.

field of American accountancy:

> Paul-Joseph Esquerre holds a unique place in American accountancy as a practitioner, author, teacher, philosopher. His humor, satire, and constructive thinking have enlivened many a meeting of the New York State Society of Certified Public Accountants, and his fame has extended far beyond the environs of the metropolis.[1]

B. Principal Contributions

As has already been implied, Esquerre, in addition to his regular practice and teaching chores, also did some writing. His first contribution to the field of accounting literature in this country, The Applied Theory of Accounts, originally appeared in 1914 and went through seven subsequent editions, five of which apparently belong to a revision of his initial volume. This work, as its title suggests, was very broad in scope, and for the most part consisted in the then conventional treatment of the various mechanisms and techniques of bookkeeping. However, one learns from various reviews[2] that in one instance especially Esquerre broke away from convention. Thus, in one chapter there appeared very valuable material for the practising accountant in a brief discussion of triple and quadruple systems of accounting, topics which the average business course often contemptuously ignored. Although his work was primarily a textbook, Esquerre managed quite well to steer away from the customary dogmatic nature of such books. In numerous instances the author directed pertinent criticisms against certain inconsistencies in accounting practice as it then existed. He

---

[1] Homer S. Pace, prefatory comments on Paul-Joseph Esquerre's address delivered before the Pittsburgh chapter of the Pennsylvania Institute of Certified Public Accountants. The American Accountant, XIII, No. 7(July, 1928), 19.

[2] W. R. Gray, Review of The Applied Theory of Accounts, by Paul-Joseph Esquerre, The American Economic Review, V, No. 2(June, 1915), 337-8.

W. H. L. (W. H. Lawton), Review of Applied Theory of Accounts, by Paul-Joseph Esquerre, The Journal of Accountancy, XXI, No. 4(April, 1916), 317.

made no claims without giving his reasons for so doing, and apparently presented a fair and clear consideration of the theory on which any controverted point was based. For example, he took issue with the time-honored rule used in the valuation of inventory, namely, cost or market, whichever is lower, and pointed out quite simply that if the object of the income statement is to show the actual profit on sales, then the actual cost of the goods sold must be the correct basis, not what they would cost at the present time or in a subsequent period. Perhaps the chief value of the work for the student of accounting practice lay in its exhaustive discussions of the specific media and processes of accounts.

In what seems to be the last of the several books which Professor Esquerre contributed to accounting literature, namely, his Accounting, which appeared in 1927, one can more readily see that his keen and ever-active mind was often ahead of the times. The book itself is largely theoretical. In fact, as one review expressed it:

> . . . In many places it carries theory to the point of being impractical--or perhaps merely inexpedient at the present time. But a wholesome disagreement with a provocative discussion is in itself ample reward for reading this book. . . . There is much . . . that should receive a full hearing, much that will probably find full acceptance in the years to come.[1]

Another review[2] also brings out this same point. It first states that this work is a plea to the accounting profession to get away from hide-bound tradition and rigid forms in auditing accounts and stating results, and that, as a matter of fact, the credit of being a pioneer along these lines is certainly due Esquerre for this work. Much more than a conventional textbook, this volume is in reality a study of the philosophy of accounting, consisting of a series of

---

[1]Review of Accounting, by Paul-Joseph Esquerre, The American Accountant, XII, No. 7(August, 1927), 50.

[2]W. H. Lawton, Review of Accounting, by Paul-Joseph Esquerre, The Journal of Accountancy, XLV, No. 3(March, 1928), 227-8.

philosophical discussions of the form and meaning of different phases of balance-sheets and financial statements on a much higher plane than is found in the ordinary text.

Furthermore, the reviews referred to above also point out several important items of accounting which have a value all their own. According to Lawton,[1] the most significant chapter of the book is that on "The Valuation of Inventories" wherein the author pays his respects to the rule of "cost or market," and contends, in the main, that actual cost is the only true and logical basis for determining the profit or loss on merchandise sold by a going concern. On the other hand, the first review mentioned above states quite positively that the most valuable material is located in the first part of the book wherein Esquerre condemns the usual form of balance sheet and income statement, another instance of his unwillingness to be tied down by tradition. While the usual balance sheet was classified according to the nature of its items, the author would have it divided rather according to the functions of the business. Thus, there would result two separate sections to the balance sheet labeled, respectively, "capital" and "operating." While this procedure was quite common to English accountants at the time, the idea was something of a novelty to American practitioners.

------

[1]_Ibid._

Harry Anson Finney

A. Biographical Sketch[1]

Harry Anson Finney was born in Postville, Iowa, November 19, 1886. He graduated from Fayette (Iowa) high schools. He then attended the University of Chicago, from which institution he received a Ph. B. Degree in 1913. The years 1915 and 1916 found him doing graduate work at Northwestern University. He also studied at the Walton School of Commerce in Chicago. He was granted a certified public accountant certificate by the state of Illinois in 1917. In this

---

[1]Jaques Cattell (ed.), Directory of American Scholars. 2d ed.(Lancaster, Pa.: The Science Press, 1951), p. 290.

"Contributors of Articles," The Accounting Review, XIX(1944), 480.

"Extensive Public Service Marks Record of Illinois Accountants," The American Accountant, XII, No. 4(May, 1927), 29.

Albert Nelson Marquis (ed.), Who's Who in America, Vol. XIII, 1924-25 (Chicago: A. N. Marquis & Company, 1924), p. 1150.

_____, Who's Who in America, Vol. XV, 1928-29(Chicago: A. N. Marquis & Company, 1928), p. 766.

_____, Who's Who in America, Vol. XVI, 1930-31(Chicago: A. N. Marquis & Company, 1930), p. 810.

Rita Perine Merritt (ed.), The Accountants Directory and Who's Who--1925 (New York: Prentice-Hall, Inc., 1925), p. 461.

Rita Perine (ed.), The Accountants' Directory and Who's Who--1920(New York: The Forty-Fifth Street Press, 1920), p. 390.

"University Notes," The Accounting Review, V, No. 3(September, 1930), 275.

Who's Who in America, Vol. XXVIII, 1954-55(Chicago: A. N. Marquis & Company, 1954), p. 868.

_____, Vol. XXVI, 1950-51(Chicago: A. N. Marquis & Company, 1950), p. 871.

connection it is of special interest that he was presented with a gold medal by the Illinois Society of Certified Public Accountants for making the highest grade in the state certified public accountant examination of the previous December. Finney also received the highest grade in an examination given by the American Institute of Accountants in May, 1919.

Finney began his teaching career as a high school commercial teacher. After that he spent some time as a professor of accounting at the Walton School of Commerce in Chicago. For the next twenty-five years, from September, 1920 until 1944, he served in the capacity of professor of accounting at Northwestern University, Evanston, Illinois.

However, Finney did not devote all his time to teaching. In 1923 he joined the Chicago branch of Haskins & Sells, certified public accountants, and remained with this firm for nearly five years. In the late 1920's he and H. P. Baumann formed their own firm of certified public accountants, Baumann, Finney & Company, of Chicago.

Finney is a member of the American Institute of Accountants, the Illinois Society of Certified Public Accountants(ex-president), the American Accounting Association, and the Delta Sigma Pi, Beta Gamma Sigma and Acacia fraternities. He was editor of the students' department of The Journal of Accountancy from 1920 until 1929 and has, as will be seen, contributed numerous books and periodical articles to accounting literature.

B. Principal Contributions

Professor Finney's works form a significant contribution to the field of accounting literature. This is especially true for one important phase of this field, namely, that of textbooks. In his writings Finney shows evidence of one of the tendencies which began to prevail in the textbook literature of the mid-twenties, namely, the tendency on the part of writers on principles to recognize and stress the underlying aims and purposes of accounting. Thus, one reviewer noted that several of his earliest works, namely, Consolidated Statements, which appeared in 1922, and also his two-volume treatise, Principles of Accounting, which appeared in 1923, the author succeeded quite well in actualizing the pedagogical principle of proceeding from the simple to the complex and little by little unfolding the subject matter in logical order.[1] Both of these works are characterized by a logical approach, thorough treatment, careful analysis, and precision in statement.

Limiting the discussion to the second book mentioned above, it is worthy of note that Finney incorporated into this two-volume work a feature which at that time seldom made its way into accounting textbook literature: an exhaustive treatment of the procedure for adjusting statements and accounts for accounting shortcomings of the past, and the various requirements of working papers by which such adjustments are analyzed and explained. According to Glover,[2] this book won a commendable position in the field as a textbook in advanced accounting and as a reference book for accountants, as was evidenced by the fact that during the short four years' interval between the first and revised editions it went through seven reprintings. Beights, in his review of the third edition of Principles of Accounting, Intermediate, said:

> For whether the text is liked or disliked, it will be admitted that this one book has wielded a very great influence on the accounting theory and practice in this country--perhaps more than any other one book.
> . . . .
> , . . . the text retains that force and authoritativeness which has long

---

[1]James P. Adams. Review of Principles of Accounting, Vols. I and II, by H. A. Finney, The American Association of University Instructors in Accounting. Papers and Proceedings, IX, No. 2(December, 1925), 157-8.

[2]Charles A. Glover, Review of Principles of Accounting, Rev. ed., Vols. I and II, by H. A. Finney, The Accounting Review, III, No. 4(December, 1928), 407-8.

made Mr. Finney's books "standards" in the field of accounting. . . . , it
will continue to be one of the outstanding texts in this field for some time
to come.[1]

In one of his later works, <u>Introduction to the Principles of Accounting</u>,
which appeared in 1932, Finney again apparently broke away from the traditional
manner of doing things by approaching the subject matter of this work via the
corporation rather than by way of the sole proprietorship. In this same treatise,
realizing that in elementary accounting courses too little attention had been
given to the recording phase of accounting, Finney laid special stress on every
student's getting thoroughly acquainted with the various steps of the bookkeeping cycle before he began the so-called theoretical study.

These works and others Finney wrote have, if only by reason of their many
editions, stood the test of time and have thus earned for their author a prominent place among the writers in accountancy not only during the latter third of
the first three decades of the twentieth century but at the present time as well

---

[1]D. M. Beights, Review of <u>Principles of Accounting, Intermediate</u>, 3d ed.,
by H. A. Finney, <u>The Accounting Review</u>, XXII, No. 1(January, 1947), 95.

Stephen Gilman

A. Biographical Sketch[1]

Stephen Gilman was born of Scotch lineage in Chicago, Illinois, June 3, 1887. He attended and graduated from the Madison, Wisconsin, High School, his parents apparently having moved to Madison a short time after his birth. He received his Bachelor of Science Degree from the University of Wisconsin in 1910. In the ensuing years he became a certified public accountant in several states, e.g., Wisconsin in 1916, and Ohio in 1919. For several years Gilman was engaged in engineering work. Later he became manager of the Credit Department of the Tennessee Coal, Iron and Railroad Company. At one time he was a member of the firm of Tanner, Gilman & Ellis, and was likewise a former vice-president of the Tanner-Gilman Schools.

By far the greater part of Gilman's life was centered around an institution named the International Accountants Society. Although the present writer has been unable to discover all the many capacities Gilman held in this organization, he has succeeded in finding definite indications that Gilman played a major role

[1]American Accounting Association, 1955 Membership Roster, (inside back cover).

"Contributors of Articles," The Accounting Review, XIX(1944), 480.

Rita Perine Merritt (ed.), The Accountants' Directory and Who's Who--1925 (New York: Prentice-Hall, Inc., 1925), p. 477.

Rita Perine (ed.), The Accountants' Directory and Who's Who--1920(New York: The Forty-Fifth Street Press, 1920), p. 403.

in it. At the beginning of the 1920's Gilman was chairman of the board and
director of this society, and by the mid-twenties he had become the vice-president. In 1943 and 1944 Gilman again served as vice-president and at the same
time held the position of educational director of the same society. According
to the 1955 Membership Roster of the American Accounting Association, Gilman
was still connected with the International Accountants Society at that late
date.

Gilman was a member of the American Statistical Association, the Illinois
Society of Certified Public Accountants, and the National Association of Cost
Accountants. Gilman was one of the initial members in the last mentioned organi-
zation, and shortly after its establishment in 1919 he served as a member of the
committees on Research and Education and also on Junior Membership. He was like-
wise a member of the Ohio Society of Certified Public Accountants and the Illi-
nois Institute of Accounts. He was among the early members of the American
Association of University Instructors in Accounting (now the American Accounting
Association), and today is numbered among that association's fifty-one Life
Members. Moreover, along with A. C. Littleton and C. R. Rorem, he served the
Association as editor of The Accounting Review from 1944 until 1946.

B. Principal Contributions

Among Gilman's contributions to accounting literature only two need be
mentioned here. The first, Analyzing Financial Statements, made its initial
appearance in 1925, and was followed by a revised edition in 1934. From various
reviews a rather good description of this work can be had.[1] In the years prior

---

[1]"Book Notices," Review of Analyzing Financial Statements, by Stephen Gilman, Harvard Business Review, IV(July, 1926), 509.

W. H. Lawton, Review of Analyzing Financial Statements, by Stephen Gilman,
The Journal of Accountancy, XLI, No. 6(June, 1926), 473-4.

to the appearance of Gilman's book interest in financial statement analysis had
been confined almost entirely to credit managers. In his work Gilman attempted
to cover the field in such a way that the needs of those others who were gradually learning to appreciate the importance of this subject might be filled.
Hence, in addition to the credit managers, Gilman had in mind general executives,
accounting officers, investors, and students of elementary accounting.

Many of the individuals included in the above enumeration, especially those
who made up the first three of the final four categories, were no longer content
with knowing the particular status of their respective enterprises at a given
date, but realized the need of asking themselves a further question, namely,
In what direction is the business drifting? The answer to this question lay in
a proper procedure and technique of analysing financial statements. Gilman
attempted to give his solution to this query by basing such an analysis not only
on the eight principal ratios then in common usage, but also by supplementing
this first step by the trend-percentage method of analyzation.

According to Prickett,[1] it is precisely in the discussion of the trend-
percentage method that the principal contribution of the book lies. In this method

J. E. McDonough, Review of Analyzing Financial Statements, by Stephen
Gilman, The American Economic Review, XVI, No. 4(December, 1926), 689-90.

Maurice E. Peloubet, Review of Analyzing Financial Statements, Rev. ed.,
by Stephen Gilman, The Journal of Accountancy, LXI, No. 3(March, 1936), 236.

A. L. Prickett, Review of Analyzing Financial Statements, by Stephen Gilman, The Accounting Review, I, No. 4(December, 1926), 95-6.

Robert Weidenhammer, Review of Analyzing Financial Statements, Rev. ed.,
by Stephen Gilman, The Accounting Review, IX, No. 4(December, 1934), 347-8.

[1]Prickett, loc. cit.

the items of the financial statement are first grouped logically in the usual manner. Then all the items of each group are shown for successive years in percentage relationship to the earliest year's balances and totals. Nevertheless, although this method and the ratio method lend themselves to using many formulas, the author is not led away by over-enthusiasm for a mere set of formulas. Again and again he reminds the reader that ratios and trends are not to be accepted blindly, and at the same time urges him always to exercise common sense.

In spite of the fact that the ever-present limitations which creep into every book that comes on the market did not escape this work, it is considered a pioneer in the field of financial statement analysis. Indeed, prior to its appearance the literature in this important phase of accounting was very scanty. Weidenhammer seems to have paid the highest tribute to Gilman's volume when he remarked that "the book deserves, to be called a classic in American accounting literature."[1]

The second work of Gilman's that warrants discussion here is his Accounting Concepts of Profit. This volume, which first appeared in 1939, was quite favorably received, a fact that is brought out clearly in several of the reviews written concerning it.[2]

Of primary value is the statement of Fiske[3] that Gilman is pioneering a

---

[1]Weidenhammer, loc. cit.

[2]Carman G. Blough, Review of Accounting Concepts of Profit, by Stephen Gilman, The Journal of Accountancy, LXIX, No. 6(June, 1940), 505.

W. P. Fiske, Review of Accounting Concepts of Profit, by Stephen Gilman, The American Economic Review, XXX, No. 2(June, 1940), 400-1.

W. A. Hosmer, Review of Accounting Concepts of Profit, by Stephen Gilman. This review was incorporated into Ross G. Walker's article, "Explorations in Accounting," Harvard Business Review, XVIII(Spring, 1940), 384-96.

[3]Fiske, loc. cit.

new area in this treatise. Blough seems to hint at the same idea in remarking that "this book is a novel departure from the usual accounting presentation. . . . Historical development has been intermingled with current controversial discussion. . . ."[1]

Further elucidation on these statements will perhaps help to clear up questions which might arise from the way they read at present. By emphasizing the importance of income treatment Gilman is in accord with one of the current trends in accounting thought, namely, the tendency to minimize the importance of the balance-sheet while at the same time placing a corresponding increase in emphasis upon the profit-and-loss statement. The excellent treatment afforded the section on inventories brings out quite well the importance of the author's method of analysis. He attempts to solve inventory problems primarily by reasoning deductively from premises and generalizations based upon them, reenforcing the premises by citations from authorities. Hence, the author has combined discussion of theoretical desirability with a fine recognition of practical expediency, since the problems themselves involve executive decisions in which both accounting and other factors are commingled. The book is therefore a valuable contribution toward a more thorough fulfilling of the responsibility of accounting in the determination of income.

---

[1] Blough, loc. cit.

Harry G. Guthmann

A. Biographical Sketch[1]

Harry George Guthmann was born in East Syracuse, New York, on December 16, 1896. He received his high school education at East Syracuse High School. He took his college training at Syracuse University and received his Bachelor of Arts Degree from that university in 1917. He then began postgraduate work at the New York University School of Commerce, and by 1920 had fulfilled the necessary requirements for and had been awarded an M.B.A. Degree. His third degree, a Ph. D., was conferred upon him in 1929 by the University of Chicago.

During the summers of 1914 and 1915 Guthmann worked as a clerk for the First National Bank in Syracuse. Later, in 1918 and 1919, he was a junior accountant with the firm of Madden and Reass in New York City. In 1919 he also served as an income tax deputy for the city of Newark, New Jersey.

Guthmann has spent the greater part of his life teaching. Almost immediately after he had received his A. B. Degree from Syracuse University in 1917, he began teaching there. He remained with his alma mater until 1922, during which time he held first the position of instructor in accounting and then that of

[1]Rita Perine Merritt (ed.), The Accountants' Directory and Who's Who--1925 (New York: Prentice-Hall, Inc., 1925), p. 490.

Rita Perine (ed.), The Accountants' Directory and Who's Who--1920(New York: The Forty-Fifth Street Press, 1920), p. 415.

Who's Who in America, Vol. XXVI, 1950-51(Chicago: A. N. Marquis & Company, 1950), p. 1089.

_____, Vol. XXVIII, 1954-55(Chicago: A. N. Marquis & Company, 1954), p. 1081.

assistant professor of finance. From 1922 to 1925 Guthmann was an associate

professor of business administration at the University of Texas. Since 1927 he

has been associated with Northwestern University; in 1935 he was elevated to the

position of professor of finance and in 1949 to that of Morrison Professor of

Finance.

Guthmann is a licensed certified public accountant in the state of New

Hampshire. At one time he was an associate member of the National Association

of Cost Accountants, a member of the American Association of University Instruc-

tors in Accounting, the Econometric Society and the American Association for the

Advancement of Science. Moreover, he served as Trustee for the Teachers In-

surance and Annuity Association from 1947 to 1951. He is presently a member of

the American Economic Association, the American Finance Association (president

in 1946), and the Phi Beta Kappa, Beta Alpha Psi, Beta Gamma Sigma, and Alpha

Kappa Psi fraternities.

B. Principal Contribution

Guthmann's principal contribution to accounting literature during the

first three decades of the present century is his The Analysis of Financial

Statements. This work originally came out in 1925, and since that time has gone

through several editions, including a Spanish edition which appeared in 1948.

This work, like Gilman's Analyzing Financial Statements, was the product of

changing times and changing ways in American accountancy. From various reviews,[1]

especially that of Couchman, one learns that at the time this book was written

[1]"Book Notices," Review of The Analysis of Financial Statements, by H. G.
Guthmann, Harvard Business Review, IV, No. 3(April, 1926), 380-1.

Charles B. Couchman, Review of The Analysis of Financial Statements, by
H. G. Guthmann, The Accounting Review, I, No. 4(December, 1926), 93-5.

A. W. Hanson, Review of The Analysis of Financial Statements, by H. G.
Guthmann, The American Economic Review, XVI, No. 2(June, 1926), 314-5.

business men were no longer satisfied to look upon financial statements in a hasty, hazy manner, but began to develop new and better methods for learning the true meaning of such statements if studied carefully. It was customary for communications written to the business world in a foreign language to be translated by experts who were familiar with the idioms and phraseologies of the language, so that the full meaning of the message might be stated correctly. Business men began to realize that financial statements, which attempt to express the conditions or the progress of the business, also need just as thorough and careful a translation if their full import is to be properly understood. Professor Guthmann's clear and concise explanations of the most efficient means for gaining the full significance of financial statements, coupled with an application of these means to particular types of business, seems to warrant its being deemed "a valuable contribution to the literature of this field."[1]

Guthmann's valuable addition to the literature on analyzing and interpreting financial statements was more than an explanation of the terms found in a balance sheet or a profit and loss account. The author explained the content of accounts in such a way that the credit man, the investor, and the business executive, not schooled in accounting, could interpret them.

The first part of the work deals with the general purpose of financial statements, their purpose, and their interpretation. This is followed by a section which sets forth analyses and interpretations of railroad companies, gas manufacturing corporations, hydro-electric power companies, mercantile and manufacturing corporations, mining companies, banks, insurance companies, and holding companies.

In his review of the revised edition of The Analysis of Financial

---

[1]Couchman, loc. cit.

<u>Statements</u>, Peloubet[1] noted that among the chapters devoted to special industries
that on mining was one of the best. While the author wisely refrained from dogmatic statements as to just what should and should not be included in the report
of a mining company, he did show the relation between the statistical information generally included in mining company reports to the financial statements,
and made it clear to the analyst or investor that it was unwise to attempt to
draw conclusions from either type of information considered separately.

The same reviewer also spoke very highly about the chapter on holding
companies, stating its value as an exposition of current practice in that field.
Aside from those criticism which inevitably accrue to a book which covers such a
wide field, Peloubet spoke very highly of this work, deeming it "an excellent
book on a difficult and widely inclusive subject . . ."[2]

Fisher's review[3] of the third edition of this work offers considerable information concerning Guthmann's standing among scholars of financial statement
analysis. Fisher quite interestingly reviewed two other similar works along
with that of Guthmann: Wall's <u>Basic Financial Statement Analysis</u>, and Myer's
<u>Financial Statement Analysis</u>. In this unique set-up the reviewer was able to
compare the three works. From a summary of the highlights of this three-in-one
review one can get a rather good view of Guthmann's principal tenets concerning
the analysis of financial statements.

Hence, Guthmann's position on the use of standard ratios, or common-size
ratios based upon industry averages, occupied a position between that of Wall

[1]Maurice E. Peloubet, Review of <u>Analysis of Financial Statements</u>, by Harry
G. Guthmann, <u>The Journal of Accountancy</u>, LXI, No. 2(February, 1936), 151-2.

[2]<u>Ibid</u>.

[3]Allan J. Fisher, Review of <u>Analysis of Financial Statements</u>, Third Edition,
by Harry G. Guthmann, <u>The Accounting Review</u>, XVIII, No. 3(July, 1943), 282-3.

and that of Myer. He included several tables incorporating such ratios, but carefully noted that such studies should be used with caution, since, although they might represent common practice, they still could be far from ideal practice. Like Myer, Guthmann was unimpressed with the concept of an index of ratios. A-mong the ratios which Guthmann did not favor were those of fixed tangible assets to net worth (which had been given a 15% weight in Wall's composite index), sales to tangible net worth (which had been given a 5% weight in Wall's index), fixed liabilities to total assets, current debt to fixed debt, and surplus to capital stock. Moreover, the ratio of plant turnover, not advocated by Myer but used by Wall, was accepted by Guthmann, though with some reservations. The sub-ject of term loans by commercial banks, with which Wall was so preoccupied, was mentioned only incidentally by Guthmann. Finally, in his discussion of holding companies he stressed the weakness of the unsupported consolidated report.

In summing up the features of the three works, the same reviewer (Fisher) remarked that, while Wall's book (written primarily from the viewpoint of the credit man) was the most personalized and stimulating of the three, and Myer's work (written from the standpoint of the accountant) was, because of its some-what new approach to statement analysis, rather limited in scope, Guthmann's work (written more from the standpoint of the business executive and the in-vestor), was the most scholarly and comprehensive.

CHAPTER II

Henry Rand Hatfield

A. Biographical Sketch[1]

Henry Rand Hatfield, the son of Rev. Robert M. and Elizabeth Ann (Taft) Hatfield, was born in Chicago, Illinois, on November 27, 1866. He received an A.B. Degree from Northwestern University in 1892 and a little over three decades later, in 1923, this same university conferred upon him an LL.D. Degree. Some

---

[1]"Accounting Hall of Fame," The Canadian Chartered Accountant, LXV, No. 4 (October, 1954), 182-3.

American Accounting Association, 1955 Membership Roster.

E. Burl Austin, "Association Notes," The Accounting Review, XXVI, No. 3 (July, 1951), 431-2.

"Dickinson, Hatfield Chosen for 1951 Awards at Ohio State's Hall of Fame," The Journal of Accountancy, XCII, No. 2(August, 1951), 135.

Fourth International Congress on Accounting, 1933, Proceedings. (London: Gee & Company, Ltd., 1933), p. xxi.

Wilmer L. Green, History and Survey of Accountancy(Brooklyn: Standard Text Press, 1930), p. 134.

Henry Rand Hatfield, "Surplus and Dividends," (1941-1942 Arthur Lowes Dickinson Lecture). (Cambridge, Mass.: Harvard University Press, 1943), 10pp.

Albert Nelson Marquis (ed.), Who's Who In America, Vol. XIII, 1924-25 (Chicago: A. N. Marquis & Company, 1924), p. 1493.

Rita Perine Merritt (ed.), The Accountants' Directory and Who's Who--1925 (New York: Prentice-Hall, Inc., 1925), p. 498.

Rita Perine (ed.), The Accountants' Directory and Who's Who--1920(New York: The Forty-Fifth Street Press, 1920), p. 420.

"University Notes," The Accounting Review, II, No. 1(March, 1927), 72; IV, No. 3(September, 1929), 209; XIV, No. 1(March, 1939), 91; XIV, No. 2(June, 1939), 201; XVII, No. 3(July, 1942), 333.

five years after receiving the A.B. Degree, i.e., in 1897, Hatfield earned a Ph.D. Degree at the University of Chicago. He was also possessor of a second LL.D. Degree, conferred upon him by the University of California in 1940.

Prior to entering the teaching profession, and even before he attended college, Hatfield spent the years 1885(6) to 1890 in the municipal bond business. He began his teaching career as an instructor in political economy at Washington University, where he remained from 1894 until 1898. He then moved to the University of Chicago, serving that institution first in the capacity of an instructor from 1898 to 1902, then as assistant professor and dean of the College of Commerce and Administration from 1902 until 1904. Professor Hatfield next moved to the University of California. He served this university in many capacities: first, as an associate professor of accounting from 1904 until 1909, then as a professor from 1909 to 1937, at which time he was promoted to professor emeritus, the position he held until the day of his death. During his many years teaching at the University of California Professor Hatfield served as dean of the College of Commerce for the years 1909-1920, 1927-1928, and also as dean of the faculties in 1916, 1917-1918, 1920-1923. According to Murphy,[1] Hatfield was responsible for the excellent accounting library at the University of California. She pointed out that he was the best example of the work of a single individual in building up an all-inclusive library for students of accounting. Because of his zeal in seeking out both rare and modern treatises in accounting the accounting library at the University of California finds no parallels on other campuses.

Furthermore, Hatfield was one of the few outstanding men in accounting to be chosen as a Dickinson Lecturer, being appointed as the 1941-1942 lecturer by the Harvard Graduate School of Business Administration. He responded to this

[1]Mary E. Murphy, "Libraries for Students of Accounting," The Accounting Review, XXIV, No. 4(October, 1948), 420-1.

privilege by delivering two lectures (on surplus and dividends) at the Harvard Graduate School of Business Administration on the twenty-first and twenty-third days of April, 1942.

In addition to his primary duties as a professor, Hatfield found time for other important matters. He served as president of Berkeley, California, Commission of Charities during the war years 1914 to 1918. At about this same time, in 1918, he served as Director of the Division of Planning and Statistics, War Industries Board. In 1929 he spent several of the summer months in Europe attending the International Congress on Commercial Education at Amsterdam, and on his return to the States in autumn of the same year he attended the Accountants' Congress held in New York. Together with Professor Himmelblau he was sent by the American Association of University Instructors in Accounting as a delegate to the Fourth International Congress on Accounting, which was held in London in 1933.

Hatfield was among the men who founded the American Association of University Instructors in Accounting, and ably served this association in its infancy, the first two years (1917 and 1918) as first vice-president, and the third year (1919) as president. He was also a member of the American Economic Association, and served as its vice-president in 1918. He was likewise a member of the Beta Theta Pi and Phi Beta Kappa fraternities, having served the latter as a senator from 1923 until 1928. Hatfield was the author of several books, two of which shall be discussed subsequently. He was also a rather frequent contributor both to American and foreign periodicals. Professor Hatfield died on Christmas Day, 1945, almost a month after his seventy-ninth birthday.

B. Principal Contributions

Although, as has been indicated, Hatfield contributed much to accounting as a teacher, he is perhaps better known as an author of works on accounting. The following discussion will attempt to demonstrate the truth of this statement. His first work, Modern Accounting, which appeared in 1909, can be considered a classic, and this for several reasons. In the first place, as has been seen in the Introduction to this dissertation, Littleton mentioned this work of Hatfield's among those appearing in the first decade of the present century, and noted that these words "may be said to mark the real beginning of American contributions"[1] to the field of accounting literature. Further proof of the excellence of Hatfield's treatise comes from the fact that the date of its writing was included in a chronological list of "Historical Dates in Accounting,"[2] as one of those dates which seemed to be significant in the development of accounting as it is known today. In his review of Modern Accounting over forty-five years ago, Walton termed it a "very excellent work" and remarked that the best evidence of his appreciation of the book perhaps lay in the fact that he recommended it to students then in advanced accounting in the School of Commerce of Northwestern University "as the best book they could obtain for collateral reading."[3] What may be perhaps the finest tribute paid to this work of Hatfield's was rendered by Dolge when, during the course of his delivery of the presentation address of the first John F. Forbes Medal (a gold medal awarded the candidate who attained the highest record each year in the certified public accountant examinations in California), he remarked: "Our beloved Dr. Hatfield set a high example many years ago in his scholarly 'Modern Accounting' and thus influenced the great flood of accounting literature which followed that epoch-making treatise. . . ."[4] A final factor determining Modern Accounting's worth to the field of American accounting literature is the fact that it went through nearly ten editions before the revised edition discussed below appeared in 1927.

---

[1]Littleton, op. cit., p. 12.

[2]The Accounting Review, XXIX, No. 3(July, 1954), 490.

[3]Seymour Walton, Review of Modern Accounting, by Henry Rand Hatfield, Ph.D., The Journal of Accountancy, X, No. 3(September, 1910), 387.

[4]"First Award of John F. Forbes Medal Made in California," The American Accountant, XIV, No. 2(February, 1929), 114.

The second work of Hatfield's to be discussed here is his <u>Accounting, Its Principles and Problems</u>. This treatise was actually a revision of his earlier classic, <u>Modern Accounting</u>, and, as Jackson remarked,[1] this work was not like modern fiction, written in a very abbreviated period of time, but appeared only when it could come forth a finished product of research and genuine scholarship. With scholarship the author combined a vision and literary style quite unusual in the literature of accounting.

From other reviews[2] one can get a better general picture of this volume. The work is an exceedingly intelligent one on accounting theory and is not to be taken lightly. Unpretentious, it sets forth in a clear, simple style the important phases of accounting. The author's method of presentation is easy to follow and grasp. Among its outstanding characteristics are frequent references to court decisions to illustrate the problems discussed. Another noteworthy feature is the eclectic nature of the volume. In many instances Hatfield gives the different viewpoints of several authorities on a given point and then proceeds with his own conclusion. Moreover, his comments and criticisms on the writings of others are tempered and for the most part convincing. He had added brief but adequate bibliographies at the end of each chapter to permit the reader to supplement his own work and to reach the authorities which he himself used.

Perhaps it was because he had this work in mind that Green included Hatfield's name in a list of thirteen writers cited as "the leading American authors who have contributed representative works on accounting during the last thirty

[1] J. Hugh Jackson, Review of <u>Accounting, Its Principles and Problems</u>, by Henry Rand Hatfield, <u>The Journal of Accountancy</u>, XLIV, No. 4(October, 1927), 308-9.

[2] Review of <u>Accounting, Its Principles and Problems</u>, by Henry Rand Hatfield, Ph.D., <u>The American Accountant</u>, XII, No. 4(May, 1927), 50.

A. W. Hanson, Review of <u>Accounting, Its Principles and Problems</u>, by Henry Rand Hatfield, <u>The American Economic Review</u>, XVII, No. 4(December, 1927), 714-5.

R. H. Montgomery, Review of <u>Accounting, Its Principles and Problems</u>, by Henry Rand Hatfield, <u>The Accounting Review</u>, II, No. 2(June, 1927), 189-93.

years (i.e., 1900-1930--mine) . . ."[1] The periodical, The American Accountant,
likewise cited the value of this work when it remarked that Hatfield "has made
a scholarly contribution to accountancy which will be a credit to himself and
to his profession."[2]

The truth of these statements was adequately proved when almost a year
after Hatfield's work appeared Beta Alpha Psi, the professional and honorary
fraternity for college students specializing in accounting, bestowed honor on
Hatfield by presenting him an award of merit as the author of the most outstanding contribution to the literature of accounting for the year ended May 1, 1928.
The award presented to Dean Hatfield was a parchment scroll, setting forth in
simple language an appreciation of his Accounting, Its Principles and Problems,
and was presented to him at a gathering in San Francisco which took the form of
a dinner on December 7, 1928. At this assemblage an officer of the fraternity
paid the following tribute to Hatfield:

> Without detracting in the least from the high merit of a number of
> other books of the year, it seems particularly fitting to express thus
> publicly an appreciation of this particular book, because in so doing one
> naturally thinks also of the man himself and of his work during the years
> past. He is not only dean of the faculties in his own university, but by
> common acclaim is dean of the teachers of accounting in this country as
> well. His "Modern Accounting" would in its day undoubtedly have brought
> its author a similar award had there been such a thing. As a scholar only
> this need be said of Dean Hatfield: he is practically the only American
> writer on accounting to show any evidence of a knowledge of continental
> European accounting literature, and one of the very first to recognize, and
> make use of the fact, that much of value and interest to students of account-
> ing is to be found in the decisions of the law courts.
>
> The executive council of the fraternity is agreed that the award is
> well placed, and to judge by the expressed choice of a large number of

---

[1]Green, op. cit., p. 134. The remaining twelve writers included C. E.
Sprague, Henry Metcalf, C. E. Woods, J. Lee Nicholson, Wm. Morse Cole, J. R.
Wildman, W. H. Bell, R. H. Montgomery, P. J. Esquerre, H. A. Finney, A. H.
Church, and R. B. Kester.

[2]Loc. cit.

practitioners and teachers as well, the selection accords with general opinion very well.[1]

---

[1]"Award of Merit for Hatfield Book Should Stimulate Authors," The American Accountant, XIV, No. 1(January, 1929), 28-9. To obviate questions concerning the procedure in selecting the best work contributed to the field of accounting literature during those particular years in which this contest affects the individuals discussed in this dissertation, it would perhaps be apropos here to set down this procedure as discussed in the article previously mentioned in this footnote. The article, page 29, states: "The procedure followed in making the award was this: First a list was obtained, from publishing houses, of the books on accounting put out in the year ended May 1, 1928. The list was printed on a reply post card, and sent to a large number of teachers of accounting and practising accountants, with the request that they indicate the books of the list they had read and that they express their choice(first, second, and third) of the most notable contributions. The replies received were tabulated, and the six books receiving the highest recognition were then named to the fraternity's grand council of six members, without indicating the results of the popular voting. The members of the council were given the summer months in which to familiarize themselves with the six books, and make a selection of the winner from among the six. In the autumn the council members reported their choice to the president of the council.

"In the popular balloting, Dean Hatfield's book was very definitely the first choice. The fraternity's council also came to the same conclusion without knowledge of the results of the other balloting except the titles of the first six books. . . .

"It is interesting to note that the first list, sent out by post card, contained the names of twenty-six works. It is an encouraging sign that in a single year there should be published twenty-six works on accounting subjects. No better indication could be asked that the profession of accountancy is growing up. . . ."

David Himmelblau

A. Biographical Sketch[1]

David Himmelblau was born in Dubuque, Iowa, on May 19, 1889. He won a B.A.

Degree at the State University of Iowa in 1909 and a B.B.A. Degree at North-

western University in 1914. He became a certified public accountant in the state

of Illinois in 1913 and in the state of Wisconsin in 1917.

---

[1]American Accounting Association, 1955 Membership Roster.

E. Burl Austin, "Association Notes," The Accounting Review, XXIV, No. 2 (April, 1949), 219-20; XXVIII, No. 1(January, 1953), 142; XIX, No. 3(July, 1954), 522.

Jaques Cattell (ed.), Directory of American Scholars. 2d ed. (Lancaster, Pa.: The Science Press, 1951), p. 421.

Fourth International Congress on Accounting, 1933, Proceedings. (London: Gee & Co. Publishers, Ltd., 1933), p. xxi.

Rita Perine Merritt (ed.), The Accountants' Directory and Who's Who--1925 (New York: Prentice-Hall, Inc., 1925), p. 508.

National Association of Cost Accountants, Year Book, 1936, Proceedings of the Seventeenth International Cost Conference(Cincinnati, Ohio, 1936), p. 103.

_____, 1951 Conference Proceedings(Chicago, Ill., 1951), p. 104.

Rita Perine (ed.), The Accountants' Directory and Who's Who--1920(New York: The Forty-Fifth Street Press, 1920), p. 426.

Frank P. Smith, "Association Notes," The Accounting Review, XXIII, No. 1 (January, 1948), 104.

"University Notes," The Accounting Review, I, No. 3(September, 1926), 100; II, No. 2(June, 1927), 209; III, No. 3(September, 1928), 330; IV, No. 3(September, 1929), 210; XIII, No. 4(December, 1938), 438; XIV, No. 3(September, 1939), 330.

"Views of Profession With Respect to Depreciation Clearly Stated," The American Accountant, XIV, No. 10(October, 1929), 538.

Who's Who in America, Vol. XXVI, 1950-51(Chicago: A. N. Marquis & Company, 1950), p. 1248.

Himmelblau began the first of his many years in teaching accounting in 1912(13) when he joined the accounting staff of the Northwestern University School of Commerce. From 1913 to 1915 he served as an instructor, from 1915 to 1917 as an assistant professor, and in 1919 was promoted to a full professor. In 1922 he was appointed chairman of the School of Commerce, in which capacity he served for almost thirty-five years. Himmelblau retired from Northwestern at the end of the 1954 spring term after forty-one years of service, most of which he spent as chairman of the Department of Accounting.

Himmelblau received his first practical experience in the Navy Department from 1917 to 1919, where he was in charge of the Cost and Financial Investigations Section of the Accounting Division of the Bureau of Supplies and Accounts. When he entered naval service in November, 1917, as an expert accountant, he held the rank of junior lieutenant, and less than a year later, in September, 1918, he was advanced to the rank of lieutenant. During his sojourn with the United States Navy Himmelblau compiled a Manual for Cost and Financial Investigations for that department.

After the war Himmelblau became a partner in the firm of Arthur Andersen & Company, where he served until 1922 when the firm of David Himmelblau & Company was established. He has remained a senior partner in this latter firm since its founding.

Professor Himmelblau was an active member in many accounting associations. He joined the American Association of University Instructors in Accounting while it was still a relatively young association. He served as its third vice-president in 1925, 1926, and 1927, as first vice-president in 1928, and as president in 1929. It was in September of this same year that Himmelblau delivered a paper entitled "Annuity Method of Depreciation Most Useful in Cost Accounting" to those assembled in New York for the Third International Congress on Accounting. In 1933 he and Professor Henry Rand Hatfield were sent as delegates of the American Association of University Instructors in Accounting to the Fourth International Congress on Accounting held in London.

Himmelblau is also a member of the Illinois Society of Public Accountants, having served as its president in 1929. He is a charter member of the National Association of Cost Accountants, a member of the American Institute of Accountants, and a member of the American Economic Association. He is likewise a former member and director of the American Society of Certified Public Accountants. He has served all of these societies and associations in many roles, especially by the timely and provocative addresses which he delivered at many of their chapter meetings.

B. Principal Contributions

Having briefly reviewed Professor Himmelblau's experiences as teacher and practitioner, it is now expedient to discuss his capacities as an editor, compiler, and especially, author. Himmelblau is both editor of and partial contributor to the Complete Accounting Course, by members of the Department of Accounting, Northwestern University School of Commerce. As a compiler not only was he responsible for his Manual for Cost and Financial Investigations for the United States Navy, but also, several years earlier, he published a compilation of certified public accountant problems and solutions entitled Solutions to 1914 Illinois C.P.A. Problems and Questions.

In addition to being co-author of several of the volumes comprising the Complete Accounting Course, Professor Himmelblau has written several books and many periodical articles. His work, Auditors' Certificates, which appeared in 1927, was among the top six books according to a popular vote taken under the auspices of the Beta Alpha Psi Accounting Fraternity in 1929, and has therefore been singled out for discussion here. Reviews of this work were quite favorable. For example, one reviewer remarked that

the early literature of American accounting has been broad and general in its treatment of the subject; thus we have had books dealing with the "principles of accounting," with "cost accounting," with "auditing," and so on. . . . But with the development of the science of the profession of accounting there has also come a demand for more specialized and technical books, . . . Professor Himmelblau's new book is an important addition to this specialized literature.[1]

This book was apparently one of the first to devote to the auditor's certificate the space and attention which it deserved. Indeed, it is quite true that this subject had long been crying for scientific analysis. Hence, Himmelblau, in publishing this fine scientific treatise, not only filled in a definite lacuna, but at the same time "made a valuable contribution to accounting literature."[2]

---

[1] J. Hugh Jackson, Review of Auditors' Certificates, by David Himmelblau, The Accounting Review, II, No. 4(December, 1927), 413-14.

Review of Auditors' Certificates, by David Himmelblau, The American Accountant, XII, No. 5(June, 1927), 48.

Roy Bernard Kester

A. Biographical Sketch[1]

Roy B. Kester was born in Cameron, Missouri, on September 11, 1882, and
was educated there, first in the public grammar and high schools, and then at
Missouri Wesleyan College. It was from this latter institution that he won an
A.B. Degree in 1902. Kester also studied at Colorado College in Colorado Springs
in 1906, and at the University of Chicago in 1907. He took further studies at
Denver University, where he received both B.C.S. (1911) and M.A. (1912) degrees,
and at Columbia University, where he received a Ph.D. Degree in 1919. In 1941
Baker University of Baldwin City, Kansas, presented him with an LL.D. Degree.

Kester began his teaching career as an instructor in mathematics at
Missouri Wesleyan Academy and College from 1902 until 1905. The years 1907 to
1915 found Kester in two more teaching positions, first at the East Denver High
School, and then at the University of Denver. From 1915 to 1949 Kester taught

---

[1]American Accounting Association, 1955 Membership Roster.

E. Burl Austin, "Association Notes," The Accounting Review, XXIII, No. 2
(April, 1948), 216.

Rita Perine Merritt (ed.), The Accountants' Directory and Who's Who--1925
(New York: Prentice-Hall, Inc., 1925), p. 535.

Rita Perine (ed.), The Accountants' Directory and Who's Who--1920(New York:
The Forty-Fifth Street Press, 1920), p. 444.

"University Notes," The Accounting Review, XIII, No. 4(December, 1938), 438.

"Varying View-Points on Principles of Valuation Presented," The American
Accountant, XIV, No. 10(October, 1929), 550.

Who's Who in America, Vol. XXVI, 1950-51(Chicago: A. N. Marquis & Company,
1950), pp. 1476-7.

at the Columbia University School of Business, serving twenty-seven of those years as a full professor of accounting. It was at Columbia that in 1936 he developed the College of Accountancy as a unit of the School of Business.

Kester also spent some time as an accounting practitioner. For a relatively short time, from 1911 to 1915, he was in the part time practice of public accounting in Denver, and was admitted to practice as a certified public accountant in Colorado in 1914. Later he was associated with the Ronald Press Company and with Boyce, Hughes & Farrell, in New York. Since 1917 he has served in the capacity of a consulting accountant.

Kester is a member of the National Association of Cost Accountants, having served as its Director of Research and Publications from 1925 to 1928. He is also a member of the American Institute of Accountants, the American Accounting Association, which he served as vice-president from 1922 to 1924 and as president in 1925, during which time the Association was still the American Association of University Instructors in Accounting, the Colorado State Society of Certified Public Accountants, of which he is an honorary life member, the New York State Society of Certified Public Accountants, having served on its Board of Directors from 1944 to 1947, and the Controllers Institute of America. Kester is likewise a member of several fraternities, namely, Beta Gamma Sigma, Acacia and Alpha Kappa Psi (past Grand President). It is worthy of note, in connection with the last named fraternity, that on December 15, 1947, Professor Kester was honored with a testimonial dinner at the University Club of Columbia by business leaders, fellow professors, and students. It was on this occasion that he was presented with the Alpha Kappa Psi Gold Award[1] for distinguished service to the fraternity.

[1]This award, established at the 1933 convention of Alpha Kappa Psi in Chicago, is a service award bestowed upon members for extraordinary services rendered the fraternity or its chapters. Cf. Alvan E. Duerr (ed.), Baird's Manual American College Fraternities, 14th ed. (The Collegiate Press George Banta Publishing Co., 1940), pp. 382-4.

In addition to his present membership in many societies and associations, it should be mentioned that Kester was a one-time member of the American Statistical Association, and of the Colorado State Board of Certified Public Accountants in 1914 and 1915, during which latter year he served as president.

B. Principal Contributions

Kester's contributions to accounting literature have been voluminous. Here, however, a discussion of his Accounting Theory and Practice will suffice, for the date of the appearance of the first of this three-volume work, in spite of its being Kester's first major publication, has subsequently been regarded as a date significant in the development of American accounting as it is known today.[1]

By consulting various reviews on the original and subsequent editions of this treatise one can learn not only its general characteristics but also the reason for its being held in such high esteem.[2]

[1] "Historical Dates in Accounting," The Accounting Review, XXIX, No. 3(July, 1954), 491.

[2] Philip H. Hensel, Review of Accounting Theory and Practice, Vol. II, by Roy B. Kester, The Accounting Review, V, No. 4(December, 1930), 335-6.

W. H. Lawton, Review of Accounting Theory and Practice, 2nd ed. rev., by Roy B. Kester, The Journal of Accountancy, XLI, No. 5(May, 1926), 390-2.

_____, Review of Accounting Theory and Practice-Advanced Accounting. 3rd rev. ed., by Roy B. Kester, The Journal of Accountancy, LVI, No. 6(December, 1933), 473-4.

_____, Review of Accounting Theory and Practice, Vol. I, 3rd ed. rev. and enlgd. by Roy B. Kester, The Journal of Accountancy, L, No. 2(August, 1930), 149-50.

_____, Review of Accounting Theory and Practice, by Roy B. Kester, The Journal of Accountancy, XXIV, No. 6(December, 1917), 488-90.

Archie M. Peisch, Review of Accounting Theory and Practice, Vol. II, 2nd ed. rev., by Roy B. Kester, The Accounting Review, I, No. 2(June, 1926), 90.

Clinton H. Scovell, Review of Accounting Theory and Practice, by Roy B. Kester, The American Economic Review, IX, No. 4(December, 1919), 830-1.

In order to avoid serious complications which might easily arise in a
general discussion of a three-volume work, it would perhaps be well to mention
that the first volume was a first-year text and was known as <u>Principles of
Accounting</u>, the second a second-year text known as <u>Advanced Accounting</u>, and the
third, a third-year text known as <u>Accounting Applications to Various Forms of
Industry</u>. In the first volume Kester aimed to provide the student with that
minimum of accounting which he (the author) rightly regarded as of equal importance with the minimum of economics demanded in the education of business or
professional men. With such an approach it was only logical to present the
results of accounting before the methods. Thus, balance sheets and profit and
loss statements precede double entry and similar technical details. In other
words, the book dealt with everyday accounting needs in a practical manner.
According to Scovell this treatise was "a creditable and practical result of
sound preparation and good teaching experience."[1]

As an author of textbooks Kester apparently was always conscious of the
many changes going on in the accounting field. This very fact is mentioned in a
review of the third edition of the first volume of the work under discussion.[2]
Thus, Kester, in the third edition of this volume, made clear the growing importance of managerial control through accounts. A most noticeable change from the
earlier editions of this treatise was the inclusion of chapters on the manufacturing corporation and the voucher system, which had formerly been treated in
the second volume of the series--surely a significant indication of rising
standards for college students in the first year course. The author's attitude
toward his reading public seems to be even more significant. In this edition he
is speaking primarily to business executives instead of students, for by this
time the executive was practically compelled to acquire some knowledge of the

---

[1]Scovell, <u>loc. cit.</u>

[2]Lawton, <u>op. cit.</u>, L, No. 2, p. 149.

subject for himself to be sure that he was getting the information he should expect from his trained accountants.

The second volume of Kester's excellent work, designated as a textbook for second-year students, dealt chiefly with the problems of valuation and presentation incident to the preparation of the balance sheet and statement of operations. Like the first volume it went through several thorough revisions. Speaking of the second revised edition Peisch has remarked that "in every respect the work is a valuable addition to the present store of accounting text material and should bring great credit to its able author."[1]

Lawton, after a somewhat thorough examination of this same edition of Advanced Accounting as a college text, notes quite clearly that

> for the practitioner it is more than that. It is a real study of accounting theory and practice in the light of the latest thought, written by one who evidently delights in his work and knows how to express himself. For logical arrangement, clearness of exposition and freedom from unnecessary irrelevance I have read nothing better. Being fairly well "fed up" with accounting literature in this line I feel entitled to speak with some conviction. . . ."[2]

In writing the third volume of the series, Accounting Applications to Various Forms of Industry, Kester collaborated with many others. Although this volume has been reprinted several times, it has never been revised.

---

[1] Peisch, loc. cit.

[2] Lawton, op. cit., XLI, No. 5, p. 392.

Joseph Jerome Klein

A. Biographical Sketch[1]

Joseph Jerome Klein, author, accountant, and lawyer, was born in New York
City on April 4, 1884. Before pursuing higher studies he attended the New York
public schools. He secured a B.S. Degree from the College of the City of New
York in 1906, with election to Phi Beta Kappa. He also won M.A. and Ph.D. degrees from New York University in the years 1909 and 1910 respectively. In 1911
he became a certified public accountant in the state of New York. He earned his
final degree, an LL.B, from Fordham University in 1923. That same year he became
a member of the New York Bar.

[1]American Institute of Accountants Fiftieth Anniversary Celebration(Concord, New Hampshire: The Rumford Press, 1938), p. xiii.

Allen Chaffee, "Dr. Joseph J. Klein, C.P.A.," The Pace Student, XI, No. 7
(June, 1926), 3-4.

Albert Nelson Marquis (ed.), Who's Who in America, Vol. XIII, 1924-25
(Chicago: A. N. Marquis & Company, 1924), p. 1868.

Rita Perine Merritt (ed.), The Accountants' Directory and Who's Who--1925
(New York: Prentice-Hall, Inc., 1925), 538.

"New York Society to Have Anniversary Dinner," The American Accountant,
III, No. 3(April, 1927), 48.

"New York State Society of C.P.A.'s Elects Officers," The Pace Student,
IX, No. 8(July, 1924), 123.

Rita Perine (ed.), The Accountants' Directory and Who's Who--1920(New York:
The Forty-Fifth Street Press, 1920), p. 447.

"Views of Profession with Respect to Depreciation Clearly Stated," The
American Accountant, XIV, No. 10(October, 1929), 540.

Who's Who in America, Vol. XXVI, 1950-51(Chicago: A. N. Marquis & Company,
1950), p. 1504.

Toward the end of the first decade of the present century, after graduation from college, Klein began teaching. He began by teaching business subjects in the high schools of new York City and also doing some lecturing at New York University. In 1911, becoming aware that as yet there were no available organized means of training commercial teachers, Klein was led to organize the first course in the subject at the College of the City of New York. Although Klein taught at City College most of his life, apparently in these early years he seems to have served not only City College but also New York University. Thus, before he had settled down permanently with City College and set up the course for training commercial teachers, he spent some time as a special lecturer and organizer of the municipal accounting lectures at the New York University School of Commerce, Accounts and Finance. Since 1914 Klein has been with the College of the City of New York, serving as a lecturer on commercial education in 1914 and 1915, on auditing and accounting systems from 1916 to 1918, and on Federal and New York State Income Tax Law and Procedure from 1919 to 1923. Since 1928 he has been an associate professor of taxation.

During the World War Klein served as an expert on the Council for National Defense, War Industries Board, in 1917 and 1918. He was also a volunteer expert for Red Cross drives and United War Work. During World War II he served as an expert consultant with the War Department and also as chairman of the price adjustment section of the North Atlantic Division, United States' Engineers, War Department, from 1942 to 1944. He is former editor of the federal and state taxes department of the New York Globe and associated newspapers. He is a senior partner of the firms of Klein, Hinds & Finke, certified public accountants, and of Klein, Finke & Austin, attorneys.

In 1950 Klein was a trustee-at-large for the New York Federation of Jewish Philanthropies. He is a former member of the Board of Higher Education for the City of New York and also of the American Society of Certified Public Accountants.

He is an honorary member of the American Institute of Accountants, a member and past president of the New York State Society of Certified Public Accountants, a member of the American Accounting Association, and the Accountants Club of America, Inc. Klein is also a member of the New York Adult Education Council, the National Tax Association, the Tax Institute, the Academy of Political Science, the Commerce and Industry Association, the American and New York State Bar Associations, the New York County Lawyer's Association, the Trade and Commercial Bar Association, Phi Beta Kappa, and various other clubs, associations, and fraternities.

B. Principal Contributions

In order to evaluate Klein as an author it will be necessary once more to rely on what his contemporaries wrote concerning several of his more noted works. In selecting the two books to be discussed here, namely, Elements of Accounting and Federal Income Taxation, it was necessary to consult reviews of several other of Klein's works to determine which books seemed to receive highest praise and had such merits as insured their continued use by teachers and students for many years after their publication. It was only after this preparatory work that the two works mentioned above were selected for discussion.

The first work, which originally appeared in 1913, and went through four or five subsequent editions, in the mind of its author was to serve as an introductory text for colleges and universities.[1] The work was written while its

---

[1]This information, like that given in connection with the other individuals treated in this dissertation, is taken almost entirely from book reviews; for discussions of the present work, cf.:

W. T. Jackman, Review of Elements of Accounting, by Joseph J. Klein, The American Economic Review, III, No. 4(December, 1913), 924-6.

Review of Elements of Accounting, by Joseph J. Klein, The Journal of Political Economy, XXI, No. 9(November, 1913), 877-8.

Earl A. Saliers, Review of Elements of Accounting, by Joseph J. Klein, The Journal of Accountancy, XVI, No. 2(August, 1913), 167.

author was a member of the faculty of New York University School of Commerce, Accounts, and Finance, and because of his experience there, coupled with assistance received from many men then prominent in the accounting profession, he was able to produce a text which apparently went far in attaining his principal purpose in writing: to bridge the chasm then existing between bookkeeping and accounting. According to Saliers[1] this book occupied "a place midway between the many elementary treatises, such as Rowe's Bookkeeping and Accountancy on the one hand, and the more advanced works, of which Hatfield's Modern Accounting is typical." According to Jackman,

> each step in the work is amply exemplified by concrete problems, so that not a single point if left in the dark. This, in such a subject, is highly commendable, . . . But, all in all, this is probably the simplest and best text that has yet appeared for the purpose it is intended to serve.[2]

In view of the above comments, it seems safe to conclude that Elements of Accounting was "a valuable contribution to accounting . . ."[3]

The second work, Federal Income Taxation, was selected for discussion principally because in the May, 1929, issue of The American Accountant, Tucker, on page 253, listed it among some thirty-five "noteworthy books" which appeared that year. Once more information about the book comes from pertinent contemporary reviews.[4] These reviews fully confirmed Tucker's choice. Klein's long

---

[1] Ibid.

[2] Jackman, loc. cit.

[3] Saliers, loc. cit.

[4] Edgar B. Kapp (ed.), Review of Federal Income Taxation, by Joseph J. Klein, The American Accountant, XIV, No. 4(April, 1929), 222-3.

E. L. Kohler, Review of Federal Income Taxation, by Joseph J. Klein, The Accounting Review, VI, No. 3(September, 1931), 245-6.

Fred Rogers Fairchild, Review of Federal Income Taxation, by Joseph J. Klein, The American Economic Review, XIX, No. 3(September, 1929), 508-9.

Stephen G. Rusk, Review of Federal Income Taxation, by Joseph J. Klein, The Journal of Accountancy, XLVII, No. 5(May, 1929), 391-2.

experience as a tax attorney, college teacher, and advisor to the Treasury Department had prepared him well for the task of producing this 2,400 page manual, which served as an aid to both the tax novice and the tax practitioner. Rusk[1] noted that, had Klein's book been released and made available at the time, his (Rusk's) responsibility as an advisor to a young entrant into the accountancy profession who had inquired of The Journal of Accountancy what books to get to master the subject of federal income taxation, would have been lightened considerably. Rusk continued: ". . . Dr. Klein has made, in my opinion, a distinctive contribution to the lore upon the subject of which his book treats."[2] The whole tone of Klein's treatise is historical, descriptive, and explanatory. His style of presentation is clear and concise. This is particularly noticeable in his explanation of the very difficult statutes of limitation. As compared with similar manuals, the author's attitude appears less critical than some, while less formally legalistic than others. Basing his words on such qualities as these, Fairchild remarked that "as a manual, the book is comprehensive, exhaustive, logically arranged, and clearly expressed. It should make a place for itself on its merits."[3]

Kohler compared this work with that of Montgomery. His well chosen words on the matter cannot be passed over:

> Since the discontinuance of Montgomery's standard work on income taxes, a new book, Federal Income Taxation, of monumental proportions and significance, has made its appearance. Dr. Klein is to be congratulated for the high standard of excellence which he has maintained throughout Federal Income Taxation. The book deserves first rank as a reference work for practitioners and even as a text-book, . . . As a stylist and interpreter Klein ranks well above Montgomery; but as a commentator and critic Montgomery must be ceded first place among all those who have thus far ventured into the field of income taxes.[4]

---

[1] Rusk, loc. cit.

[2] Ibid.

[3] Fairchild, loc. cit.

[4] Kohler, loc. cit.

Although Klein was aided in the production of this work by many able assistants, for it is not a work which any man could have prepared single-handed, nevertheless, according to Kapp,[1] its author's touch, that of a master, is very perceptible throughout. The same reviewer gives the following encomium of Dr. Klein and his work:

> So long as it is absolutely necessary that we have an income tax it is indeed fortunate that we have a Dr. Klein. . . . .
> . . . .
> The accountancy and legal professions have much to be grateful for in this volume. It goes a long way toward clarifying a subject noted for its abstruseness and will undoubtedly form a mile-stone on the long road toward an adequate understanding of the federal income tax.[2]

---

[1] Kapp, loc. cit.

[2] Ibid.

Ananias Charles Littleton

A. Biographical Sketch[1]

Ananias Charles Littleton was born on December 4, 1886, in Bloomington, Illinois. He graduated from the Bloomington High School in 1905. Apparently unable to pursue a higher education immediately, he worked several years as a station agent and telegraph operator for the Chicago & Alton Railroad Company. After several years at this work Littleton had apparently earned sufficient funds for further schooling, and he eventually won A.B. and A.M. degrees from the University of Illinois in 1912 and 1918 respectively. The delay in receiving the Master's Degree was perhaps due partially or in toto to the fact that

[1]American Accounting Association, 1955 Membership Roster.

E. Burl Austin, "Association Notes," The Accounting Review, XXVI, No. 3 (July, 1951), 430; XXVIII, No. 2(April, 1953), 293; XXX, No. 2(April, 1955), 326.

R. L. Dixon, "Association Notes," The Accounting Review, XVII, No. 3(July, 1942), 334.

Harry D. Kerrigan, "University Notes," The Accounting Review, XVI, No. 3 (September, 1941), 319.

Rita Perine Merritt (ed.), The Accountants' Directory and Who's Who--1925 (New York: Prentice-Hall, Inc., 1925), p. 554.

Rita Perine (ed.), The Accountants' Directory and Who's Who--1920(New York: The Forty-Fifth Street Press, 1920), p. 459.

"University Notes," The Accounting Review, II, No. 4(December, 1927), 425; III, No. 1(March, 1928), 81; VI, No. 2(June, 1931), 158; VI, No. 3(September, 1931), 247; VIII, No. 2(June, 1933), 183; IX, No. 2(June, 1934), 200; X, No. 1 (March, 1935), 130; XII, No. 3(September, 1937), 335; XIV, No. 4(December, 1939), 464.

Who's Who in America, Vol. XXVI, 1950-51(Chicago: A. N. Marquis & Company, 1950), p. 1640.

Littleton went to work for three years after receiving the A.B., this time with Deloitte, Plender, Griffiths & Company, a firm of public accountants in Chicago. He received his Illinois certified public accountant certificate on October 2, 1919.

It was in 1915, three years before he received his Master's Degree, that Littleton began his long teaching career at the University of Illinois. From 1919(1920) to 1922 he served as assistant dean of the College of Commerce. In 1922 he was appointed to the position of assistant director of the Bureau of Business Research, in which capacity he served for twenty years before resigning in 1941. In June, 1931, Professor Littleton received a Ph.D. Degree in Economics from the University of Illinois. His thesis was "The Historical Foundations of Modern Accounting." Later that same year he was promoted to the rank of professor of accounting, the position which he held until quite recently, when he was promoted to the position of professor emeritus.

It is worthy of note that in 1953, when exercises commemorating the Fiftieth Anniversary of the founding of courses in business took place at the University of Illinois, Littleton, together with other members of the teaching staff who had been responsible for the initiation, development, and growth of these courses, was awarded an appropriately engraved plaque. Also worthy of note is the fact that the Alpha Kappa Psi award for 1954, for outstanding contributions to the field of accounting, was presented to A. C. Littleton at the Banquet Session of the Annual Convention.[1]

Littleton is a member of the American Institute of Accountants and the Illinois Society of Certified Public Accountants. He served the former as a member of the committee on Accounting Procedure for several years, and also ably

[1]This cash award for a Life Membership in the American Accounting Association is made through the Association, the one to receive it being selected by the Association, not by Alpha Kappa Psi.

served the latter, especially as a member of its Educational Committee for some time. Littleton is likewise a Life member of the American Accounting Association, which he has served in numerous capacities: in 1936 as vice-president; in 1937, 1939-42 as co-director of research; in 1943 as president; and in 1943-47 as Editor of The Accounting Review. Littleton, also a member of the Beta Gamma Sigma, Beta Alpha Psi, and Delta Chi fraternities, is an author of note and has contributed many articles and book-reviews to various accounting journals.

B. Principal Contributions

As an author Professor Littleton has definitely made very important contributions to the field of accounting literature. The publication date of his earliest work, An Introduction to Elementary Accounting, which appeared around 1919, has been remembered as an important date in the development of accounting as it is known today.[1]

Littleton's second work, Accounting Evolution to 1900, made its initial debut into the field of accounting literature in 1933. The work is very well-known and has been favorably received both in the United States and abroad. Once again the discussion is based on several sources, particularly book reviews.[2]

Littleton dedicated this particular treatise to Henry Rand Hatfield, and in so doing seems to have taken Professor Hatfield's classic article "An

---

[1]Cf. "Historical Dates in Accounting," The Accounting Review, XXIX, No. 3 (July, 1954), 491. However, in connection with this fact it is most perturbing to note that there are apparently no available reviews of this work of Littleton's, by which one can determine the reasons why it has been selected to be held in such significance.

[2]R. A. Bryant, Review of Accounting Evolution to 1900, by A. C. Littleton, The Accounting Review, X, No. 4(December, 1935), 411-2.

Herbert C. Freeman, Review of Accounting Evolution to 1900, by A. C. Littleton, The Journal of Accountancy, LVI, No. 11(November, 1933), 389-91.

Review of Accounting Evolution to 1900, by A. C. Littleton, The American Accountant, XVIII, No. 10(October, 1933), 316-7.

"University Notes," The Accounting Review, X, No. 1(March, 1935), 130.

Historical Defense of Bookkeeping" as the inspiration and model for his own
work. Moreover, he included it in abridged form as the first chapter of his
book. Realizing full well that accountancy had its own peculiar development,
the author endeavored to reveal something of the pattern which diverse forces
had been weaving in the growth of bookkeeping and accounting, through the inter-
mingling of economic forces, business institutions, industrial methodology, and
social growth, with men's ambitions, ideals, plans, and failures.

The first part of the book, consequently, embodies a brief reconstruction
of the long evolutionary struggle to devise and perfect a tool of expression and
measurement, viz., proprietary double-entry bookkeeping, while the second part
summarily sketches the circumstances surrounding the expansion of simple cleri-
cal bookkeeping processes into an important field of knowledge, namely, accountancy. Concerning this second part, Freeman comments that "Professor Littleton
presents, as no other writer has done, a study of the development of accounting
thought and practice in the nineteenth century."[1]

Littleton's approach to his subject is that of analysis and synthesis of
significant developments and trends in bookkeeping and accountancy, rather than
that of merely cataloging events in chronological order. In other words, his
approach is not only that of the historian, but of the interpreter of history as
well. Because of these factors the result was a profoundly arresting and un-
usually significant work, affording all accountants a work delightful in its
clear, pungent presentation and its clever selection of illustrative material.

In proof of the wide acceptance gained by Accounting Evolution to 1900 it
may be noted in conclusion that Littleton was awarded the scroll presented by
the Grand Chapter of Beta Alpha Psi, national honorary accounting fraternity,
because his work was esteemed the most noteworthy contribution to accounting
literature during the year which ended May 1, 1934.

---

[1]Freeman, loc. cit.

Although during the last two decades by far the greater part of Littleton's writings took the form of periodical articles, nevertheless he has made
several other significant contributions to accounting literature. The first, a
more general contribution, embraces his untiring efforts in accounting research
at the University of Illinois. He was largely responsible for the various
"Research Bulletins" published by that university. The second, a more specific
contribution, was An Introduction to Corporate Accounting Standards, which
Littleton wrote in collaboration with Professor William A. Paton of the University of Michigan. This work, first published in 1940 by the American Accounting
Association, because of its great stimulus to the general discussion of accounting principles, among other things, was considered by Brundage to be one of the
milestones in accountancy during the first half of the twentieth century.[1]

In conclusion it is interesting to note that at Ohio State University's
eighteenth Annual Institute of Accounting, held in May, 1956, Littleton was
1956's sole nominee for the Accounting Hall of Fame citation.[2]

---

[1]Percival F. Brundage, "Milestones on the Path of Accounting," Harvard
Business Review, XXIX, No. 4(July, 1951), 71-81.

[2]"Accounting Hall of Fame," (News Report) The Journal of Accountancy, CI,
No. 6(June, 1956), 6.

James Oscar McKinsey

A. Biographical Sketch[1]

James Oscar McKinsey was born in Gamma, Missouri, on June 4, 1889. He won
a Pd.B. Degree from State Teachers College, Warrensburg, Missouri, in 1912, an
L.L.B. Degree from the University of Arkansas in 1913, a Ph.B. Degree from the
University of Chicago in 1916, and an A.M. Degree from the same university in
1919. He also held a B.C.S. Degree from St. Louis University. In 1919 he became a certified public accountant in the state of Illinois.

McKinsey began his teaching duties as a high school instructor, and remained in this role for five years. He joined the faculty of the University of
Chicago in 1917, and for the next three years served there as an instructor and
assistant professor of accounting. From 1920 to 1921 he was a lecturer on
accounting at Columbia University. In the mid-twenties McKinsey returned to the
University of Chicago, this time in the capacity of an associate professor of

---

[1]American Accounting Association, 1955 Membership Roster.

Albert Nelson Marquis (ed.), Who Was Who in America, Vol. I, 1897-1942
(Chicago: The A. N. Marquis Company, 1942), p. 817.

Rita Perine Merritt (ed.), The Accountants' Directory and Who's Who--1925
(New York· Prentice-Hall, Inc., 1925), p. 576.

"Ohio Society of C.P.A.'s," The Pace Student, IX, No. 11(October, 1924),169

Rita Perine (ed.), The Accountants' Directory and Who's Who--1920(New
York: The Forty-Fifth Street Press, 1920), p. 476.

Hiram T. Scovill, "Reflections of Twenty-Five Years in the American Accounting Association," The Accounting Review, XVI, No. 2(June, 1941), 167-75.

"University Notes," The Accounting Review, I, No. 4(December, 1926), 101;
III, No. 2(June, 1928), 229.

accounting. In 1926 he was promoted to the rank of full professor, and served
in this capacity until 1935, although in 1928 his professional work as an
organization counsellor and accountant had forced him to reduce his university
work to teaching only two courses.

While McKinsey seems to have spent a large portion of his time in the role
of an educator, he likewise spent considerable time as an accounting practitioner.
He seems to have gotten his first practical experience while serving as a private
and later as a lieutenant in the Ordnance Department, United States Army, from
1917 to 1919. For the next several years he was a member of the firm, Frazer
and Torbet, C.P.A.'s, and New York resident manager. In 1925(26) he severed his
connections with this firm in order to open offices under the firm name of James
O. McKinsey and Company, and remained a senior partner with this company until
1935. From then until 1937, the year of his death, he served as Chairman of the
Board for Marshall Field & Company. He was also a director for the Chicago
Corporation, the Kroger Grocery and Baking Company, the Selected Shares Corporation and Woodlawn Hospital. He was also a member of the board of trustees of the
Armour Institute of Technology, a member of the board of managers for the Chicago
Y.M.C.A., a member of the board of directors for the Central Y.M.C.A. College,
and a member of the transportation committee of the Chicago Association of Com-
merce.

McKinsey held membership in several accounting associations: namely, the
American Institute of Accountants, the Illinois Society of Certified Public
Accountants, the National Association of Cost Accountants, and the American
Association of University Instructors in Accounting, which he served as president in 1924. It is interesting to note that at the 1937 meeting of this last-
mentioned association Professor Scovill introduced a motion that the Association
express its deep sorrow at the death of Mr. McKinsey. As a result of that motion
the following resolution was adopted:

Resolved: That the American Accounting Association hereby record its profound sorrow at the death of Mr. James O. McKinsey, former president of the Association. As president and in many other capacities his leadership and devotion to the ideals of the Association resulted in noteworthy contributions to the progress of the teaching and accounting professions in the United States.[1]

B. Principal Contributions

Despite the fact that Professor McKinsey was a very busy man in his double role of accounting teacher and accounting practitioner, he nevertheless found time to write several books and numerous periodical articles. It seems safe to state that he was a pioneering type of individual. This statement is corroborated by what Howard Greer of Ohio State University said in one of the many discussions at the Ninth Annual Meeting of the American Association of University Instructors in Accounting held at Chicago in December, 1924. In a discussion concerning present-day tendencies and trends in accounting literature, Greer bemoaned the fact that most of the men in the teaching profession had prior to that time done little more than look around themselves, see what was going on, and had merely gathered together in writing, etc., what they had thought to be the best of the practice with which they had come in contact. Very few had forged ahead of the current and struck out in new directions, had actually developed something new and scientifically sound to which accountancy could lay claim. Then Greer added the following significant words: ". . . Mr. Paton, Mr. McKinsey, and Mr. Bliss have made notable contributions in this direction."[2] The fact that Professor McKinsey had definitely struck out in new directions is evidenced by the titles of some of his books and articles, e.g., "Accounting as an Administrative Aid," "Approach to the Study of Municipal Accounting Problems,"

[1] American Accounting Association, "Convention Report--Proceedings of the 22nd Annual Convention," (Atlantic City, N. J., December 27-29, 1937), The Accounting Review, XIII, No. 1(March, 1938), 97.

[2] Howard C. Greer, "Discussion," The American Association of University Instructors in Accounting, Papers and Proceedings of the Ninth Annual Meeting (Chicago, Ill., 1924), pp. 89-90.

"Expense Budgets," etc., and in particular by his works Budgetary Control and Managerial Accounting, which have been singled out for special discussion here.

According to several reviewers,[1] the first of these two works, Budgetary Control, which appeared in 1922, was the most satisfactory and first exhaustive treatise on commercial or business budgets to come to their notice. Its purpose was to set forth a comprehensive and detailed exposition of a method of coordinating the primary business functions. The discussion of the meaning of budgetary control, the interdependence and interrelation of business activities and of the need for a balancing or coordinating of them, the installation of budgetary control and its effect upon the major business functions, the various types of budgets, etc., were some of the highlights of the work.

According to McKinsey, business, broadly speaking, had only three major functions, viz., that of selling, of producing or manufacturing, and of financing. These major functions were to be served by the two great tools of management, namely, accounting and statistics. Thus, budgetary control was to be a combination of accounting and statistics. From this it followed that administrative control necessitated the use of estimates. The preparation and use of the estimated balance sheet and statement of profit and loss were explained as the means of presenting the anticipated results of the budget period.

As Jackson expressed it:

> Professor McKinsey has . . . . covered the field of budgetary control for a commercial enterprise, . . . with remarkable clearness; in simple language he has presented the principles that control a most difficult and elusive phase of business management--the coordination or balancing of the functional activities of a business enterprise. . . .[2]

---

[1] J. Hugh Jackson, Review of Budgetary Control, by J. O. McKinsey, The American Economic Review, XIII, No. 2(June, 1923), 315.

Francis Oakey, Review of Budgetary Control, by J. O. McKinsey, The Journal of Accountancy, XXXV, No. 1(January, 1923), 65.

[2] Jackson, loc. cit.

However, the second work, _Managerial Accounting_, which came out in 1924, appeared to be the more important of the two. According to Hatfield[1] the accounting treatises of the then present generation, unlike those of previous centuries which combined theory with much information and advice dealing with business procedure rather than with accounting, were focused upon accounting theory in such a way that they really wrestled with the many unsettled problems in the field. Valuation, the apportionment of depreciation, how to tell an asset from an expense and, ever and above all, the determination of profits were such problems demanding settlement. These works were rigidly and boldy scientific as never before, at least to the extent that they attempted to formulate a definite body of knowledge which dealt with a specific limited sphere.

The present treatise, however, while learned and scientific, transcends those limitations which authors of the twentieth century had generally felt, and once more accounting became more than accounting. Thus, _Managerial Accounting_ was not satisfied merely to tell how transactions are to be recorded in order to meet the needs of the manager; it told what ought to be done, and how it should be done, in order to make it worthy of record in the books of account. It told how various responsibilities should be divided before stating how to keep accounts which measure responsibility. It described the nature of operations first, then proceeded to tell in detail how to record these operations. Yet the book should not mistakenly be looked upon as a work on business management or salesmanship rather than accounting. Although properly named _Managerial Accounting_, it nevertheless dealt with accounting as related to business life, and not merely as something enclosed between the covers of a ponderous ledger.

In Reighard's opinion, the outlook on the accounting process recorded in this volume was

---

[1]Henry Rand Hatfield, Review of _Managerial Accounting_, by James O. McKinsey, _The Journal of Accountancy_, XXXIX, No. 5(May, 1925), 432-3.

much needed in instructional work in this field in contrast with the wealth of material which exists along the lines of public accounting, costing, analysis, and theory. It is the best presentation in a single volume of the possibilities of aid to management through the operations of the accounting staff which the reviewer has seen.[1]

In summing up the over-all value of this work, another reviewer noted that "the bulk of the work is sound, interesting, illuminative and original."[2] Reighard deemed it a "most commendable piece of work," one that would "doubtless be a factor in influencing accounting thought and literature."[3] Finally, according to Paton, "there is no doubt that in Managerial Accounting the author has done a very creditable piece of work, particularly in view of the fact that this is a pioneering effort. . . ."[4]

---

[1]John J. Reighard, Review of Managerial Accounting, by James O. McKinsey, The Accounting Review, I, No. 2(June, 1926), 94-6.

[2]Hatfield, loc. cit.

[3]Reighard, loc. cit.

[4]W. A. Paton, Review of Managerial Accounting, by J. O. McKinsey, The Journal of Political Economy, XXXIII, No. 4(August, 1925), 470-2.

Robert H. Montgomery

A. Biographical Sketch[1]

Robert H. Montgomery, accountant, lawyer, educator, and author, was born
on September 21, 1872, at Mahanoy City, Pennsylvania, the son of a Methodist
minister. Although his education in boyhood was constantly interrupted by a

[1]"Accountant Aids Study of Reduction of War Profits," The American Accountant, XVI, No. 4(April, 1931), 110.

"Accountants Club Members Guests of President," The American Accountant,
XII, No. 6(July, 1927), 25.

"Accounting Hall of Fame," The Canadian Chartered Accountant, LXV, No. 4
(October, 1954), 182-3.

American Institute of Accountants, American Institute of Accountants
Fiftieth Anniversary Celebration 1937(Concord, New Hampshire: The Rumford Press,
1938), pp. 25, 27, 29.

"American Institute of Accountants--Annual Meeting Held in St. Louis on
September 15, 16, 17, and 18," The Pace Student, IX, No. 11(October, 1924),166-7.

American Institute of Accountants, Officers & Committees, Trial Boards,
State Boards of Accountancy, State Societies of CPA's, Minutes of Annual Meeting,
Awards, 1954-1955(New York: The American Institute of Accountants, 1954), p. 34.

E. Burl Austin, "Association Notes," The Accounting Review, XXVI, No. 3
(July, 1951), 431.

John L. Carey (ed.), "Col. Robert H. Montgomery," The Journal of Accountancy, XCV, No. 6(June, 1953), 677-8.

Allen Chaffee, "Colonel Robert H. Montgomery," The Pace Student, XI, No. 8
(July, 1926), 8-9.

"Colonel Carter New President of Accountants Club," The American Accountant, XV, No. 2(February, 1930), 83.

"Colonel Montgomery Defines Professional Responsibilities," The American
Accountant, XII, No. 9(October, 1927), 5-10, 58-61.

"Colonel Robert H. Montgomery, . . . ," The Pace Student, VIII, No. 6(May,
1923), 82.

succession of moves from one locality to another, he nevertheless managed to secure his formal education at public and night school. However, circumstances made it necessary for him to begin working for a living at the age of fourteen. At sixteen he became office boy for John Heins, in Philadelphia, who at that time was president of the American Association of Public Accountants and one of the prominent accountants in this country. Heins, in an age when no schools existed in which accountancy might be learned, trained his staff rigorously. Thus, his office was the best training school that a young accountant could have had. There seemed to be just the right blend of Dutch and Irish in young

C. W. DeMond, Price, Waterhouse & Co. In America (New York: The Comet Press, Inc., 1951), pp. 113, 140, 257.

"Fortieth Anniversary Celebrated by American Institute," The American Accountant, XII, No. 10(November, 1927), 13.

Fourth International Congress on Accounting, 1933. Proceedings(London: Gee & Co., Publishers, Ltd., 1933), pp. xxi-xxii.

L. Gluick, "What's Wrong With Our Textbooks?" The Accounting Review, XXII, No. 1(January, 1947), 36-8.

J. Brooks Heckert, "Accounting Hall of Fame," The Accounting Review, XXV, No. 3(July, 1950), 260-1.

"Honor Conferred on R. H. Montgomery by Roumanian Minister," The American Accountant, XV, No. 8(August, 1930), 382.

"International Congress Indicates Advanced Status of Profession," The American Accountant, XIV, No. 9(September, 1929), 467-8.

"International Congress of Accountants," The American Accountant, XIII, No. 6(June, 1928), 27.

International Congress on Accounting, 1929. Proceedings(New York: The Knickerbocker Press, 1930), pp. xvff.

Albert Nelson Marquis (ed.), Who's Who in America, Vol. XIII, 1924-25 (Chicago: A. N. Marquis & Company, 1924), p. 2298.

Rita Perine Merritt (ed.), The Accountants' Directory and Who's Who--1925 (New York: Prentice-Hall, Inc., 1925), p. 587.

"Montgomery Heads Joint Committee of Congress of Accountants," The American Accountant, XIII, No. 2(February, 1928), 52.

"New York State C.P.A. Society Holds Special Conference," The Pace Student, VIII, No. 12(November, 1923), 191.

Montgomery's ancestry, for it was not long before he was promoted. Just ten years later, in 1898, he became a junior partner in that same firm, which by that time had become Heins, Whelen, Lybrand & Company. Moreover, in 1899 Montgomery became a charter member of the Pennsylvania Institute of Certified Public Accountants.

Soon after he became a partner in the firm just mentioned, Montgomery volunteered as a private and served in the Porto Rican Campaign of the Spanish-American War, in Battery A.of the Philadelphia Light Artillary. He also served in the Pennsylvania National Guard from 1898 until 1902. When he returned to the States after the war he took up the study of law during his evenings, and in 1900 was admitted to the bar in Philadelphia County, Pennsylvania. In 1902, with Montgomery in charge, the New York office of Lybrand, Ross Bros, & Montgomery, Accountants, was opened. That same year, at the age of twenty-nine, he was one of the two delegates sent by the Pennsylvania Institute of Certified Public Accountants to a convention in Washington, D.C., which resulted in the formation of the Federation of Societies of Public Accountants in the United

Homer S. Pace (ed.), "Editorial Comment," The American Accountant, XVIII, No. 9(September, 1933), 261-2.

_____, "International Convention of Accountants," The Pace Student, XI, No. 6(May, 1926), 2.

_____, "The Editor's Page," The American Accountant, XII, No. 9(October, 1927), Inside front cover.

Rita Perine (ed.), The Accountants' Directory and Who's Who--1920(New York: The Forty-Fifth Street Press, 1920), p. 484.

"Roumania to Confer Decoration on Colonel Robert H. Montgomery," The American Accountant, XV, No. 3(March, 1930), 118.

Nicholas A. H. Stacey, "The Accounting Hall of Fame," The Accountant, CXXXI(July 31st, 1954), 108.

"The New York State Society of Certified Public Accountants," The Pace Student, XI, No. 11(October, 1926), 6-9.

Who's Who in America, Vol. XXVI, 1950-51(Chicago: A..N. Marquis & Company, 1950), p. 1925.

States of America.

In 1904 Montgomery was admitted to the bar in New York. For some time thereafter he specialized in public utility accounts, but his legal training subsequently led him to make taxation his great specialty. That same year, 1904, at the First International Congress of Accountants in St. Louis, Montgomery read a paper entitled: "The Importance of Uniform Practice in Determining the Profits of Public Service Corporations Where Municipalities Have the Power to Regulate Rates." In 1906 Montgomery was retained to install a new system of accounts for the New York State Hospitals. In 1909, he and the late Francis F. White, of Deloitte, Plender, Griffiths & Co., were selected by the New York State Chamber of Commerce to examine and report on the accounting system of the city of New York.

In 1905 the Federation of Societies of Public Accountants merged with the American Association of Public Accountants (founded 1887). Montgomery took an active part in the affairs of this association, and was elected president in 1912 and 1913. In 1916 the association was reorganized as the American Institute of Accountants, and Montgomery played a leading role in its development. In 1921, the American Society of Certified Public Accountants was set up. Montgomery fought vigorously for a merger of the Institute and the Society, and his energetic efforts to that end, coupled with his great personal influence, were largely responsible for the successful consummation of the merger in 1936. He served as vice-president of the American Institute of Accountants in the year 1927-1928, and was its president from 1935 until 1937.

Meanwhile, Montgomery had served as president of the New York State Society of Certified Public Accountants from 1922 to 1924, having been accepted into that society in 1914, twelve years after he had come to New York. During his presidency he originated the "all-day-conference" and the "technical-committee" idea. It was during his term also that a code of professional conduct was adopted, to which the practitioners of New York State readily subscribed. In addition, he provided the Society, as a personal gift, with a foundation for a technical library.

Although Montgomery was primarily an accounting practitioner, he spent a number of years in teaching work. Thus, he was one of the three or four Philadelphia accountants to underwrite the evening school of the University of Pennsylvania (The Wharton School of Finance and Commerce) and to teach the first classes. He was assigned to teach auditing. Montgomery also taught at New York University as an instructor in accounting before he came to Columbia in 1912. where, in the School of Business, he was to teach for almost two decades. He served that institution as an instructor in economics from 1912 to 1914, as an assistant professor of accounting from 1914 to 1919, as a full professor of accounting from 1919 to 1923, and as professor of income tax procedure and accounting from 1924 until 1931. He also served as a member of the Administrative Board of the School of Business from 1919 to 1931.

During World War I Montgomery was commissioned a lieutenant colonel of the United States Army, in March, 1918. From the previous January he had been chief of the section on organization and methods of the Office of the Director of Purchases; he became, for the year ending April, 1919; organizer and member of the War Department Board of Appraisers; he was War Department representative on the price-fixing commission of the War Industries Board; and he served as chief of the price-fixing section of the Purchases, Storage and Traffic Division of the General Staff.

Several other important facts in Montgomery's life should be listed. First, in 1923, at the request of the Polish Government, he spent three months in Poland investigating the business possibilities of that country. Further, it is particularly interesting to note Montgomery's active participation in a number of International Accounting Congresses. Mention has already been made of the congress held in St. Louis in 1904. In 1926 Montgomery headed a delegation from the New York State Society of Certified Public Accountants to the international gathering in Amsterdam, Holland. He played an extremely active role as president of the Third International Congress of Accountants, which met in New York in September, 1929. In recognition of his service as president of this third congress, and also of the courtesies extended to the representatives of Roumania in attendance at the congress, on June 17, 1930, Montgomery was given the Royal Roumanian Decree of Commander of the Crown by Charles A. Davila, Roumanian Minister to the United States. In 1933, Colonel Montgomery was one of the thirteen delegates sent by the American Institute of Accountants to the Fourth International Congress on Accounting in London. At this same congress he also represented the Porto Rico Institute of Accountants.

In 1931 Montgomery was made executive secretary of The War Policies Commission erected by the Secretary of War, Patrick Jay Hurley, to obtain the views of industry, veterans organizations, labor and capital, as well as the War, Navy, and other departments of the government, on the subject of taking the profits out of war. He also served as director of research and planning under the N.R.A.

In addition to those which have already been mentioned, Montgomery was a member of several other accounting and legal associations and societies, of which only a few will be mentioned here. Worthy of special note is the fact that he was an authorized certified public accountant in three states, namely, New York, Missouri, and Pennsylvania. He was a member of the American Economic Association, the Academy of Political and Social Sciences, the American Association of University Instructors in Accounting, and the Accountants' Club of America, which he served as president for the first three years of the club's existence (1927-28-29). Editor John L. Carey, writing in the June, 1953, issue of The Journal of Accountancy one month after Montgomery's death (May 2, 1953), summed up the sentiments of thousands of certified public accountants in the following eulogistic words:

Never did Colonel Montgomery play a passive part. Wherever he was, he said what he thought. He was often a controversial figure. But he could accept defeat without rancor, and victory with grace. He was a born leader, a strong, determined, persistent man, ready to fight at any time for his convictions. But to his friends, at the same time, he was kind and gentle, encouraging, helpful, thoughtful, loyal.

To many accountants Robert Montgomery symbolizes the profession itself-- its humble beginnings, its struggles, its successes, its recognition. He has left an imprint on American accounting that will never be erased. His death leaves an empty place that can never be refilled.[1]

B. Principal Contributions

One cannot relate the events of Montgomery's life as an outstanding practitioner, lawyer, and educator, and consider his biography complete. Although he stood head and shoulders above many in the things just mentioned, this is equally true of Montgomery the author. He played a leading role in founding The Journal of Accountancy in 1905. Later, in 1912, he wrote the first American book on auditing, and in 1917 one of the first authoritative books on income tax accounting.

His work on auditing, Auditing Theory and Practice, has, in the minds of many,[2] contributed considerably to accounting thought and practice in the United

---

[1]Carey, op. cit., p. 678.

[2]American Institute of Accountants, loc. cit.

Wm. Morse Cole, Review of Auditing Theory and Practice, 2nd ed., by R. H. Montgomery, The American Economic Review, VII, No. 1(March, 1917), 130-2.

Herbert C. Freeman, Review of Auditing Theory and Practice, by R. H. Montgomery, The Journal of Accountancy, XIV, No. 4(October, 1912), 341-5.

Wilmer L. Green, History and Survey of Accountancy(Brooklyn: Standard Text Press, 1930), p. 134.

Henry Rand Hatfield, Review of Auditing Theory and Practice, by R. H. Montgomery, The Journal of Political Economy, XXI, No. 8(October, 1913), 781.

"Historical Dates in Accounting," The Accounting Review, XXIX, No. 3(July, 1954), 491.

W. H. Lawton, Review of Auditing Theory and Practice, 1916 ed., by R. H. Montgomery, The Journal of Accountancy, XXI, No. 6(June, 1916), 478-80.

Thomas Warner Mitchell, Review of Auditing Theory and Practice, by R. H. Montgomery, The American Economic Review, III, No. 2(June, 1913), 382-4.

States. For many years prior to the appearance of this work, the standard handbook on auditing had been Lawrence R. Dicksee's Auditing. This, together with
Pixley's work of the same name, constituted the major portion of the literature
on this subject outside of periodical writings, both being English publications.
Then, in 1905, Montgomery brought out an American edition of Dicksee's Auditing,[1]
but he left out many parts which had applied particularly to British conditions
and rewrote other parts in order to bring them into harmony with American experience and ideas. This revision served the accounting public fairly well for the
next seven years. However, the American concept of the scope of an audit and
American practice in general had been so different from those of the British that
for some time there had been felt a need for a book on auditing written entirely
from the American viewpoint. Auditing Theory and Practice, which, according to
Gluick,[2] has for over a generation been properly known as the "Auditor's Bible,"
was an attempt to remedy that need.

In this work the author breaks down the whole field of accounting into
constructive accounting, bookkeeping, inspective accounting, and interpretative
accounting. This last is the most important, for all the others exist for it.
Thus, it would not be sufficient for the auditor to check, verify, and state that
the accounts are correct. He must be able to tell a connected and lucid story as
revealed to him by the figures; in other words, he had become, or should have become if he thoroughly grasped the principles of auditing set forth in this book,
a translator, or better still, an interpreter.

Throughout the work Professor Montgomery gave many arguments to support his

Review of Auditing Theory and Practice, 2nd ed., by R. H. Montgomery, The
Journal of Political Economy. XXVI, No. 7(July, 1916), 734.

[1]According to DeMond, op. cit., p. 113: "This book was made possible
through Dickinson's influence in securing from Dicksee permission for an American
edition of his work."

[2]Gluick, loc. cit.

plea for an interpretation of the facts clear enough for the man for whom the audit is made to understand. Thus, in the words of Cole, "Montgomery's Auditing is standard; and it is so largely because it puts emphasis where emphasis belongs--on intelligence and judgment, as contrasted with mechanical checking, in audits."[1] Another outstanding accounting teacher, Hatfield, in his review of the work under discussion, seems to have accurately summarized the general consensus of opinion about the book. He notes:

> The primacy among treatises on auditing, which until the present has been held by Dicksee's work, now passes to Montgomery's Auditing Theory and Practice. Mr. Montgomery has previously rendered a valuable service as editor of the American edition of Dicksee. The present volume is, however, no mere revision or rearrangement of another's work, but an independent treatise, scholarly, comprehensive, masterly. It is a happy blend of well-sustained theoretical writing and practical suggestions based on the author's professional experience. . . .
> Throughout the work the author takes an advanced position on the question of professional ethics. This is not merely in the short section professing to deal formally with that much-discussed topic, but more valuably in the passages scattered throughout the book, where in discussing matters of theoretical interest he always stands clearly for professional honor and personal integrity.[2]

The high esteem in which the work was held by accountants, whether teachers or practitioners, has not proved to be ephemeral. Even today this work continues to be praised by all who peruse its pages. For example, in 1949, The American Institute of Accountants presented an award to Robert H. Montgomery "for outstanding service to the profession over the years and for his writings as typified by the seventh edition of his book, 'AUDITING.'"[3] Furthermore, Montgomery's writing of Auditing Theory and Practice in 1912 was included in a chronological listing of dates which are significant to the development of accounting as it is known today. This list, entitled "Historical Dates in Accounting," appeared in the July, 1954, issue of The Accounting Review, page 491.

While Montgomery was very well-known for his contribution to auditing theory

---

[1] Cole, loc. cit.

[2] Hatfield, loc. cit.

[3] American Institute of Accountants, op. cit., p. 34.

and practice, he was also a most celebrated author of income tax manuals. This
is evidenced by the fact that from 1917 to 1929 he contributed almost yearly a
new and up-to-date edition of his Income Tax Procedure.

The present century was still in her teens when she witnessed the various
enactments of income tax laws by the United States Congress, viz., the federal
income tax laws of October 3, 1913 and of September 8, 1916. The American people
were unfamiliar with the underlying ideas of the nature of income and of income
taxation. This naturally caused much of the confusion which many a taxpayer
found in his efforts to understand the law and subsequent modifications of it.
Plehn[1] noted that the reason for this ignorance lay in the fact that as a people
Americans were habitually inclined to think of a man's wealth in terms of capital
rather than in terms of income. They had had considerable practical experience
in valuing property, but comparatively meager experience in rating income.

Such an habitual state of mind, coupled with the taxpayers' eagerness for
light on the income tax afforded an opportunity which was seized upon by many
writers. Hence, many books and pamphlets on this subject were offered to the
public. Plehn[2] placed Montgomery's work among the best of these writings, and at
the same time remarked that the work was essentially a manual for the accountant.
To describe the initial and subsequent volumes of this handbook Freeman's words
seem to fit quite well. He said in part that the book "might perhaps be described
as a guide to income tax practice in the light of the most recent developments of
the art. . . ."[3]

Montgomery's annual contribution to the subject of federal taxation contained the law itself, regulations, interpretations, court decisions, board of

---

[1]Carl C. Plehn, Review of Income Tax Procedure, 1918, by Robert H. Montgomery, The American Economic Review, VIII, No. 2(June, 1918), 380-5.

[2]Ibid.

[3]H. C. F., Review of Income Tax Procedure, 1917, by Robert H. Montgomery,
The Journal of Accountancy, XXVIII, No. 2(February, 1917), 157.

tax appeals decisions, and the author's own comments and elucidations of the numerous phases of the law. According to Rusk,[1] Montgomery's works on the matter of federal taxation were liked by many because he was courageous and outspoken. He did not hesitate to point out the defects of the laws, and, quite often, he saw the defects long before others. Thus, if the law was defective Montgomery pointed out the defect, and in this way notified the taxpayer in advance to protect his own interests in the matter.

There is no doubt that Montgomery's Income Tax Procedure was well thought of and used by many. Thus, one reviewer referred to it as "the annual classic on the American income tax . . ."[2] Several years subsequent to the discontinuance of this standard work on income taxes, and in spite of the appearance of new and learned writers in the field of income taxation, Kohler expressed the view of many in saying that "as a commentator and critic Montgomery must be ceded first place among all those who have thus far ventured into the field of income taxes."[3]

Montgomery was given perhaps the highest praise bestowed upon any accountant when in 1950 he was one of the first three living North Americans to be elected to the Accounting Hall of Fame at Ohio State University. If anyone has filled to completion the qualifications for election to this honored position, among which are contributions to accounting literature, public speaking before professional and other groups, public service and previous honor awards in the profession, and honorary degrees conferred by universities, it most certainly was Robert H. Montgomery, accountant, lawyer, educator, and author.

---

[1]Stephen G. Rusk, Review of Income Tax Procedure, 1927, by Robert H. Montgomery, The Journal of Accountancy, XLIII, No. 3(March, 1927), 232-3.

[2]Francis J. Clowes, Review of Income Tax Procedure, 1925, by Robert H. Montgomery, The Journal of Accountancy, XXXIX, No. 3(March, 1925), 235.

[3]E. L. Kohler, Review of Federal Income Taxation, by Joseph J. Klein, The Accounting Review, VI, No. 3(September, 1931), 245.

George Hillis Newlove

A. Biographical Sketch[1]

George Hillis Newlove was born at Crystal, North Dakota, December 16, 1893, and later was educated at Bathgate High School. He won a Ph.B. Degree at Hamline University, St. Paul, Minnesota, in 1914, an A.M. Degree at the University of Minnesota in 1915, and finally a Ph.D. Degree from the University of Illinois in 1918. That same year he was awarded a certified public accountant certificate by the state of Illinois and in the following year by the state of North Carolina.

Newlove began his teaching career while he was working toward his Ph.D. Degree at Illinois, serving there in the capacity of instructor in accounting from 1916 to 1918. During the next few years, from 1919 to 1923, Newlove served as dean of the Washington, D.C. School of Accountancy. From 1923 to 1928 he served as an associate professor of accounting at Johns Hopkins University in Baltimore. In addition to his teaching duties while in the nation's capital and

[1]American Accounting Association, 1955 Membership Roster.

Jaques Cattell (ed.), Directory of American Scholars, 2nd ed.(Lancaster, Pa.: The Science Press, 1951), p. 687.

Harry D. Kerrigan, "University Notes," The Accounting Review, XV, No. 4 (December, 1940), 541.

Rita Perine Merritt (ed.), The Accountants' Directory and Who's Who--1925 (New York: Prentice-Hall, Inc., 1925), p. 600.

Rita Perine (ed.), The Accountants' Directory and Who's Who--1920(New York: The Forty-Fifth Street Press, 1920), p. 494.

"University Notes," The Accounting Review, II, No. 3(September 1927), 300; III, No. 1(March, 1928), 82; III, No. 2(June, 1928), 230.

Who's Who in America, Vol. XXVIII, 1954-55(Chicago: A. N. Marquis & Company, 1954), p. 1980.

Baltimore, Newlove spent several years, 1921 to 1925, as a senior auditor for the Income Tax Unit, United States Department of the Treasury. In 1928 he severed his connections with Johns Hopkins to become a professor of accounting at the University of Texas, where he has remained until the present.

During World War I Newlove served in the United States Navy as a lieutenant junior grade, Pay Corps, from February, 1918, until July, 1919. A former member of the American Economic Association, he is at present a member of the National Association of Cost Accountants and the American Accounting Association. The latter association still went by the name of the American Association of University Instructors in Accounting when Newlove served it as vice president in 1931 and 1932, and as president in 1933. He is also an honorary of the Beta Alpha Psi and Beta Gamma Sigma fraternities.

B. Principal Contributions

By the end of the second decade of the present century, due in great part to federal and state income tax laws and the consequent need for more accurate financial statements, there was a rapid increase in the number of candidates for certified public accountant examinations. Recognizing that such aspirants constituted an audience of very respectable size, Newlove compiled his C.P.A. Accounting, the first edition of which appeared in 1920. The work was intended to serve as an aid to potential accountants who faced the arduous task of preparing for and taking a certified public accountant examination. It could not be taken up by anyone and studied to pass this rigid examination. Rather, the several volumes comprising the work simply furnished an excellent review for the accountant already well-schooled.

Once again it is necessary to rely upon the observations of contemporary reviewers to learn about the more important aspects of the book under discussion.[1]

---

[1]John L. Carey, Review of C.P.A. Accounting, 2nd ed., by George Hillis Newlove, The Journal of Accountancy, XLI, No. 4(April, 1926), 314.

Thus, after having classified the various subjects of accounting, the author first presented a very brief but adequate summary of accounting principles, which were accompanied by supporting references to reliable and accepted authorities in accounting matters. Following this were questions from the certified public accountant examinations of various states, and finally, longer problems and their solutions, again gleaned from past certified public accountant examinations.

The value which this work had for candidates for the certified public accountant examination, for accountants desiring to brush up on the theoretical side of accounting, and finally, for accounting instructors, must have been considerable; for, in less than ten years after the work's original appearance it went through three subsequent editions, and had increased from three to four volumes in size. One reviewer of a subsequent edition contented himself with merely describing the contents of the book, stating that there are cases "when it is possible to appreciate the magnitude of a work only by scrutiny of its constituent parts. . . . No comment is necessary to show the wealth of material in these books, or their value for review and for reference."[1]

A second and final work set apart for investigation here is Consolidated Balance Sheets. According to various reviewers,[2] in this work, which came out

---

J. L. C., Review of C.P.A. Accounting, 3rd ed., by George H. Newlove, The Journal of Accountancy, XLVI, No. 6(December, 1928), 475.

Edgar B. Kapp (ed.), Review of C.P.A. Accounting, 3rd ed., by George H. Newlove, The American Accountant, XIII, No. 1(December, 1928), 42.

Walter E. Parks, Review of C.P.A. Accounting, 3rd ed., by George Hillis Newlove, The Accounting Review, IV, No. 4(December, 1929), 266.

Review of C.P.A. Accounting, 2nd ed., by George H. Newlove, The American Accountant, XII, No. 5(June, 1927), 47-8.

[1]J. L. C. loc. cit.

[2]F. W. Thornton, Review of Consolidated Balance Sheets, by G. H. Newlove, The Journal of Accountancy, XLIII, No. 1(January, 1927), 66-7.

"Book Notices," Review of Consolidated Balance Sheets, by George Hillis Newlove, Harvard Business Review, V, No. 3(April, 1927), 380.

around 1926, Newlove directed his efforts to the mechanical rather than the
theoretical aspects of consolidations; i.e., he specifically intended the work to
be a guide-book to practice, rather than a presentation of principles. He gives
the "how" of procedure and almost completely excludes the "why." Filbey keenly
observes that

> an interesting feature is the solution of each problem by both the "cost
> value method" and the "actual value method." . . . This dual treatment should
> result in a much better understanding of the principles involved in the con-
> solidated balance sheet, not only on the part of the student and the casual
> user of the book, but in many cases also on the part of the instructor in
> accounting. Perhaps even an occasional author of an accounting text . . .
> would find in this feature of the book considerable food for thought and an
> occasion for revising his views on the subject.[1]

Thus, in addition to being one of the most complete treatments of consolidated
statements that had been published up to 1926, the work was also considered as
"an important contribution to a relatively new and important phase of accountancy
work."[2]

Edward J. Filbey, Review of Consolidated Balance Sheets, by George H. Newlove, The Accounting Review, II, No. 2(June, 1927), 195-6.

Review of Consolidated Balance Sheets, by G. H. Newlove, The American
Accountant, XII, No. 2(March, 1927), 43.

[1]Filbey, loc. cit.

[2]Review of Consolidated Balance Sheets, loc. cit.

CHAPTER III

Jerome Lee Nicholson

A. Biographical Sketch[1]

Jerome Lee Nicholson was born at Trenton, New Jersey, on September 24, 1863. While still very young he went to Pittsburgh, where he received a common-school and business-college education. Still a youngster, he found it necessary to get a job and earn his living.

He started as an office boy for the Keystone Bridge Company of Pittsburgh, and soon won a promotion to the engineering department. It was in this particular department that Nicholson found his life work, for it was here that he developed his first liking for cost accounting--a branch of accounting in which he specialized and in which he rendered very effective service to hundreds of business organizations, to the government during the war period, and to literally thousands of students of accountancy.

Nicholson spent his spare time in the study of accountancy, and when the

_____

[1]"Historical Sketch of National Association of Cost Accountants," The American Accountant, XIII, No. 6(June, 1928), 6-7.

"Major Jerome Lee Nicholson," The Pace Student, X, No. 2(January, 1925), 27-8.

Albert Nelson Marquis (ed.), Who's Who in America, Vol. XII, 1922-23 (Chicago: A. N. Marquis & Company, 1922), p. 2314.

National Association of Cost Accountants, Year Book, 1920(New York: Press of J. J. Little & Ives Company, 1921).

Rita Perine (ed.), The Accountants' Directory and Who's Who--1920(New York: The Forty-Fifth Street Press, 1920), p. 495.

opportunity presented itself, in 1884, he accepted an accounting position offered him by the Pennsylvania Railroad Company. He remained in this position for a year, and in 1885 came to New York, where for the next four years he acted first as a bookkeeper and later as a traveling salesman for Katz & Company. Having long contemplated entering the professional practice of accountancy on his own, in 1889 he started practice under the name of J. Lee Nicholson. Later, it was found expeditious to take in other accountants as partners, and the firm name was changed to J. Lee Nicholson and Company. During those years of the firm's existence it rendered very valuable accounting service to a large number of business organizations, particularly to manufacturing organizations in the development of cost systems and procedures.

During World War I Nicholson served the United States Government in several capacities. In 1917 he was appointed as chief of the Division of Cost Accounting (cost on war contracts), Bureau of Foreign and Domestic Commerce. He next served with the Federal Trade Commission as a consulting cost specialist. Finally, on November 15, 1917, he was commissioned a major in the Ordnance Department, and carried the title of Supervising Cost Accountant. Until January, 1919, Nicholson, by reason of his expert knowledge of costs, rendered very important service to the government in the clearing up of cost-plus contracts which were executed during the war. Thus, in the summer of 1917 he was chairman of a conference of delegates from the War, Navy, and Commerce Departments, the Federal Trade Commission, and the Council of National Defense. This conference in a pamphlet issued July 31, 1917, made certain recommendations regarding government contracts.

Nicholson took a very active interest in accounting societies. For more than twenty years he was a member of the New York State Society of Certified Public Accountants, and for several years served as its first vice-president. He was a former member of the American Association of Public Accountants, and at the time of his death was a member of the American Institute of Accountants, the successor of the American Association of Public Accountants. In 1919 Nicholson called a meeting in Buffalo, New York, from which resulted the National Association of Cost Accountants. At that meeting he was chosen temporary chairman, and was subsequently elected first president of the Association.

Nicholson likewise rendered great service to accounting in the field of education. In 1911 he lectured on cost accounting at New York University, and from 1912 to 1917 he served as an instructor and lecturer on cost accounting at Columbia University. Not many years after the World War he established the J. Lee Nicholson Cost Accounting Institute in Chicago. At that time, this was apparently the only school in the country devoted exclusively to the teaching of cost accounting.

B. Principal Contributions

Nicholson was, in addition, a writer and speaker on cost accounting. He was the author of a considerable number of articles on this subject which appeared in trade publications from time to time. He also wrote several books on cost accounting which found favor as textbooks and reference works in schools and colleges teaching accountancy. It is particularly worthy of note that his first volume, Factory Organization and Costs, which appeared in 1909, was the "first American treatise on cost accounting proper, dealing with the subject from an accountant's point of view."[1]

As a concluding remark it needs be said that Green, in his History and Survey of Accountancy,[2] includes Nicholson among those leading American authors who contributed representative works on accounting during the first three decades of the present century.

---

[1]L. G., Review of Factory Organization and Costs, by J. Lee Nicholson, C.P.A., The Journal of Accountancy, VIII, No. 1(July, 1909), 222.

[2]Wilmer L. Green, History and Survey of Accountancy(Brooklyn: Standard Text Press, 1930), p. 134.

William Andrew Paton

A. Biographical Sketch[1]

William Andrew Paton, economist and accountant, was born at Calumet, Michigan, on July 19, 1889. He attended Michigan State Normal College during the

---

[1]American Accounting Association, 1955 Membership Roster.

E. Burl Austin, "Association Notes," The Accounting Review, XXV, No. 4
(October, 1950), 461; XXIX, No. 1(January, 1954), 154.

Jaques Cattell (ed.), Directory of American Scholars(Lancaster, Pennsylvania: The Science Press, 1951), pp. 721-2.

"Contributors to the January Number," The Accounting Review, XXIV, No. 1
(January, 1949), 2.

J. Brooks Heckert, "Accounting Hall of Fame," The Accounting Review, XXV,
No. 3(July, 1950), 260-1.

Harry D. Karrigan, "University Notes," The Accounting Review, XV, No. 2
(June, 1940), 330.

Rita Perine Merritt (ed.), The Accountants' Directory and Who's Who--1925
New York: Prentice-Hall, Inc., 1925), p. 611.

William Andrew Paton, "Recent and Prospective Developments in Accounting
Theory,"(Boston: Harvard University Press, 1940), iii.

Rita Perine (ed.), The Accountants Directory and Who's Who--1920(New York:
The Forty-Fifth Street Press, 1920), pp. 503-4.

"Report of the 1953 President," The Accounting Review, XXIX, No. 2(April,
1954), 299.

Hiram T. Scovill, "Reflections of Twenty-Five Years in the American
Accounting Association," The Accounting Review, XVI, No. 2(June, 1941), 167-75.

"University Notes," The Accounting Review, I, No. 2(June, 1926), 101-2;
IV, No. 3(September, 1929), 210; VIII, No. 4(December, 1933), 373; XI, No. 3
(September, 1936), 315; XII, No. 3(September, 1937), 335; XIII, No. 3(September,
1938), 332.

Who's Who in America, Vol. XXVIII, 1954-55(Chicago: A. N. Marquis & Company, 1954), p. 2076.

school years 1907-08 and 1911-12. Not long thereafter he enrolled at the University of Michigan, and eventually won three degrees from that university, an A.B. in 1915, an A.M. in 1916, and finally, in 1917, a Ph.D. Degree. He is also the possessor of a Litt.D. Degree, which was conferred upon him in 1944 by Lehigh University of Bethlehem, Pennsylvania. He likewise holds a certified public accountant's certificate in the state of Michigan.

Paton began his teaching career at Michigan in 1915, and served that university as an instructor in economics until 1916. After teaching from 1916 to 1917 at the University of Minnesota, he returned to the University of Michigan. Since that time, with the exception of several short intervals, he has held the positions of assistant professor, 1917 to 1919, associate professor, 1919 to 1921, and professor of accounting, 1921 until the present. Since 1947 he has been the Edwin Francis Gay Professor of Accounting and professor of economics at the University of Michigan. He has served as a visiting professor at several other universities, namely, the University of California, 1921, 1937-38, and the University of Chicago, 1924. In 1940 Paton was the outstanding man in accounting appointed to deliver one or more lectures at the Harvard Graduate School of Business Administration. So successfully did he perform this commission that he was designated Dickinson Lecturer for that year. The lectures delivered by Professor Paton in the spring of 1940 were entitled "Recent and Prospective Developments in Accounting Theory."

During World War I Paton was with the Bureau of Research and Statistics, War Trade Board, in 1918. In 1919 he served with the Income Tax Unit of the Bureau of Internal Revenue. It appears that Paton also spent some years as an accounting practitioner, for in 1926 he and a Professor Ross formed a partnership to practice public accounting, with offices in the State Savings Bank Building, Ann Arbor, Michigan. This partnership apparently lasted for several years, for Paton obtained a leave of absence from the 1929 spring semester at the University of Michigan in order to engage in professional work and writing.

Paton likewise took an active interest in various economic and accounting societies. Thus, he served as vice-president of the economics section of the Michigan Academy of Science, 1920-21. He is at present a Fellow of the American Academy of Arts and Sciences, a member of the American Economic Association, the Michigan Association of Certified Public Accountants, the American Institute of Accountants, which he served as councilor from 1935 to 1937, and the Phi Beta Kappa, Phi Kappa Phi and Beta Gamma Sigma fraternities. Paton's membership in the American Accounting Association dates back almost to 1916 when its predecessor, the American Association of University Instructors in Accounting, was organized at Columbus, Ohio. Throughout subsequent years he has served that association in various capacities; as secretary-treasurer in 1920, as third vice-president in 1921, as president in 1922, as editor of The Accounting Review from 1926 to 1928, and finally, as Director of Research, from 1937 to 1939. At present he is one of this association's fifty-one Life Members. In this connection it is of interest to note that Paton won this life membership in the American Accounting Association as the Alpha Kappa Psi award for 1953 for outstanding contributions to the field of accounting. This cash award, made to the one selected by the American Accounting Association, was presented to Professor Paton by Edward G. Eriksen, member of the Grand Council of Alpha Kappa Psi at the annual meeting in Chapel Hill, North Carolina.

B. Principal Contributions

As an author Paton is outstanding. However, before beginning an actual discussion of his more important works, it might wbe well to quote the following poignant remarks of Professor Walker:

> Professor Paton, for one, has always shown a stimulating daring in challenging what is called "standard practice"--and always with the effect of causing those of us who are engaged in just doing things to stop and ask whether what we are doing is either logical or "practical." His early writings were groundbreakers if there ever were any, and they gave him unique credits in the ledger of accounting accomplishments. He has repeatedly

demonstrated in his thinking, in his handling of the well-worn topics of everyday accounting, that rare something or other which we call "background," and which always gives the reader the agreeable feeling that the writer's conclusions have real parentage in scholarship. . . .[1]

This same general idea regarding Paton was stated some fifteen years previous by Professor Greer[2] when, in a discussion concerning the then current tendencies and trends in accounting literature, he included Paton among those very few teachers in the profession of accounting who had at that relatively early date forged ahead of the current and struck out in new directions, developing something definitely new and scientifically sound to which accountancy could lay claim. Discussions of several of Paton's works will be helpful in showing that these words are de facto true.

The facts mentioned above are brought out quite well in Lawton's review of Paton's Accounting Theory with Special Reference to the Corporate Enterprise, which appeared in 1922. The following words have special pertinence here:

> As its sub-title indicates, the author of Accounting Theory reverses the traditional attitude of Sprague, Hatfield, et al., which views the business enterprise from the proprietary standpoint and, basing the theory on sole proprietorship, seeks to apply it to all other forms of ownership. Instead, Dr. Paton adopts the managerial point of view as exemplified in corporate ownership and endeavors to apply it to other forms. In order to do this he adopts the premise that a business enterprise is a distinct entity "although not without important qualifications." . . .[3]

From various reviews of his Accounting,[4] which came out in 1924, it is also

---

[1]Ross. G. Walker, "Explorations in Accounting," Harvard Business Review, XVIII, No. 3(Spring, 1940), 385.

[2]Howard C. Greer, "Discussion," The American Association of University Instructors in Accounting. Papers and Proceedings of the Ninth Annual Meeting (Chicago, Ill., 1924), IX, No. 1(February, 1925), 89-90.

[3]W. H. Lawton, Review of Accounting Theory, with Special Reference to the Corporate Enterprise, by William Andrew Paton, The Journal of Accountancy, XXXV, No. 4(April, 1923), 313.

[4]"Book Notices," Review of Accounting, by W. A. Paton, Harvard Business Review, IV, No. 2(January, 1926), 254.

A. W. Hanson, Review of Accounting, by W. A. Paton, The American Economic Review, XV, No. 1(March, 1925), 120.

quite evident that in this treatise the author's mind continued to reach out in
new directions. Thus, he continued to stress the formula for bookkeeping first
laid down in the aforementioned work, i.e., assets equal equities, as against
that made familiar by Sprague, assets equal liabilities plus proprietorship.
Paton likewise continued to give special attention to the topic "appreciation,"
and according to Hatfield the author's treatment was a "masterly" one. The same
reviewer continued:

> This has from the beginning been a feature in his accounting theory.
> Professor Paton was perhaps the pioneer in boldly coming out for consistent
> treatment of fluctuations in value as against the current, falsely-called
> conservative practice. . . .[1]

The same is true in Paton's Essentials of Accounting, which appeared in
1938. In this volume the author spoke out in favor of the combined form of income and surplus statement, which at the time was not yet common in published
reports. A new feature in this work was the discussion of the effect of changes
in the price level on capital and income. The author maintained that in order
to fulfill his function as an interpreter of the essential economic conditions
of an enterprise for the assistance of investors and the management, the accountant cannot remain blind to the limitations of conventional accounts and reports
in the face of the varying dollar. This being true, there remained the practical
problem of effectively reporting such changes. In concluding her review of this
work, Virginia Jenness remarked that it was "unmistakably a valuable contribution
to accounting literature."[2]

Henry Rand Hatfield, Review of Accounting, by W. A. Paton, The Journal of
Accountancy, XL, No. 5(November, 1925), 389-90.

J. T. Madden, Review of Accounting, by W. A. Paton, The American Association of University Instructors in Accounting, Publications, IX, No. 2(December,
1925), 158-60.

Theodore O. Yntema, Review of Accounting, by W. A. Paton, The Journal of
Political Economy, XXXIII, No. 4(August, 1925), 478-9.

[1]Hatfield, loc. cit.

[2]Virginia Jenness, Review of Essentials of Accounting, by W. A. Paton,

Paton has made another notable contribution to accounting literature in his role as editor of the Accountants' Handbook, which first appeared in 1932 as the second edition of a work of the same title edited originally in 1923 by Dr. Earl A. Saliers. Paton was much more than mere editor of this volume, for he was indubitably its principal contributor. The paramount value of the work is evidenced by its widespread use among accountants.

In addition to his longer arresting works on accounting, Paton has likewise contributed considerably to accounting, economic, and current periodicals. These articles were written in the same thought-provoking manner displayed in his more extensive writings, and one of them, "Accounting Policies of the Federal Power Commission," which appeared in the June, 1944, issue of The Journal of Account-ancy, earned for its author an award for its being "the most significant and valuable article of the year, . . ."[1]

For his contributions to accounting literature, his numerous speaking appearances before professional and other groups, and for many other weighty reasons, in 1950 Professor Paton was elected as one of the first three living North Americans to the Accounting Hall of Fame at Ohio State University.

---

incorporated into Ross G. Walker's "Explorations in Accounting," Harvard Business Review, XVIII, No. 3(Spring, 1940), 394.

[1]American Institute of Accountants, Officers & Committees, Trial Boards, State Boards of Accountancy, State Societies of CPA's, Minutes of Annual Meeting, Awards, 1954-1955(New York: American Institute of Accountants, 1954), p. 33.

Charles Forrest Rittenhouse

A. Biographical Sketch[1]

Charles Forrest Rittenhouse was born at Deersville, Ohio, October 3, 1880, and attended Deersville Academy. He won an A.B. Degree from Scio College in 1902, and a B.C.S. Degree from Northeastern University in 1914. He became a licensed certified public accountant in the state of Massachusetts in 1915 and in the state of New Hampshire in 1918.

Rittenhouse was formerly an instructor in the commercial branches of the

[1]American Accounting Association, 1955 Membership Roster.

American Institute of Accountants Fiftieth Anniversary Celebration, 1937 (Concord, New Hampshire: The Rumford Press, 1938), pp. xiii, 29.

"Elected Chairman of Board," The American Accountant, XVII, No. 4(April, 1932), 127.

Fourth International Congress on Accounting, 1933. Proceedings(London: Gee & Co., Ltd., 1933), p. xxi.

Rita Perine Merritt (ed.), The Accountants' Directory and Who's Who--1925 (New York: Prentice-Hall, Inc., 1925), p. 637.

National Association of Cost Accountants, Year Book, 1926. Proceedings of the Seventh International Cost Conference(Atlantic City, New Jersey, 1926), p. 5.

"Officers Reelected in Massachusetts," The American Accountant, XII, No. 7 (August, 1927), 50.

Rita Perine (ed.), The Accountants' Directory and Who's Who--1920(New York: The Forty-Fifth Street Press, 1920), p. 524.

"University Instructors in Accounting Hold Annual Meeting," The Pace Student, IX, No. 4(March, 1924), 58.

"What National and State Societies Have Accomplished in Year," The American Accountant, XIV, No. 5(May, 1929), 263.

High School of Commerce, Boston, Massachusetts. Later, in the same city he
served in the role of an associate professor at Simmons College. He had also
been a professor of accounting and head of the Accounting Department of the
College of Business Administration of Boston University. In addition to his
teaching duties Rittenhouse also worked as an accounting practitioner, and
served for many years as senior partner to Charles F. Rittenhouse & Co., Certified Public Accountants.

Rittenhouse was among those relatively few men who were associated with the
American Association of University Instructors in Accounting during its formative
years. It was more than likely due to men like him that the association eventually grew to be so well-recognized in accounting circles, particularly in those
circles made up of accounting teachers on the collegiate level. Rittenhouse
served the association well in those early years, as third vice-president in
1918, as second vice-president in 1919, as first vice-president in 1921 and 1922,
and finally, as president in 1923. Such dutiful service to and interest in the
problems faced by this youthful accounting society is ample evidence of Rittenhouse's prominence as an accounting teacher.

Rittenhouse was also very active in the Massachusetts Society of Certified
Public Accountants, and served that organization in the capacities of vice-
president, in 1926 and 1927, and president, in 1928. In 1933 he represented
the same society at the Fourth International Congress on Accounting, which was
held in London that year. Also a member of the National Association of Cost
Accountants, he served as president of the Boston Chapter for the year 1926-27.
He is an honorary member of the American Institute of Accountants. Moreover, he
was among the thirteen delegates sent by the Institute to London in 1933 to attend
the Fourth International Congress on Accounting. In 1936 he was elected first
vice-president of the American Institute of Accountants. In 1932 Governor Ely of
Massachusetts appointed him to serve on the Board of Registration of Certified

Public Accountants of that state. Once appointed, he was subsequently elected
to serve as chairman of the board for the same year.

B. Principal Contributions

By far the majority of Rittenhouse's works were textbooks and were in the
main written in collusion with another accounting teacher, Percy. However, there
seems to be nothing in particular to distinguish these works from many other
texts which began to appear in great numbers toward the end of the second decade
of the present century. True, nearly all of them received reviews in the current
periodical literature of the time. From these about all that need be mentioned
is the fact that Rittenhouse was apparently always on sound ground, and by
emphasizing accounting principles did to some degree contribute to the literature
of accounting text and problem books which provided for the tenderfoot and
advanced student alike the practical preparation needed for advancement both in
higher schooling in accountancy and in accounting practice.

Earl Adolphus Saliers

A. Biographical Sketch[1]

Earl Adolphus Saliers was born at Attica, Ohio, April 25, 1884. He received his early education from public schools. He earned a B.S. Degree from Heidelberg College in 1908, and an M.A. Degree from Ohio State University in 1910. During the summer of 1910 he studied at the University of Wisconsin, and in the fall of the same year enrolled in the University of Pennsylvania, from which institution he won a Ph.D. Degree in 1911.

Saliers began his career as an accounting teacher almost immediately after finishing his higher training on the university level. Hence, from 1911 to 1915

---

[1]American Accounting Association, 1955 Membership Roster.

E. Burl Austin, "Association Notes," The Accounting Review, XXVII, No. 3 (July, 1952), 397.

Jaques Cattell (ed.), Directory of American Scholars, 2d ed.(Lancaster, Pennsylvania: The Science Press, 1951), p. 817.

Robert L. Dixon, Jr., "Association Notes," The Accounting Review, XXII, No. 3(July, 1947), 326-7.

Harry D. Kerrigan, "University Notes," The Accounting Review, XV, No. 2 (June, 1940), 299; XVI, No. 2(June, 1941), 230; XVI, No. 4(December, 1941), 445.

Rita Perine (ed.), The Accountants' Directory and Who's Who--1920(New York: The Forty-Fifth Street Press, 1920), p. 535.

"University Notes," The Accounting Review, IV, No. 2(June, 1929, 145; V, No. 4(December, 1930), 339; VI, No. 4(December, 1931), 328; VII, No. 2(June, 1932), 151; XII, No. 2(June, 1937), 207; XII, No. 4(December, 1937), 454.

Who's Who in America, Vol. XXVI, 1950-51(Chicago: A. N. Marquis & Company, 1950), pp. 2394-5.

he served as an instructor in accounting at Lehigh University. He spent the
1915-1916 academic year at Yale University in the same capacity, and in 1916
was promoted to the position of assistant professor. He held this position until
1922, at which time he entered the service of the Ronald Press Company as a member of its editorial staff. After a year with this firm Saliers returned to the
teaching profession, this time as an associate professor of accounting at Northwestern University. Within a year's time he was promoted to the position of
professor, and remained in this role until 1927. In 1927 and 1928 Saliers again
left teaching, this time to serve as associate editor of the Book Division of
A. W. Shaw Company, Chicago. He spent the year 1928-1929 in writing and research.
Finally, in 1929, he accepted the position of professor and head of the Accounting Department in the newly organized School of Business Administration at the
University of Louisiana, and has held this position until quite recently.

During World War I Saliers was a Production Expert with the Bureau of Air-
craft Production from April to September, 1918. He then served as a distinguished
accountant with the S.A.T.C. from October, 1918, until June, 1919.

Professor Sailers took an active part in many accountancy and economic
societies and associations. He was one of the original members of the American
Association of University Instructors in Accounting, and served as third and
second vice-president respectively during the first two years of the Association's
existence, i.e., in 1917 and 1918. He was also an honorary member of the
Louisiana Society of Certified Public Accountants, a member of the American
Accounting Association, the Southern Economic Association, the American Institute
of Accountants, the National Commonwealth Teachers Federation, the Southern Busi-
ness Educators Association, the Southwestern Social Science Association, the Civil
Legion, the National Rifle Association, and the Beta Gamma Sigma, Beta Alpha Psi,
Delta Sigma Pi, Phi Kappa Phi, and Pi Gamma Mu fraternities. For many years
Professor Saliers was a foreign correspondent of the Société de Comptabilité de
France (The Accounting Society of France).

B. Principal Contributions

As an author and editor Saliers made many contributions to the literature
of accountancy. Those works of his which, due to their more obvious importance,
have been selected for discussion here, form only a relatively meager portion of
his total contribution. According to Bauer,[1] Saliers' Principles of Depreciation,
which appeared in 1915, was "the first comprehensive work on depreciation presented by an American writer, and for this reason alone is interesting." Although
parts of this pioneering effort on Saliers' part seemingly had received rather
inadequate treatment, nevertheless the work stood the test of time and went
through several major revisions, the last being published in 1939 under the title
Depreciation, Principles and Applications.

Further evidence of Saliers' role as a pioneer in accounting literature,
especially with regard to textbooks, is found in his Accounts in Theory and
Practice, which appeared in 1920. It would seem pertinent at this point to set
down in summary form a few of the ideas which Lawton[2] expressed in his review of
this work. He stressed the fact that in those years which rounded out the second
decade of the present century there were increasing numbers of books on accounting
being written by educators rather than by professional practitioners. Such was a
logical and natural corollary of the fact that an ever-growing number of accounting courses were being instituted in colleges and universities at that time.
This was due in part to the increase in the number of young students who intended
to make accountancy their profession, and also, seemingly more important, to the
growing awareness everywhere that knowledge of the principles of accounting is a
very necessary part of the equipment for any business or profession. Hence, in
departments other than those which dealt primarily with business courses these

---

[1]John Bauer, Review of Principles of Depreciation, by Earl A. Saliers, The
American Economic Review, VI, No. 1(March, 1916), 129-31.

[2]W. H. Lawton, Review of Accounts in Theory and Practice, by Earl A. Saliers,
The Journal of Accountancy, XXX, No. 6(December, 1920), 471-2.

subjects began to be included as subsidiary but necessary ones. Concrete evidence of this was shown in the establishment of a new industrial engineering course at Columbia University which included the study of accounting, business law, corporation finance, and factory cost.

From the above it naturally followed that members of the teaching staff of the accounting departments of various colleges and universities began to write books. Although such books were simply textbooks, it would have been a mistake to pronounce them superfluous because they merely taught what had been established as standard by professionals. These authors, Saliers' included, were practically pioneers blazing the pedagogical trails of accountancy. Just as active practitioners had after long years standardized theory and practice, so also was there need for the educators to standardize the methods of teaching them.

Saliers can also be called a pioneer for his role as general editor of the Accountants' Handbook, the first edition of which appeared in 1923. This concise compendium of information pertaining to accounts and related subjects was not intended as a replacement for other textbooks and specialized discussions of the several subjects contained in it, but rather as a supplementary reference book which would bring to the reader the information he needed and used most often. The following extracts of Rittenhouse's review seem to give both a satisfactory general summary of the work and also the high esteem with which it had quickly become regarded:

> The primary aim has been to prepare for accountants and others concerned with accounting procedure a handbook of information similar to the handbooks which have been in use for years by engineers, physicians and lawyers and which have become almost indispensable in these professions. . . .
> The work is not limited to strictly accounting material. A digest of many allied subjects is included. . . . Furthermore these subjects are not dealt with in a superficial manner as might easily have happened in a work of this kind. Lacking a textbook on any one of them, one could find almost any principle relating thereto stated and analyzed in a manner sound in substance and easy of comprehension.
> While essentially a compilation, there are many instances of originality of treatment. The selection, arrangement, and classification of the material is in itself ample proof of able scholarship and untiring research. . . .
> The editor of this work, assisted by an able staff of special

contributors and fostered by publishers who have brought out so many standard works in the field of accounting, has made a valuable and lasting contribution to the accounting profession. . . .[1]

---

[1]Charles F. Rittenhouse, Review of Accountants' Handbook, by Earl A. Saliers The American Association of University Instructors in Accounting, Publications, IX, No. 2(December, 1925), 168-70.

D. R. Scott

A. Biographical Sketch[1]

D. R. Scott was born at Monticello, Missouri, October 24, 1887. He won an
A.B. Degree and a B.S. Degree in Journalism from the University of Missouri in
1910. He was a Fellow in Economics at this university, 1910-1911, and was Austin
Scholar at Harvard, 1916-1917. He was elected a Fellow in Economics at the
University of Chicago for the 1911-1912 school year, but later resigned. In 1930
Scott won a Ph.D. Degree from Harvard University.

In 1912 Scott went to work as a reporter with the Detroit Times, but apparently newspaper-work was not his calling, for in 1914 he resigned his position
with the Times in order to teach, a career which he was to pursue the remainder
of his life. Scott spent all of his nearly forty years teaching career at the
University of Missouri. He served the university as an instructor in economics
and accounting from 1914 to 1917; he was promoted to the rank of an assistant
professor in 1919, and served as a full professor from 1920 until his death in

_____

[1]American Accounting Association, 1955 Membership Roster.

E. Burl Austin, "Association Notes," The Accounting Review, XXIX, No. 3
(July, 1954), 523.

Jaques Cattell (ed.), Directory of American Scholars, 2d ed.(Lancaster,
Pennsylvania: The Science Press, 1951), p. 837.

Rita Perine (ed.), The Accountants' Directory and Who's Who--1920(New York:
The Forty-Fifth Street Press, 1920), pp. 540-1.

"University Notes," The Accounting Review, VI, No. 2(June, 1931), 159.

Who's Who in America, Vol. XXVIII, 1954-55(Chicago: A. N. Marquis & Company, 1954), p. 2381.

February, 1954. In 1931, at Missouri, when accounting work, which prior to that time had been taught in the Department of Economics, was transferred to a new department of Accounting and Statistics, Scott was named chairman of this new department.

Scott was a member of several accounting and economic associations. He was a member of the American Economic Association, the American Association of University Instructors in Accounting and its successor, the American Accounting Association, which he served as third vice-president in 1941. He was likewise a member of the Kappa Tau Alpha, Beta Gamma Sigma, Alpha Pi Zeta, and Alpha Kappa Psi fraternities. During World War I Scott spent fifteen months as a statistician in the statistical branch of the General Staff, United States Army.

B. Principal Contributions

Scott's contributions to the literature of accountancy in the United States include two books and some fifteen or twenty periodical articles. The first of his longer works, Theory of Accounts, appeared in 1925. From several reviews[1] of the work one can get some general notions about it. In this first work there appeared certain general ideas which the author later embodied in his second work. Thus, a considerable part of the volume treated matter which was more or less foreign to the field of accounts, for the author believed that the best college preparation an individual could have for a special field of work like accounting was a good theoretical training in his specialty supplemented by similar training in as many related fields as his limited time permitted. The reviewers were very hesitant about fully accepting the author's ideas in this regard, for they apparently saw something creeping in which would break from accepted traditions on the matter. Yet, apart from this apparent hesitancy, the material of the work was

[1]Earl A. Saliers, Review of Theory of Accounts, by D. R. Scott, The Accounting Review, I, No. 2(June, 1926), 90-1.

Frank W. Thornton, Review of Theory of Accounts, by D. R. Scott, The Journal of Accountancy, LXI, No. 4(April, 1926), 313.

considered quite "safe, sane and modern."[1]

Scott's second and final work, The Cultural Significance of Accounts, appeared in 1931, and was certainly a bold pioneering effort, if there ever was one. This is brought out clearly by the reviews of this book.[2] Prior to the appearance of this work it had been customary to evaluate accounting in terms of its usefulness to the individual business enterprise. That accounting could influence and in turn be influenced by the basic social philosophy and social organization was an aspect of the subject which had received little thought and about which still less had been written. Thus, due to the great desirability of a statement of the significance of accounts in the larger field of economic relationships, Professor Scott took upon himself the ambitious effort of attempting to show the function which accounts actually have in the cultural organization of society.

The role of accounting in modern society is developed by tracing the changes in cultural patterns from the Middle Ages down to modern times. The underlying philosophy or points of view which made such development possible is sought and examined critically. Scott also presents a statement of the significance of accounts from an historical point of view. These and all the other various ideas expressed by the author orientated toward and supported his thesis that accounting was tending to become the hub of social life and economic organization. He contended that as regulation, cooperation, and monopoly tended to supplant free competition, the importance of the market as a factor of economic control declined

[1]Thornton, loc. cit.

[2]Henry Rand Hatfield, Review of The Cultural Significance of Accounts, by D. R. Scott, The Journal of Accountancy, LIV, No. 3(September, 1932), 230.

G. E. Lukas, Review of The Cultural Significance of Accounts, by D. R. Scott, The Accounting Review, VII, No. 1(March, 1932), 80-1.

R. A. Stevenson, Review of The Cultural Significance of Accounts, The American Economic Review, XXIII, No. 2(June, 1933), 286-9.

In addition, the decadence of the market was accompanied by the ascendency of accounting as the chief factor of control. As a result it might be expected that in the future the theory of market control would be supplanted by a new theory which would develop out of accounting theory. As a further result, the market, the law, and politics would all be subordinate to the new social philosophy which necessarily had to precede the predicted changes.

Of the three men who reviewed this novel work, Hatfield seems to have summed up and evaluated it best:

> The author's fundamental argument is that accounting, as a branch of statistics, is destined to "control" economic activities taking the place of "market control." Coincident with this shifting of control is the establishment of an underlying objective, scientific philosophy and the shelving of all previous conventional economic theory.
> . . . .
> The author attempted a stupendous task in trying to find an economico-philosophical interpretation of society. Praise may be due him, not for complete success in his efforts, but because, as an accountant, he has written a book which transcends mere accounting. This work, though different in scope and treatment, resembles Cummings' [Canning's] Economics of Accountancy in attempting flights previously untried. Pioneering aviators, even though failing to reach their goal deserve commendation for their efforts. So do these authors, whose works may serve as a stimulus to their successors.[1]

[1]Hatfield, loc. cit.

Clinton Homer Scovell

A. Biographical Sketch[1]

Clinton Homer Scovell, a native of New Hampshire, was born in Manchester, July 15, 1876. In 1903 he won an A.B. Degree from Harvard University, and in the following year a master's degree. Scovell's first work in accounting was with the Great Northern Railroad and United States Smelting, Refining and Mining Company. In 1907 he entered public practice with the firm of Gunn, Richards & Company, in New York. In November, 1908, he became a partner of Harvey S. Chase & Company of Boston. Several years later, in December, 1910, he organized the firm of Clinton H. Scovell & Company. On October 1, 1916, the firm name became Scovell, Wellington & Company, Mr. Wellington having become a partner on August 1, 1913. At the time of his death, December 31, 1926, Scovell was senior partner of the firm, which by that time had eight partners and had offices operating in New York, Chicago, Philadelphia, Cleveland, Syracuse, and Springfield, Massachusetts.

Scovell was accredited a certified public accountant in New York State in

---

[1]"Clinton Homer Scovell, 1876-1926," The American Accountant, XII, No. 1 (February, 1927), 31.

Rita Perine Merritt (ed.), The Accountants' Directory and Who's Who--1925 (New York: Prentice-Hall, Inc., 1925), p. 658.

National Association of Cost Accountants, Year Book, 1924. Proceedings of the Fifth International Cost Conference(Springfield, Massachusetts, 1924), p. 3.

_____, Year Book, 1925. Proceedings of the Sixth International Cost Conference(Detroit, Michigan, 1925), p. 3.

Rita Perine (ed.), The Accountants' Directory and Who's Who--1920(New York: The Forty-Fifth Street Press, 1920), p. 542.

"Prizes for Cost Essays," The Pace Student, XI, No. 5(April, 1926), 11.

1909 and in Massachusetts the following year. At the time of his death he held
membership in a number of accounting organizations, among which were the American
Institute of Accountants, and Societies of Certified Public Accountants of New
York, Massachusetts, and Illinois. Moreover, he had for many years served as a
director of the National Association of Cost Accountants and was its second vice-
president in 1924-25, and president in 1925-26. In connection with this association just mentioned, it is interesting to note that in 1926 Scovell donated to the
association $1,500 which was to be disbursed under the rules of a prize essay
competition. He contributed liberally from his time and money to educational
institutions also, and was president of the Boston School of Physical Education
when he died.

B. Principal Contributions

Scovell was a pioneer in the field of cost accounting and exhibited great
interest in advancing this form of accounting, as is evidenced by his contributing
to its literature two books, Cost Accounting and Burden Application, and Interest
as a Cost. The first volume appeared originally in 1916 and went through several
subsequent editions prior to its author's untimely death. According to FitzHugh,[1]
Scovell, in his attempt to examine the elements of cost, to define principles, and
to describe methods of procedure in the development of a cost accounting practice
--particularly with respect to the determination of overhead charges or burden,
made a most valuable addition to the literature on that particular subject. Both
FitzHugh and another reviewer[2] remarked that a noteworthy characteristic of this
work, even though written by a practicing accountant, was that it laid emphasis
upon principles rather than upon specific methods. The entire book dealt with

---

[1]M. M. FitzHugh, Review of Cost Accounting and Burden Application, by Clinton
H. Scovell, The American Economic Review, VII, No. 1(March, 1917), 137-9.

[2]Review of Cost Accounting and Burden Application, by Clinton H. Scovell,
The Journal of Political Economy, XXV, No. 6(June, 1917), 639-40.

principles and laid down general lines of procedure, and at no point were accounting forms, concrete illustrations, or specific methods set forth. The author simply separated cost and burden into their elements and considered them in relation to each other and to the business as a whole.

According to FitzHugh, perhaps the most important and to that time the least written about subject in the entire work was what the author designated as "unearned burden." Scovell advocated analyzing burden in such a manner that the part that was due to unused capacity for manufacturing might be kept separate from that due to used capacity, and, thereby, show more clearly the effect of varying volumes of business, and help in determining manufacturing and selling policies. In this first work the author also discussed at some length interest charged to cost, a subject very closely connected with unearned burden. This topic, incidentally, as shall be seen, was expounded at much greater length in the second work mentioned above, and will be discussed in greater detail below.

FitzHugh concluded his review of this work as follows:

> The work is a valuable contribution to the literature on the subject of cost accounting, and comes at a very opportune time, when managers everywhere are giving more thought than ever before to obtaining accurate and reliable cost data. . . .[1]

Scovell's second work, Interest as a Cost, appeared in 1924, a relatively short time before his death. From what constitutes a considerable number of reviews for any book one can get a rather satisfactory appraisal of this work.[2] At the time the book first appeared economists generally considered interest on capital invested in plant and other fixed assets as a cost of doing business.

---

[1]FitzHugh, loc. cit.

[2]"Book Notices," Review of Interest as a Cost, by Clinton H. Scovell, Harvard Business Review, III, No. 2(January, 1925), 255-6.

Frank H. Knight, Review of Interest as a Cost, by Clinton H. Scovell, The Journal of Political Economy, XXXIII, No. 4(August, 1925), 468-70.

George O. May, Review of Interest as a Cost, by Clinton H. Scovell, The Journal of Accountancy, XXXVII, No. 6(June, 1924), 475-6.

Although accountants had recognized the validity of this theory, they had usually been unwilling to legitimize interest as a cost by putting it on the cost books or cost records. In the fact of such practice a small group of accountants had been persistent in the belief that costs can be shown on the books only when interest is included. Scovell was recognized at the time as the leading advocate among this minority group of accountants who called for the inclusion of interest, on owned as well as borrowed capital, as an element in cost in manufacturing and merchandising. In this volume the author aimed at treating the question exhaustively, arguing his own position from every angle and attempting to answer all possible objections. By his discussion of the economic, accounting, and legal phases of the problem, the author indeed contributed to accounting literature a concise resume of the subject, for prior discussions of it had been widely diffused among a great number of sources. However, although the work apparently did not extract the topic from the realm of controversy, by reviving a question which had been actively debated by accountants and economists several years prior, it did pave the way for some learned and constructive discussions in the future, as is evidenced by the content of the reviews it received. In conclusion, the book can perhaps be best described in the words of Professor Paton as "certainly provocative."[1]

W. A. Paton, Review of Interest as a Cost, by Clinton H. Scovell, The American Economic Review, XV, No. 2(June, 1925), 321-6.

Review of Interest as a Cost, by Clinton H. Scovell, The Pace Student, IX, No. 11(October, 1924), 176.

[1]Paton, loc. cit.

Charles Ezra Sprague

A. Biographical Sketch[1]

Charles Ezra Sprague, banker, teacher, and writer on accountancy, was born at Nassau, New York, October 9, 1842, the son of the Rev. Ezra Sprague and his second wife. At the age of fourteen Charles entered Union College, Schenectady, New York, where he took all prizes for which he was eligible and was elected to Phi Beta Kappa at graduation in 1860. Later he received the degrees of M.A. and Ph. D. from Union University. In 1910, Olivet College in Michigan presented him with a Litt. D. Degree.

In May, 1862, after teaching at Greenwich Union Academy for some time, Sprague enlisted in the Union Army and saw active service during the Civil War until he was wounded at Little Round Top during the battle of Gettysburg. For meritorious service in that battle he was made a colonel in March, 1864. He served in his native state's National Guard, 1870-72, and 1897-1901, and during the latter period served as assistant postmaster-general for the state of New York.

---

[1]Helen Jo Scott Mann, "Charles Ezra Sprague," Dictionary of American Biography, XX Vols. & Supplement(New York: Charles Scribners' Sons, 1935), Vol. XVII, pp. 471-2.

Albert Nelson Marquis (ed.), Who's Who in America, Vol. VII, 1912-13 (Chicago: A. N. Marquis & Company, 1912), p. 1974.

_____, Who's Who In America, Vol. VIII, 1914-15(Chicago: A. N. Marquis & Company, 1914), p. 2208.

Charles E. Sprague, The Philosophy of Accounts, 5th ed.(New York: The Ronald Press Company, 1923), pp. iii-xxi.

The Committee on History, "Charles Ezra Sprague--Public Accountant," The New York Certified Public Accountant, XXII, No. 7(July, 1952), 430-2.

From 1864 until 1870 Sprague taught at Yonkers Military Institute, Peekskill Military Academy, and Poughkeepsie Military Academy. He wrote a considerable number of articles on military tactics, and because of his knowledge of British and Prussian military methods, he was asked to assist the commandant of the United States Military Academy in revising the book of tactics used there.

Sprague's career as a banker began in 1870. At that time his ability as an interpreter--he spoke sixteen languages--brought him a position as a clerk with the Union Dime Savings Bank in New York City. In 1877 he became secretary, then treasurer, and in 1892 president, the position he held at the time of his death. Savings bank bookkeeping owes a great deal to the various systems he devised or adapted for it. He seemed always to be searching for new and more efficient ways of performing routine tasks. Thus, he introduced the use of the small check book and pass book and the loose-leaf ledger. He likewise designed the first machine for the making of ledger entries, and worked out amortization methods which subsequently found wide usage in savings banks.

During his years as clerk at the Dime Savings Bank Sprague became a skilled accountant. This experience, together with that gained from his connections with the periodical The Bookkeeper(which was known later, July, 1883 to June, 1884, as the American Counting Room) of which for the first three years of the 1880's he was contributor and editor, experience received from several years' public accountancy work, and finally, experience acquired by frequent lectures before and during a year's service as president of the Institute of Accounts (1886), were major factors in his preparation for the more spectacular services he rendered accountancy during the last ten or fifteen years of his life. As early as 1885 Sprague was listed as a public accountant in the New York Directory. Of his later service the one of which the least is known was his relationship to the earliest effort in the world to provide specialized formal education for the public practice of accounting. The Committee on History of the New York Society of Certified Public Accountants presents the facts thus:

Early in 1892, the American Association of Public Accountants sent to the Regents of the University of the State of New York, a petition for a charter for a College of Accounts. A hearing thereon was held in Albany on June 8, 1892, when those who met with the Regents Committee included fourteen officers and members of the Association, Melvin Dewey, Secretary to the Regents (in many ways corresponding to the present Commissioner of Education) and a long-time friend of Dewey, Charles E. Sprague. There are no records of his participation in the meeting--he seems to have been only an observer--but it also seems that he may have told his friend Dewey that the purpose was important, but the proposal then made was too ambitious. If so it is highly probable that Dewey passed the advice on to the Regents.[1]

Sprague also introduced from Great Britain the system of a board of examiners for public accountants, and served as chairman of the New York board from 1896 until 1898.

Sprague had considerable influence in the establishment of the New York University School of Commerce, Accounts, and Finance in 1900, and found time in the midst of numerous other activities to teach evening classes there as a professor of accountancy from 1900 until his death.[2] Since his particular subject was without methods, texts, or other materials, Sprague himself provided them for his students. Thus, between 1900 and 1910 he wrote The Accountancy of Investment (1904), Extended Bond Tables (1905), Problems and Studies in the Accountancy of Investment (1906), Tables of Compound Interest (1907), Amortization (1908), The Philosophy of Accounts (1908), and Logarithms to 12 Places (1910).

B. Principal Contributions

Sprague's The Philosophy of Accounts, a work which went through five editions in less than fifteen years, has been honored quite recently. The date of its original appearance has been included in the recent published chronological list of dates which are reputed to have had great significance in the development of present-day accounting.[3]

---

[1]The Committee on History, op. cit., p. 432.

[2]For further information concerning Sprague's tireless efforts in this regard, cf. Joseph French Johnson's excellent article in Sprague, op. cit., pp. v-vii.

[3]"Historical Dates in Accounting," The Accounting Review, XXIX, No. 3

According to Hatfield,[1] prior to the appearance of this book American works on accounting and bookkeeping had almost without exception been mere practical manuals, and were neither scientific nor theoretical treatises. What meager theory had found its way into such works had been not only fragmentary, but often misleading and of no practical worth. Sprague broke with this line of theory, traditional with American writers, and in general agreed with the theory then current in Germany known as the theory of Hügli and Schäer.

Thus, it was characteristic of Sprague's work to insistently seek the reasons for any action. Sprague was more interested in the principle than in the mechanics--with the "why" rather than the "how." However, procedure was by no means neglected, and in a marked degree his book makes clear the regular steps through which the transactions--for whose record the accounts are created--should be successively, logically, and accurately expressed. Although abstract principles or abstract rules find little place in his work, nevertheless, the student is led to see the "wherefore" as a preliminary to each successive record up to the last.

At the turn of the present century the conventional explanation of accounting theory was to treat each account as though it represented an actual relationship of debtor and creditor, carrying out the principle by a forced and unnatural personification. Connected with this was the formulation of a rule of thumb for debiting and crediting, which in its most extreme form appeared in the common formula "Debit all that comes in and credit all that goes out." In his treatise, however, Sprague rejected the principle that there was in all cases a debtor-- either assumed or real--and pointed out that the various accounts, instead of uniformly presenting the single relationship of debtor and creditor, were

---

(July, 1954), 490.

[1]Henry Rand Hatfield, Review of The Philosophy of Accounts, by Charles E. Sprague, The Journal of Accountancy, VII, No. 5(November, 1908), 67-9.

essentially different in their nature and were to be divided into contrasting groups. With such an understanding of the nature of accounts the uniform formula for debiting and crediting naturally failed. Hence, the author clearly showed that "debit" had an entirely different significance in one set of accounts from what it had in another.

Sprague's system of classifying accounts also differed from the traditional view. For some very strange reason most American texts had clung to the antique and illogical classification of accounts as "real, personal and fictitious." The author abandoned this in favor of merely two groups, namely, Specific Accounts, i.e., those indicating assets and liabilities, and Proprietorship Accounts, i.e., those indicating capital and profit-and-loss. Sprague broke away from the traditional view once more by pointing out that accounting forms were not necessarily fixed and absolute. He was of the mind that these forms might be deviated from when anything was to be gained by such action.

These significant cleavages from the traditional American viewpoint, coupled with others of lesser import, furnish evidence enough that this work was indeed that of a brilliant pioneer in accountancy. Summing up the greatness of this treatise, Hatfield correctly called it a "masterly little treatise, with which no other American work can properly even be compared, with which even the wide literature of Germany can furnish but few rivals."[1]

Lawton, in his review of the fifth edition of this major contribution to accounting literature in this country, points out that the word "classic" often refers to a book that has fallen into that limbo of literature where everyone speaks of it with awe and nobody reads it. However, the reviewer is quick to note that such is not the case in the practical professions. He continues:

> In the practical professions, however, classic still retains an honored and honorable meaning. In each of them some pioneer has blazed a trail of broad principles, marking the path that must be followed by future generations,

---

[1]Hatfield, loc. cit.

trails that humbler workers may smooth and broaden, as woodland and prairie trails have been transformed into smooth pikes and shining rails, but whose general direction cannot be changed.

Such conception must accompany the crowning of the late Professor Sprague's Philosophy of Accounts as a classic. . . .[1]

Sprague was indeed an outstanding man, not only in accountancy, but in banking as well. Nor did his successors forget the fact; for in May, 1953, he was awarded posthumously the distinctive honor of election to Ohio State University's Accounting Hall of Fame.[2]

---

[1] W. H. Lawton, Review of The Philosophy of Accounts, by Charles E. Sprague, The Journal of Accountancy, XXXV, No. 1(January, 1923), 67-8.

[2] "Accounting Hall of Fame Names Andrews; W. A. Paton Presents Citation," (Current Notes) The Journal of Accountancy, XCVI, No. 1(July, 1953), 16.

Ross Graham Walker

A. Biographical Sketch[1]

Ross Graham Walker, a native of Athens, Michigan, was born August 31, 1891.
He received an A.B. Degree from the University of Michigan in 1920, and an honorary A.M. Degree from Harvard University in 1938. In 1920 Walker began his teaching career as an instructor in economics at the University of Michigan. He remained at Michigan for two years. In 1924, apparently having busied himself in
some other occupation after resigning from the University of Michigan, he once
more resumed teaching, this time as a professor of commerce at the State University of Iowa. In 1926 Walker left this Midwest campus and headed east to assume
the duties of assistant professor of accounting at the Harvard Graduate School of
Business Administration. Although by 1931 Walker had risen to the position of an
associate professor at the Graduate School, he nevertheless seemed to have things
other than teaching in mind, at least pro tem, for in that year he left Harvard's
accounting department in order to become treasurer and director of the Hamilton
Woolen Company, of Southbridge, Massachusetts. He remained in this capacity,
concurrently serving as vice-president and director of the Southbridge Savings
Bank, until 1935. Walker returned to Harvard in 1936, and since then has been a
professor of business administration in the graduate school of that subject.

During World War I Walker served as a sergeant in the Headquarters Attach-
ment of the 14th Division, United States Army. Since 1928 he has served as a

---

[1]"University Notes," The Accounting Review, I, No. 2(June, 1926), 101; VI,
No. 2(June, 1931), 158.

Who's Who in America, Vol. XXVIII, 1954-55(Chicago: A. N. Marquis & Company,
1954), p. 2769.

consultor in management economics and industrial accounting. He is presently a trustee in the Controllership Foundation. He is also a member of the Controllers Institute of America, having served this institution as chairman of the Committee on Education from 1944 until 1948. He is likewise a member of the Phi Beta Kappa and Alpha Tau Omega fraternities.

B. Principal Contribution

Although in comparison with most of the other accounting teachers and practitioners discussed herein Walker has contributed a somewhat meager portion to accountancy literature, nevertheless, his major contribution, Problems in Accounting Principles, which appeared in 1929, was of considerable importance. In order to understand the practical value of this work, it is necessary to set down in general outline various reasons which seem to have been responsible, in part at least, for the writing of the book.[1] Lawton, in his review of the work, sets forth several very cogent reasons. He remarked that accounting theory and the principles of various other facets of accounting could be learned easily in a short time by any bright high school graduate. In contrast, however, a knowledge of practical accounting could be attained only by practical experience. Hence, state certified public accountant laws required one or more years of actual employment in public accounting as a preliminary to the certified public accountant examination. Such a theory might have been correct back in the mid-teens and early twenties, but seemed rather doubtful at the time the book appeared; for, due to the fact that only the largest public accounting firms handled a wide variety of businesses while the remainder tended to specialize according to locality or personal fitness, the candidate could rarely obtain the broad practical

[1]Edgar B. Kapp (ed.), Review of Problems in Accounting Principles, by Ross G. Walker, The American Accountant, XIV, No. 9(September, 1929), 491-2.

W. H. Lawton, Review of Problems in Accounting Principles, by Ross G. Walker, The Journal of Accountancy, XLVIII, No. 5(November, 1929), 394-5.

H. F. Taggart, Review of Problems in Accounting Principles, by Ross G.

training needed to cover the range of average certified public accountant examination papers. The only logical conclusion was that in the future the ranks of certified public accountants would be filled largely by graduates from standard business schools, and as a corollary, that training in accounting had to be supplied through laboratory work.

Professor Walker's Problems in Accounting Principles was an example of how one important business school was handling this important laboratory work. The volume constituted perhaps the first formal attempt to apply the case method to elementary accounting instruction. It was not a textbook in the ordinary sense. True, the topics considered covered the usual territory of the elementary text, but in arrangement and importance assigned they differed decidedly from the ordinary treatise. Considerably more attention was devoted to matters of interpretation and analysis than to technique. The whole theory of the case book was not merely to give the student a bit of information and then explain why such was so. The book attempted rather to present typical business conditions and allowed the student to explore and find his own way in the field of accounting. This process of exploration was guided by classroom instruction and discussion so that when an accounting truth did appear out of a given problem its true application would be clear.

Such was Walker's attempted solution to the problem of the lack of well-rounded practical accounting experience needed by the individual who was soon to appear before his local Certified Public Accountant Board of Examiners. Although the "case" method had been employed in courses in marketing, industrial finance, and business economics at Harvard Business School for many years, Walker was the first to overcome the obstacles peculiar to its being used in accounting. In general it may be said that the work was received quite favorably. For example, Taggart remarked: "The work cannot but be considered an important addition to

---

Walker and P. B. Coffman, The American Economic Review, XX, No. 1(March, 1930), 120-1.

accounting literature."[1] That the book was well thought of by many in the field

of accounting is very evident from the fact that as a result of a popular vote

it ranked among the top six contributions to accountancy literature for the year

ended May 1, 1929.[2]

---

[1]Taggart, loc. cit.

[2]Cf. "Wildman-Powell Book Designated as Most Notable of Year," The American Accountant, XV, No. 2(January, 1930), 18.

John R. Wildman

A. Biographical Sketch[1]

John Raymond Wildman was born at Yonkers, New York, March 15, 1878. He was educated at Yale University and New York University, and held Sc.B., B.C.S. (cum laude) and M.C.S. degrees. While attending the latter university Wildman won an accounting prize. He served during the Spanish-American War both in the United States and Porto Rico, and in various operations incident to American organization in Porto Rico from 1898 to 1900. During these years and until 1905 Wildman was a government disbursing officer, and in 1904 served as general manager of the Porto Rican Teachers' Expedition to the United States. From 1905 until 1909 Wildman served on the New York staff of Haskins and Sells.

Wildman's teaching career was confined to the years 1909 to 1923, during which time he served as an instructor in accounting and professor of accounting at New York University. His final five years teaching were combined with professional practice, for he rejoined the firm of Haskins and Sells on December 1, 1918, where, in subsequent years, among other capacities he held those of director

---

[1]American Accounting Association, 1955 Membership Roster.

"Convention Report," American Accounting Association, Proceedings of the Twenty-Third Annual Convention(Detroit, Michigan, December 28-30, 1938), 80.

Rita Perine Merritt (ed.), The Accountants' Directory and Who's Who--1925 (New York: Prentice-Hall, Inc., 1925), p. 715.

Rita Perine (ed.), The Accountants' Directory and Who's Who--1920(New York: The Forty-Fifth Street Press, 1920), p. 588.

"Views of Profession with Respect to Depreciation Clearly Stated," The American Accountant, XIV, No. 10(October, 1929), 542.

of professional training and director of Technical Procedure. Once he had laid teaching aside, Wildman apparently continued with this firm until the time of his death in September, 1938.

During his lifetime Wildman was a certified public accountant of various states. He was a member of the New York State Society of Certified Public Accountants, the Society of Certified Public Accountants of the State of New Jersey, the American Society of Certified Public Accountants, the American Institute of Accountants, the National Association of Cost Accountants, the American Economic Association, and the American Statistical Association.

Not mentioned in the above enumeration was the American Association of University Instructors in Accounting. Wildman had a very special connection with this association. He was numbered among that small gathering which met in December, 1916, at the Deschler Hotel in Columbus, Ohio, in order to establish the association. Those present at that initial gathering elected Wildman as first president of the American Association of University Instructors in Accounting, and from that time onward he spent a great amount of time in promoting and furthering its causes. Scovill, during the twenty-third annual convention of the Association, which met just several months after Wildman's death, seems to have expressed most aptly the sentiments of not only those who knew him well but also of the accounting profession as a whole:

> To his foresight and interest probably more than to those of any other one individual may be attributed the formation of the Association twenty-three years ago. . . . Up to the time of his death, however, in September, 1938, he maintained an interest in the welfare of the Association and was always willing to assist in an advisory manner in promoting its ideals and purposes.
>
> In view of his intimate relationship with, and keen interest in the Association, and in view of the esteem in which he was held by the members, be it thereby
>
> Resolved: That in the death of John R. Wildman, Accounting education and the Accountancy profession have lost a practical thinker, an excellent teacher, a profound scholar, a reliable author and a valued leader in professional thought and conduct.[1]

---

[1]"Convention Report," loc. cit.

B. Principal Contributions

Of the books written by Wildman only two will be discussed here. The first, Principles of Auditing, appeared originally in 1916, and was followed several years later by a second edition. Since Montgomery's Auditing had appeared just several years previous, such a thing as a new book on auditing seemed, at first thought, almost a presumption. However, as several reviewers[1] remarked, once one had scanned several pages of its contents he learned that the title was apparently a misnomer. Professor Cole suggested that a more appropriate title would have been "The Technique of Auditing," for most of the chapter headings suggested processes rather than principles. Principles were enunciated here and there, but what the book really contained was a mass of detailed instructions of what to do before, during and after an audit. Although the young auditor could and should learn audit technique by practical experience, nevertheless this book, representing a type of accounting literature which was comparatively rare in those early years, provided him with an opportunity to learn the customary details before he would actually be called upon to use them.

Elwell, writing over a decade later, remarked how well Wildman's work had been received and pointed out in particular the great influence it had had on subsequent auditing textbook writers:

> The reviewer believes that John R. Wildman was the first American accounting instructor to publish an auditing text in which the student was given a specific detailed procedure to be followed. Wildman's "Principles of Auditing" was published at least eleven years ago and marked a distinct advance in the type of text material available for accounting majors. The publication of so many auditing texts within the past few years in which Wildman's basic idea has been used and developed proves the soundness of the method. Instructors generally, therefore, may well place another mark to the credit of the first president of The American Association of University Instructors in Accounting, a gentleman whose vision, judgment, and knowledge

---

[1]William Morse Cole, Review of Principles of Auditing, by John Raymond Wildman, The American Economic Review, VI, No. 3(September, 1916), 644-7.

W. H. Lawton, Review of Principles of Auditing, by John Raymond Wildman, The Journal of Accountancy, XXII, No. 2(July, 1916), 70-1.

of the subject has meant so much for accounting instructional methods in this country.[1]

Wildman's most important contribution to accountancy literature during this period, Capital Stock Without Par Value, which appeared in 1928, was written in conjunction with Weldon Powell, at that time also connected with Haskins and Sells.[2] Of the reviews written on this work, Kapp's review appears to have summarized its content very well. The following are several of his remarks:

> The present volume . . . combines in its discussion the studious back-ground of the theorist with the eminent soundness of the practitioner.
> The authors have sought to simplify the subject rather than to becloud it with too-refined distinctions and dissertations. . . . The authors stress the similarities rather than the differences between par and no-par shares, from the view-point of the accountant; the fundamental concept back of both types of shares is that of capital.
> . . . .
> Early in the book four fundamental principles are set up, namely that capital is a complex of invested values, that divisible surplus arises from profitable utilization of assets, that capital may not be distributed in the guise of profits, and that dividends may be paid out of earned surplus only. After the discussion which is based upon these principles, the authors conclude that "common shares without par value, when used rationally and in accordance with sound economic principles, have advantages which outweigh those shares having par value," and that "preferred shares without par value are unsound in principle." It is further their belief that "stated capital and stated value per share are fictions for which there is no economic warrant."[3]

Professor Jackson lauded the work highly:

> Pages could be written concerning the good things that are contained in this volume. After a somewhat careful perusal of it, the reviewer is of the

---

[1]F. H. Elwell, Review of Auditing Procedure, by DeWitt C. Eggleston, The Accounting Review, II, No. 1(March, 1927), 67.

[2]Cf. "Wildman-Powell Book Designated as Most Notable of Year," The American Accountant, XV, No. 1(January, 1930), 19. Mr. Powell, also a certified public accountant, was a native of Indiana. He received his education at Indiana University and the University of Illinois, graduating from the latter in 1922 with a B.S. Degree. He returned to Illinois as an instructor in accounting, at the same time taking graduate work in accounting and economics, and received an M.S. Degree in 1923. His thesis for the master's degree at the University of Illinois was on the subject, "No-Par Stock."

[3]Edgar B. Kapp, (ed.), Review of Capital Stock Without Par Value, by John R. Wildman and Weldon Powell, The American Accountant, XIV, No. 3(March, 1929), 158.

opinion that it is one of the simplest, most sensible statements on accounting matters that has appeared in recent years. This coupled with the fact that it deals with a much-debated and elusive subject, assures it a permanent place in the literature of accounting.

The commendable thing about the volume is that first things are put first, or, to state the matter differently, important things are those which are emphasized. . . .[1]

The utmost praise redounded upon the co-authors of this work when, during the annual convention of the American Association of University Instructors in Accounting, held in Washington, December 27 and 28, 1929, Professor A. C. Littleton, in behalf of Beta Alpha Psi, the professional and honorary fraternity for college students specializing in accounting, presented to them scrolls of honor for having made in the writing of Capital Stock Without Par Value the most notable contribution to accounting literature during the year ending May 1, 1929.[2]

---

[1]J. Hugh Jackson, Review of Capital Stock Without Par Value, by John R. Wildman and Weldon Powell, The Accounting Review, IV, No. 4(December, 1929), 263.

[2]Cf. "Wildman-Powell Book Designated as Most Notable of Year," loc. cit.

CONCLUSION

Having discussed at length the prevalent thoughts and tendencies in accounting literature in the Introduction, and having proceeded at greater length in discussing the particular individuals who seem to have been to a great degree responsible for the existence of these tendencies in Chapters I, II, and III, it is now expedient to attempt appropriate conclusions.

If one carefully checks the educational background of the various men spoken of in the foregoing chapters he can readily discern that in nearly all instances each received a college education, and in many cases continued his higher schooling until he won either a master's or doctor's degree. Thus, of the twenty-six individuals discussed in the previous chapters twenty-three possessed bachelor's degrees, sixteen, master's degrees, and ten, doctor's degrees. Moreover, only two of the leading American accountants, namely, Montgomery and Nicholson, never attended college. Indeed, two-thirds of the twenty-four men who did attend college held graduate degrees. Furthermore, seven, namely, Cole, Finney, Himmelblau, Newlove, Paton, Saliers, and Scott are listed in the Directory of American Scholars, while all but six were listed in the Who's Who in America and the Who's Who, nineteen in the former, one (Dickinson) in the latter. Moreover, Guthmann, Hatfield, Klein, Paton, Sprague, and Walker were members of Phi Beta Kappa. Saliers was a member of Pi Gamma Mu, the national Social Science Honorary Society, while Wildman was a member of the Delta Mu Delta Scholarship Society.

In view of the above facts it is easy to realize why these men earned for themselves such an honorable name among their teaching and practicing confreres

138

in accounting. Their intellectual abilities, coupled with their firm determination to excel in scholastic activities, no doubt served well as a kind of boot-training for the work in which they were later engaged. They knew by hard experience the many stumbling blocks along the road to the attainment of higher scholastic degrees; and in overcoming these earlier difficulties they adequately prepared themselves for combatting those which were to come later.

It is highly logical that only men of such caliber could serve accountancy as eager yet prudent pioneers, blazing new trails in accounting thought and literature during the early years of the present century. Moreover, to their fine educational background was frequently added many years of valuable experience in both teaching and practicing accounting. Thus, of the twenty-six men, ten can be considered almost exclusively as accounting teachers, two as connected wholly with accounting practice, and the remaining fourteen as having spent considerable time both in teaching and in practice. Furthermore, only six were not certified public accountants. Of the twenty holders of certified public accountant certificates, several were licensed by more than one state.

All these merits stood these outstanding American accountants in good stead when it came to writing down the combined thought of classroom and office. Moreover, their frequent contact with others well-known in accounting educational and professional circles gave them an opportunity to air their views, as well as to imbibe the views and comments offered by others, who were often extremely conversant with problems then faced by educator and professional alike. While the latter were confronted with myriad day-by-day problems by their clientele, the former, realizing the growing need for educating young accounting apprentices both in the theory and practice of accounting, were constantly faced with problems in revising subject matter so as always to present the most up-to-date views in both theory and practice.

These and many other reasons indicate that these men were outstanding pioneers in accounting literature. They were actual witnesses to changes, and because of these changes saw the needs arising in American accountancy at the turn of the century. However, they were not content to stand on the sidelines with eyes half-closed and mouths agape at what was taking place. Their fertile minds sought out and found solutions for the many problems. When they themselves did not formulate them, they accurately recorded their findings as reporters and witnesses of what others were doing to solve the problems. To write as these men did required not only a keen insight into the many current problems but also a subtle foresight of what the future would demand.

The latter half of the Introduction to this dissertation was concerned primarily with a discussion of the tendencies in accounting literature most prominent during the period under review. In that discussion mention of particular works to illustrate these tendencies was purposely omitted. It seemed that only after the principal works had been discussed summarily in the subsequent three chapters could these books be properly appraised and said to exemplify a certain tendency.

However, before listing examples of the several important tendencies in accounting literature, it must first be noted that whether a work is fundamentally theoretical or practical, there is almost inevitably a commingling of the two orders in every work. While this observation might prove less true in instances when material of a practical nature is added to a treatise which is primarily theoretical, it nevertheless holds true with remarkable consistency for works written primarily for accounting practice. Any practical work must almost always include at least the basic theory in order to insure the working out of problems in the most accurate manner. Hence, in all the works called upon to exemplify a certain tendency, there is included, to a lesser or greater degree depending upon the type of work, some admixture of both theoretical and practical aspects.

The tendency among the theoretical works toward a philosophical or logical approach is well-exemplified by Cole's Accounts, Their Contruction and Interpretation, Sprague's The Philosophy of Accounts, Hatfield's Modern Accounting, and Esquerre's The Applied Theory of Accounts. Quite naturally the tendency to avoid the mercantile point of view worked its way into those works which ex professo dealt with industrial accounting. Nicholson's Factory Organization and Costs and Scovell's Cost Accounting and Burden Application are patent examples of this particular leaning in the literature of the time. Stephen Gilman's Accounting Concepts of Profit was a later treatise discussing many of the ideas which, during the previous decade or longer, had advocated that greater attention be given to income accounting.

There are also many examples of works which tended to lay the greater stress on the practical aspect of accounting. Suffice it here to single out for the different categories only those which appear to be the more important. Paton's Accounting Theory with Special Reference to the Corporate Enterprise, Bell's two-volume work Theory and Practice of Accounting: Use in Managerial Control, Gilman's Analyzing Financial Statements, McKinsey's Managerial Accounting, and especially Bliss's two works, namely, Financial and Operating Ratios in Management and Management Through Accounts, are all excellent works written primarily to aid management in their control of day-to-day business activities. Among the works which served as an aid to those engaged in public accounting are Montgomery's Auditing, Eggleston's Auditors' Reports and Working Papers, Himmelblau's Auditors' Certificates, Wildman's Principles of Auditing, and also the many detailed income-tax manuals which began to appear yearly after the income tax amendment became effective on February 25, 1913. Among the many authors of tax manuals Montgomery and Klein deserve special mention.

Eggleston's two works, Municipal Accounting and Wall Street Procedure are examples of works dealing at length with special classes of business. Many text-books could be cited, but a few examples should suffice. Klein's Elements of

<u>Accounting</u>, Dickinson's <u>Accounting Practice and Procedure</u>, Kester's <u>Accounting</u> <u>Theory and Practice</u>, Littleton's <u>An Introduction to Elementary Accounting</u> and the many works of Finney and others furnished the student with adequate texts with which to prepare himself for work in the field of accountancy.

Nearly all the works just mentioned, together with the many periodical articles written in the same vein or along similar lines, formed a considerable amount of material on the various aspects of accounting. In fact, there was almost too much being written for one to read it all. No doubt the individual educator or practitioner found it next to impossible to keep up even on the more important changes in accounting theory and practice. Hence, the accounting teacher or professional wishing to learn the latest methods of accounting theory and procedure, as well as all currently successful practices in what was quickly becoming a vast field, was faced with an endless task. One work, however, Salier's <u>Accountants' Handbook</u>, which was similar to those previously issued for doctors and lawyers, gave to the accounting teacher and practitioner alike a handy reference manual containing a good percentage of necessary knowledge. This momentous work first appeared in 1923. Subsequent editions of it were revised and brought up to date under the able editorship of Paton. In compiling this work both men were aided of necessity by many learned contributors and collaborators.

These writings, in addition to the others discussed in the body of this dissertation, form a relatively small but important representation of the total contributions made to accounting literature by the twenty-six men selected for recognition. Hence, the general purpose for which this study was initially made, namely, to find out who the pioneers were and what contributions they actually made, seems almost complete. Nevertheless, the enumeration in Appendix F of other books and periodical articles contributed by these men to accounting thought during the first three decades of the twentieth century fills out that aim more completely.

At this point several concluding observations should be made concerning the esteem with which these men were held by both contemporary and subsequent leaders in accounting. It ought to be noted first that contemporary reviewers of these works seem most fair in their appraisal of them and their authors. This opinion gathers greater strength when several reviewers of the same work coincide in their impressions about its relative merits or weak points. Thus, when several well-known reviewers in chorus-like fashion agree that a particular author should be highly commended for a particular publication, there is solid evidence for dreaming that individual of outstanding ability. It is all the more convincing when such evidence is available not merely for one but for several works written by the same author. All this evidence converges upon the conclusion that a certain writer is outstanding and of superior talent. Yet, this recognition together with laudatory comments from fellow educators or practitioners, as well as that given by reviewers of subsequent editions of a particular work, seems comparatively meager praise for men whose writings were not only responsible for forming the principal aspects of accounting thought in their own day but also sowed the seeds of many of the foremost aspects of accounting thought and practice at the present time.

This paucity of recognition may no doubt in certain respects be due to the comparative youth of the accounting profession in the United States. Just like a youngster who has grown up so rapidly that he doesn't have time to take stock of all that occurred while he was actually going through the process of maturity, so accounting and accountants in America, because of their relatively rapid progress in attaining maturity, did not take time out to look back and see in detail what it had gone through and who had so ably guided it in its process of maturation. One would like to think--and there seems to be good reason for so doing-- that this was not because of neglect or forgetfulness, but rather because of a constant endeavor to keep moving ahead.

Nevertheless, accountants, both educators and professionals alike, have within the past several decades or so taken proper steps toward bestowing recognition upon those who took such an important part in making accounting literature in the United States what it is today. The majority of these steps forward have been mentioned within the body of this dissertation. However, to obtain a more complete picture of the attempts to recognize those worthy of praise for their outstanding contributions to accounting literature, it seems apropos at this time to trace at least sketchily the main phases of these endeavors. Since several appendices have been included below to give the reader more exact information about what certain organizations and individuals have accomplished along these lines during the past quarter-century or longer, only a brief summary of these accomplishments needs be set forth here.

Believing that special recognition given a man by fellow members in a particular field naturally tends to enkindle in that man an ardent desire to strive for greater perfection in his particular work, Beta Alpha Psi,[1] National Accounting Fraternity, from 1928 until 1936 presented annual awards to the authors or co-authors of the most notable contributions to accounting literature. Of the men spoken of in this present work Hatfield was selected as winner of this award in 1928, co-authors Wildman and Powell in 1929, and Littleton in 1933.

World War II interrupted the presentation of awards by Beta Alpha Psi for outstanding contributions to accounting literature. For several reasons this highly commendable practice was not resumed after the war. One was that in 1944 a system of awards was initiated by the American Institute of Accountants.[2] Although in the majority of cases these awards have been presented to those engaged in professional and governmental accounting work, nevertheless on several occasions awards have been granted to a particular individual or individuals for

---

[1]For further information, cf. Appendix A, p. 147.

[2]Cf. Appendix B, p. 150.

contributing what the awards' committee estimated to be the most important and valuable book or article in the field of accounting during a particular year. Of special note is that an award was given Robert H. Montgomery in 1949 for outstanding service to the accounting profession over the years and for his writings.

A second and more important reason for Beta Alpha Psi's discontinuing its award program was the establishment at Ohio State University in 1950 of the Accounting Hall of Fame.[1] This Hall of Fame, which has as its principal purpose the honoring of living North Americans who have made outstanding contributions at any time to the field of accounting, has also honored posthumously those whose contributions would have warranted election had it been established earlier. It is most interesting to note that among the special qualifications demanded for eligibility the criterion accorded first place is worded "contribution to accounting literature." Of the men treated in the foregoing chapters six, namely, Montgomery, Paton, Dickinson, Hatfield, Littleton, and Sprague have won election to the Accounting Hall of Fame.

In 1952, Alpha Kappa Psi,[2] professional fraternity in commerce and business administration, established an annual award in the form of a life membership in the American Accounting Association, which was to be presented to that particular individual who, by reason of his contributions to accounting, was selected by the Association. Of the four who have received this award to the present time two, namely, Paton and Littleton, have been discussed in this dissertation.

An Article entitled "Historical Dates in Accounting,"[3] which appeared in the July, 1954, issue of The Accounting Review, while concerned principally in setting down in chronological order certain important dates in accounting, in so doing recognized on six occasions accounting treatises whose appearance was of

[1]Cf. Appendix C, p. 152.
[2]Cf. Appendix D, p. 156.
[3]Cf. Appendix E, p. 158.

definite import in the history of accounting in the United States. The six works cited were the following: The Philosophy of Accounts (Sprague--1908), Accounts-- Their Construction and Interpretation (Cole--1908), Modern Accounting (Hatfield-- 1909), Auditing Theory and Practice (Montgomery--1912), Accounting Theory and Practice (Kester--1917), and Elementary Accounting (Littleton--1919). This enumeration bears mute but eloquent testimony to the greatness of their authors.

These final paragraphs have indicated the attempts which have been made to give proper recognition to those deserving it by reason of their outstanding contributions to accounting literature. Whereas the Beta Alpha Psi awards were bestowed solely because of outstanding literary contributions, the later awards and commendations were given for more than literary work alone. This is not to say, however, that the other forms of encomium overlooked so important an aspect as a person's total contributions to the field. Undoubtedly on many occasions when an award was given the determining factor was that the person selected had accomplished excellent work in the literary phase of the field of accounting.

In conclusion it can safely be stated that all these means of recognition are, after all, only a gentlemanly way of rendering deep appreciation to those who had performed their role well, and extend to younger and less experienced men and women in the field of accounting the incentive to labor assiduously to do all in their power to maintain the high standards set by their prominent predecessors.

APPENDIX A

Beta Alpha Psi Awards

Beta Alpha Psi,[1] National Accounting Fraternity for college students specializing in accounting, from 1928 to 1936 presented awards for the most notable contributions to the literature of accounting.[2] The procedure used in selecting
the best work of a particular year seems to have been a most satisfactory one.

---

[1]"Beta Alpha Psi, a professional accounting fraternity, was organized
February 12, 1919, at the University of Illinois. Its purpose as expressed in
its constitutions is 'to encourage and foster the ideal of service as the basis
of the accounting profession, to promote the study of accounting with a view toward securing the highest ethical ideals; to act as a medium between professional
men, instructors, students and others who are interested in the development of
the study or profession of accountancy; to develop high moral, professional, and
scholastic standards in its members; and to encourage cordial intercourse among
its members of the profession of accountancy.'" Alvan E. Duerr (ed.), Baird's
Manual American College Fraternities, 14th ed.(Menasha, Wisconsin: The Collegiate
Press George Banta Publishing Company, 1940), p. 390.

[2]For further information, cf. the following articles:

"Award of Merit for Hatfield Book Should Stimulate Authors," The American
Accountant, XIV, No. 1(January, 1929), 28-30.

"Book on Economics of Accountancy Chosen as Best of Year," The American
Accountant, XVI, No. 1(January, 1931), 22-3.

"Popular Vote Being Taken to Choose Best Accounting Book of Year," The
American Accountant, XV, No. 7(July, 1930), 323.

"To Choose Best Book," The American Accountant, XVI, No. 6(June, 1931),
184-5.

"What Was Best Book on Accounting Published During Year?" The American
Accountant, XIV, No. 7(July, 1929), 383-4.

"Wildman-Powell Book Designated as Most Notable of Year," The American
Accountant, XV, No. 1(January, 1930), 18-9.

First, a list of the accounting books published during the year was drawn up in May from book reviews published during the year and from a canvass of the publishing houses. This list was submitted to teachers and accountants for their votes of first, second, and third ranking. When these returns were all in, the results were tabulated by the president of the fraternity's Grand Council, and from the results the six or seven books were selected which had received the greatest preference in the general voting.

This list of six or seven was then submitted to the six professional men who constituted the fraternity's Grand Council. No one but the president knew the ranking of the six or seven books according to the popular balloting; the list was submitted in alphabetical form by authors. The council members then familiarized themselves with the selected books and separately voted for their first and second choices as the most notable contribution. The vote of the council was the deciding factor; the popular vote only governed the selection of those books which eventually received intensive consideration.

The award presented to individual winners was a parchment scroll which set forth in simple language an appreciation of the winner's book. The scroll was executed in hand engrossed lettering in which the initial capitals were beautifully illuminated colors after the manner of manuscripts of the medieval period.

The primary purpose of this endeavor by students in accounting was in a modest way to encourage the production and use of good technical books.

From 1928 to 1936 Beta Alpha Psi awards for the most outstanding contributions to accounting literature were made to the following:

> Henry Rand Hatfield, for Accounting--Its Principles and Problems.
> John R. Wildman and Weldon Powell, for Capital Stock Without Par Value.
> John R. Canning, for The Economics of Accountancy.
> William B. Castenholtz, for The Control of Distribution Costs and Sales.
> A. P. Richardson, for The Ethics of a Profession.
> A. C. Littleton, for Accounting Evolution to 1900.
> National Committee on Municipal Accounting, for work in this field.

The second World War interrupted the presentation of awards by the fraternity for outstanding contributions in the field of accounting literature. After the war the giving of awards was not resumed, since the Ohio State Hall of Fame and the American Institute of Accountants began at or shortly after that time to provide suitable recognition for such achievements. At present most of the Beta Alpha Psi awards are given to honor accountants for outstanding practical work and organizational work by presenting them with honorary membership in the organization.

APPENDIX B

American Institute of Accountants Awards

Shortly before the end of World War II the American Institute of Accountants set up a special committee on annual awards. Based upon the recommendations of this committee the American Institute has continued to present annual awards for outstanding public service to the accounting profession and for the most significant and valuable article on an accounting subject published in a particular fiscal year. These awards have normally been presented at the annual meeting of the American Institute of Accountants.[1]

Since 1944 the following have received awards for either one or the other of the things specifically mentioned above:

```
1944--J. Harold Stewart
       George Oliver May
       William A. Paton
1945--Victor H. Stempf
       E. L. Kohler and W. W. Cooper
1946--Arthur H. Carter
       Maurice E. Peloubet
1947--T. Coleman Andrews
1948--Edward A. Kracke
       N. Loyall McLaren
1949--Hiram T. Scovill
       Robert H. Montgomery
1950-and 1951 (No Awards.)
1952--Samuel J. Broad
       Percival F. Brundage
1953--Carman G. Blough
       Mark E. Richardson
```

---

[1]"Official Decisions and Releases," The Journal of Accountancy, LXXX, No. 6 (December, 1945), 492.

1954--Maurice H. Stans
1955--Saul Levy
    Lloyd Morey[1]

---

[1]American Institute of Accountants, <u>Officers & Committees, Trial Boards,</u>
<u>State Boards of Accountancy, State Societies of CPA's, Minutes of Annual Meeting,</u>
<u>Awards, 1954-1955</u>(New York: American Institute of Accountants, 1954), pp. 33-4.

APPENDIX C

Accounting Hall of Fame[1]

In 1950 the Department of Accounting at the Ohio State University established an Accounting Hall of Fame to which are elected living North Americans who
have made outstanding contributions to the field of accounting--public, private,
governmental, or educational. Additional elections are also made to honor posthumously those whose contribution would have warranted election if this Hall of
Fame had been established earlier. Among the criteria for selection are the
following:

1. Contribution to accounting literature.
2. Public speaking before professional and other groups.
3. Service to accounting organizations of a professional character.
4. Recognition as an authority in a particular field.
5. Public service.
6. Previous honor awards in the profession and honorary degrees conferred
   by universities.

---

[1]"Accounting Hall of Fame Names Andrews; W. A. Paton Presents Citation,"
The Journal of Accountancy, XCVI, No. 1(July, 1953), 16.

"Accounting Hall of Fame," The Canadian Chartered Accountant, LXV, No. 4
(October, 1954), 182-3.

E. Burl Austin (ed.), "Association Notes," The Accounting Review, XXVI,
No. 3(July, 1951), 431; XXVIII, No. 4(October, 1953), 594; XXIX, No. 3(July,
1954), 523.

"Dickinson, Hatfield Chosen for 1951 Awards at Ohio State's Hall of Fame,"
The Journal of Accountancy, XCII, No. 2(August, 1951), 135.

J. Brooks Heckert, "Accounting Hall of Fame," The Accounting Review, XXV,
No. 3(July, 1950), 260-1.

Nicholas A. H. Stacey, "The Accounting Hall of Fame," The Accountant,
CXXXI, (July 31, 1954), 108.

The faculty of the Department of Accounting appoints a Nominating Board of forty-five, consisting of fifteen public accountants, fifteen industrial and governmental accountants, and fifteen accounting educators. Appointments to the Nominating Board run for three years (except for the initial appointments), and one-third of each class is appointed each year in order to maintain the full membership of the Board.

Nominations are made by the Board, and from these a list of ten names receiving the highest nominating vote is resubmitted to the Board for final vote. Election to the Hall of Fame is declared on the basis of those receiving the highest preferential vote in the final ballot. Should any member of the Nominating Board be included in the preliminary nomination and be among the ten receiving the highest vote, he is not permitted to participate in the final ballot. The Department of Accounting at the University determines only the number of persons to be honored in a single year. Those so honored are the ones receiving the highest majorities in the final ballot.

Accountants elected to the Hall of Fame are invited to attend the annual Institute on Accounting sponsored each May at the University. An appropriate scroll is presented at the banquet session and a framed photograph is mounted in the halls of the College of Commerce and Administration. Persons elected to the Accounting Hall of Fame to date are as follows:

1950

Living at Time of Election
George Oliver May — Price Waterhouse & Company
Robert Heister Montgomery — Lybrand, Ross Bros. & Montgomery
William Andrew Paton — University of Michigan

1951

Deceased at Time of Election
Arthur Lowes Dickinson — Price Waterhouse & Company
Henry Rand Hatfield — University of California

1952

Deceased at Time of Election
    Elijah Watt Sells   Haskins & Sells
    Victor Hermann Stempf   Touche, Niven, Bailey & Smart

1953

Living at Time of Election
    Thomas Coleman Andrews   U.S. Commissioner of Internal Revenue

Deceased at Time of Election
    Arthur Edward Andersen   Arthur Andersen & Company
    Joseph Edmund Sterrett   Price Waterhouse & Company
    Charles Ezra Sprague   Dime Savings Bank

1954

Living at Time of Election
    Carman George Blough   Director of Research, American Institute
                             of Accountants
    Samuel John Broad   Peat, Marwick, Mitchell & Company
    Hiram Thompson Scovill   University of Illinois

Deceased at Time of Election
    Thomas Henry Sanders   Harvard School of Business Administration

1955

Living at Time of Election
    Percival Flack Brundage   Bureau of the Budget

1956

Living at Time of Election
    A. C. Littleton   University of Illinois

Although the Accounting Hall of Fame has filled a definite need in granting proper recognition to those in the field of accounting deserving of it, research on this particular point shows that it seems not to have been sufficiently publicized. The following words taken from an editorial in the October, 1954, issue of The Canadian Chartered Accountant will supply proof for this somewhat startling statement:

> We were very much astonished the other day to learn from The Accountant, which as everyone knows is published in England, that Ohio State University has established an Accounting Hall of Fame for American Accountants which has been in existence since 1950. Our surprise was less at the existence of the Hall of Fame than at the source of the information, a British publication. . . .[1]

This quotation impresses upon one the important fact that the Accounting Hall of Fame has not yet been sufficiently advertised, especially since it took

---

[1]"Accounting Hall of Fame," op. cit., p. 182.

over four years for our neighbors to the north to hear about it, and, to make matters worse, not from an American but an English publication!

APPENDIX D

Alpha Kappa Psi Award[1]

In 1952, Alpha Kappa Psi,[2] professional fraternity in commerce and business administration, established an annual award in the form of a life membership in the American Accounting Association, to honor individuals who have made outstanding contributions to the field of accounting. This annual award is given through the American Accounting Association. It is a cash award used to purchase a life membership in the association, and the person to receive it is selected by the association, not by Alpha Kappa Psi. The following gentlemen have been honored with this award:

---

[1]R. C. Cox, "Report of the Annual Convention," The Accounting Review, XXXI, No. 1(January, 1956), 120.

"Report of the President," The Accounting Review, XXX, No. 2(April, 1955), 326.

"Report of the 1952 President," The Accounting Review, XXVIII, No. 2, (April, 1953), 269.

"Report of the 1953 President," The Accounting Review, XXIX, No. 2(April, 1954), 299.

[2]"Alpha Kappa Psi, the first professional fraternity in commerce, was founded on Oct. 5, 1904, in the School of Commerce, Accounts, and Finance at New York University and incorporated under the laws of the state of New York on May 20, 1905.
. . . .
"The objects of the fraternity are to further the individual welfare of its members; to foster scientific research in the fields of commerce, accounts and finance; to educate the public to appreciate and demand higher ideals therein; and to promote and advance in institutions of collegiate rank courses leading to degrees in business administration." Cf. Alvan E. Duerr (ed.), Baird's Manual American College Fraternities, 14th ed.(Menasha, Wisconsin: The Collegiate Press George Banta Publishing Company, 1940), pp. 382-5.

156

1952--Maurice H. Stans
1953--William A. Paton
1954--A. C. Littleton
1955--Carman G. Blough

APPENDIX E

Historical Dates in Accounting[1]

The following is a modification of a chronological list of dates which
appear to be significant in the development of accounting as it is known today.
According to the authors[2] of this list, a knowledge of the historical value of
these dates will give anyone interested in accounting a better understanding of
the subject. The list commences with the date 4500 B.C., at which time taxes
were levied and collected in the Babylonian Empire, and terminates with the date
1953, the year in which the American Institute of Accountants published the CPA
Handbook, and also revised and restated their Accounting Research Bulletins. The
following dates, from 1900 to 1930, point out the highlights in accounting in the
United States for the first three decades of the present century, and are of
special interest in that they coincide with the limits of the present dissertation:

   1900 New York University organized the School of Commerce, Accounts and
        Finance.

---

[1]"Historical Dates in Accounting," The Accounting Review, XXIX, No. 3(July,
1954), 486-93. The reference included in the present appendix has been modified
considerably to fit this study.

[2]This enumeration was prepared by George Abs, Clayton Grimstad, Robert Hay,
W. Asquith Howe, William La Place, Francis J. McGurr, and William Serraíno. The
project was completed in an accounting seminar under the direction of Professor
W. B. Jencks, College of Commerce and Administration, Ohio State University.
Ibid., p. 486.

1902 The firm of Lybrand, Ross Bros., & Montgomery was formed in New York.
1902 The Federation of Societies of Public Accountants in U.S. was formed.
      Its chief purpose was to secure the passage of a federal act regu-
      lating accountancy.
1902 The first important consolidated balance sheet was issued by U.S.
      Steel.
1903 The firm of Ernst & Ernst was formed in Cleveland.
1904 The first International Congress of Accountants was held in St. Louis.
1904 Cost accounting was being taught in the University of Pennsylvania
      and New York University.
1905 The Federation of Societies of Public Accountants, formed in 1902,
      merged into the American Association of Public Accountants, formed
      in 1887. The society advocated federal regulation of public ac-
      countancy.
1905 The first issue of the Journal of Accountancy was published.
1905 This year marked the beginning of state laws establishing uniform
      systems of accounts for public utilities.
1906 The Uniform Sales Act was approved by the Commission on Uniform State
      Laws.
1906 Accounting systems were being taught at New York University.
1907 The Treasury Department changed from single entry to double entry
      bookkeeping.
1907 The accounting profession started to set up rules of professional
      conduct.
1908 Sprague wrote The Philosophy of Accounts.
1908 Cole wrote Accounts--Their Construction and Interpretation. The
      "Where Got--Where Gone" statement was introduced. He advocated
      settling up sales and purchases net, and showing discounts lost.
1909 Henry Rand Hatfield wrote Modern Accounting.
1909 The first United States corporation excise tax law, measured by in-
      come, was enacted.
1910 Massachusetts made it compulsory for all savings banks in the state
      to be audited by certified public accountants once a year.
1910 The University of Pennsylvania offered a bachelor's degree with a
      major in accounting. New York University offered a master's degree
      with a major in accounting.
1911 Kansas passed a "Blue Sky" law, requiring the licensing of securities
      brokers.
1912 Montgomery wrote Auditing Theory and Practice.
1913 The Sixteenth Amendment became effective.
1913 The 1913 Revenue Act was passed on October 3, 1913 . . . effective
      March 1, 1913.
1913 The Federal Reserve banking system was established.
1914 The Uniform Partnership Act was approved by the Commission on Uniform
      State Laws.
1916 The American Association of University Instructors in Accounting was
      organized in Columbus, Ohio.
1916 The American Association of Public Accountants changed its name to
      American Institute of Accountants.
1917 The first estate tax was enacted.
1917 The Revenue Act of 1917 imposed the first excess profits tax.
1917 The American Institute of Accountants and the Federal Reserve Board
      collaborated to issue the "Approved Methods for Preparation of Balance
      Sheet Statements," with the objective of standardization of the audit
      and audit report.
1917 Roy B. Kester wrote Accounting Theory and Practice.

1917   The first American Institute of Accountants examination was given.

1918   The Uniform Conditional Sales Act was approved by the Commission on Uniform State laws.

1919   The National Association of Cost Accountants was organized at Buffalo, New York.

1919   The case of Landell vs. Lybrand, pointed out that the accountant had no liability to third parties unless he was grossly negligent since there was no contract with the third party.

1919   Beta Alpha Psi, an accounting fraternity, was formed at the University of Illinois.

1919   A. C. Littleton wrote Elementary Accounting.

1920   The Federal Power Commission Act introduced regulatory accounting.

1921   The American Society of Certified Public Accountants was organized in Washington.

1921   The Revenue Act of 1921 permitted the use of the lower of cost or market as a means of pricing inventory.

1921   New Mexico was the 48th state to recognize a public accounting statute.

1921   The first Accountant's Index was published.

1921   The Government Accounting Office was established.

1922   The federal budget system was inaugurated.

1923   The District of Columbia, Alaska, and Hawaii and the Philippine Islands passed CPA laws.

1923   The American Association of University Instructors in Accounting and the American Institute of Accountants set up committees on education.

1924   The Board of Tax Appeals was set up by the Revenue Act of 1924.

1924   The Alabama Certified Public Accountant law was upheld by the United States Supreme Court.

1925   Michigan granted accountants the right of privileged communication with their clients.

1926   The Accounting Review was published quarterly.

1926   The Revenue Act of 1926 provided a special method of reporting income from installment sales.

1927   In the case of Ipswich Mills vs. Dillon, the court held that public accounts were the sole owners of their working papers unless the contract of employment stated otherwise.

1928   New York passed a law requiring a CPA candidate to be a college graduate to sit for the examination after January 1, 1938.

1929   The American Institute of Accountants set forth rules of professional conduct.

1930   The National Association of Cost Accountants "Topical Index" was published.

APPENDIX F

Individual Contributions to Accounting Literature--1900-1930

The present appendix enumerates the books and periodical articles which the individuals discussed in the body of this dissertation contributed to accounting literature during the first thirty years of the present century. Since the present writer is primarily interested in when these contributions first appeared and who actually made them, it is permissible to depart from the usual bibliographical procedure.[1]

In compiling this enumeration the present writer has employed almost entirely The Accountants' Index and its subsequent supplements. The Index to the Accounting Review, The Journal of Accountancy Index, and H. C. Bentley's Bibliography of Works on Accounting by American Authors, Vol. II, were likewise of considerable assistance.

Spurgeon Bell

Books:

Accounting Principles, Their Use in Business Management. New York: The Macmillan Company, 1921.
A Report on Accounting Administration for Correctional Institutions. Prepared for the Illinois Efficiency & Economy Committee. Chicago: The Windermere Press, 1914.
Theory and Practice of Accounting: Use in Managerial Control. 2v. Chicago: American Technical Society, c1922.

Periodical Articles:

"Comments on the Municipal Budget," (In American Association of University Instructors in Accounting. Publications, December, 1925, p. 136-9.)

---

[1]Whenever a title appears a second time, as is the case in the event of a revised edition, it is not enumerated for obvious reasons.

"Fixed Costs and Market Price," Quarterly Journal of Economics, (May, 1918),
507-24.
"Limitations of a Functional Basis for the Classification of Accounts and Items,"
(In American Association of University Instructors in Accounting. Pro-
ceedings, 1922, p. 150-65.)
"Research Work at Ohio State University," Accounting Review, (March, 1926),
39-42.
"Specialized Courses in Accounting," (In American Association of University
Instructors in Accounting. Proceedings, 1919, p. 71-8.)

James H. Bliss

Books:

Financial and Operating Ratios in Management. New York: The Ronald Press Co.,
1923.
Management Through Accounts. New York: The Ronald Press Co., 1924.
Bliss and Alger Bookkeeping and Accounting Theory and Practice Complete. Saginaw,
Mich.: Bliss Publishing Company, c. 1923. (In collaboration with Francis
R. Alger.)

Periodical Articles:

"Capital Requirements and Control," Management and Administration,(December, 1923),
705-8.
"Cost Accounting in Manufacturers' Associations," (In Chamber of Commerce of the
United States. Proceedings Second Conference on Uniform Cost Accounting,
Hotel Astor, New York City, March 25, 26, 1924, p. 47-9); Extract. Illinois
Manufacturers' Costs Association Monthly Bulletin, (February 13, 1925), 1-2.
"Cost Methods in the Packing Industry," New York, April 15, 1922. 16p. (National
Association of Cost Accountants, Official Publications, v. 3, no. 14).
"Costs and Accounting Methods in Industry," Manufacturers' News, (January 12, 19,
26, 1922).
"Costs and Accounting Methods in the Packing Industry," Administration, (March,
1922), 279-90.
"Interpretation of the Financial Statement," (In American Association of Univer-
sity Instructors in Accounting. Proceedings, 1922, p. 57-65).
"Management Ratios," Management Handbook, 1924, p. 235-58.
"Methods of Analyzing Financial Report," Management and Administration, (March,
1924), 299-304.
"Operating and Financial Ratios Characteristic of Industries," Management and
Administration, (February, 1924), 155-60.
"Story Told by the Financial and Operating Statements," Management and Administra-
tion, (January, 1924), 25-30.

William Morse Cole

Books:

Accounting and Auditing. Minneapolis: Cree Publishing Co., 1910.
Accounts: Their Construction and Interpretation. Boston: Houghton Mifflin, 1908.
Bookkeeping, Accounting, and Auditing. Chicago: Washington Institute, c1914.
Chicago: Lincoln Institute of Business, c1921.
Cost Accounting for Institutions. New York: The Ronald Press Co., 1913.
Problems in the Principles of Accounting. Cambridge, Mass.: Harvard University
Press, 1915.

Solutions and Answers for the Fundamentals of Accounting. Boston: Houghton
    Mifflin Company, c1921. (In collaboration with Anne Elizabeth Geddes.)
The Fundamentals of Accounting. Boston: Houghton Mifflin, 1921. (In collabora-
    tion with Anne Elizabeth Geddes.)

Periodical Articles:

"Accounting Methods for Determining Costs and Prices," Bulletin of the American
    Economic Association, (April, 1911), 124-35.
"Confusion in Accountancy Terms," Australasian Accountant and Secretary, (August,
    1927), 249-53.
"Confusion of Terms," Journal of Accountancy, (March, 1927), 192-8. Licentiate
    in accountancy, (June, 1927), 141-7.
"Income Statements for Institutions," Journal of Accountancy, (February, 1913),
    79-89.
"Institution Accounting and Records," Journal of Home Economics, (November,
    1910), 572-81.
"Interest on Investment in Equipment," Journal of Accountancy, (April, 1913),
    232-6.
"Problem in Joint Costs," Harvard Business Review, (July, 1923), 428-37. Paper
    Trade Journal, (August 2, 1923), 53-6.
"Problem in Joint Costs," New York, October 1, 1923. 13p. (National Association
    of Cost Accountants, Official Publications, v. 5, no. 2.)
"Rise of Accountancy," Journal of Accountancy, (February, 1909), 295-6.
"Uniform Accounting for Institutions," Journal of Home Economics, (February, 1912)
    39-50.

Arthur Lowes Dickinson

Books:

Accounting for Modern Corporations. Chicago: American Technical Society, 1922.
    (In collaboration with William M. Lybrand and Frank Herbert MacPherson;
    earlier editions published by the American School of Correspondence,
    Chicago, in 1909 and 1919, were not issued for general distribution.)
Accounting Practice and Procedure. New York: The Ronald Press Co., 1914.

Periodical Articles:

"Accountancy Practice and Procedure," (In Cyclopedia of Commerce, Accountancy,
    Business Administration. 1910, v. 7. p. 239-80).
"Accounting Practice and Procedure," a paper to be presented at the annual meet-
    ing of the American Association of Public Accountants, Atlantic City, New
    Jersey, October 20-23, 1908. 47p. American Institute of Accountants,
    Yearbook, 1908, p. 188-254. Accountant, (December 12, 1908), 740-58.
    Incorporated Accountants' Journal, 1908-9, p. 51. Journal of Accountancy,
    (October-December, 1908), 415-25; 7-18; 96-110.
"Accounting Practice and Procedure," (In Accountancy and Business Management.
    1920. v. 4. p. 289-330).
"American Association of Public Accountants," Accountant, (November 28, 1925),
    845-6.
"Construction, Use and Abuse of Cost Accounts," Accountant, (October 23, 1926),
    566-74. Journal of Accountancy, (July, 1927), 1-20. Canadian Chartered
    Accountant, (November, 1928), 147-67. Public Accountant, (January-February,
    1929), 218-26; 235-47.
"Corporation Profits," (In Accountancy and Business Management. 1920. v. 4.
    p. 247-87).

"Economic Aspect of Cost Accounts and Its Application to the Accounting of
Industrial Companies," Journal of Accountancy, (March, 1911), 325.
"Duties and Responsibilities of the Public Accountant with Regard to New Issues
of Stocks and Bonds," Journal of Accountancy, (November, 1905), 16-27.
"Duties and Responsibilities of the Public Accountants," Accountant, (July 26,
1902), 745-51. Commerce, Accounts and Finance, (April, 1902), 23-7.
"Economic Aspect of Cost Accounts and Its Application to the Accounting of In-
dustrial Companies," Journal of Accountancy, (March, 1911), 325.
"Fallacy of Including Interest and Rent as Part of Manufacturing Cost," Journal
of Accountancy, (December, 1911; August, 1913), 588-93; 89-98.
"Interest and Sinking Funds," Accountant, (October 10, 1891), 715-20.
"Life Assurance Accounts," Accountant, (1887), 455, 464.
"Notes on Some Problems Relating to the Accounts of Holding Companies," Accountant,
(May 19, 1906), 647-9. Journal of Accountancy, (April, 1906), 487-91.
"Profession of the Public Accountant," Accountant, (May 27, 1905), 650-8. Auditor,
(1905), 165, 185.
"Profits of a Corporation," (In Cyclopedia of Commerce, Accountancy, Business
Administration, 1910, v. 6, p. 255-97).
"Profits of a Corporation; with discussion," Federation of Societies of Public
Accountants in the United States of America. Official Record of the Congress
of Accountants Held at the World's Fair, Saint Louis, September 26th, 27th
and 28th, 1904, p. 171-203. Accountant, (October 22, 1904), 442-53. In-
corporated Accountants Journal,(1904-5), 34.
"Publicity in Industrial Accounts with a Comparison of English and American
Methods," Accountant, (October 4, 1924), 469-90. Journal of Accountancy,
(October, 1924), 254-74.
"Relation Between the Accountant and the Banker," Journal of Accountancy, (May,
1909), 55-7.
"Some Special Points in Accountancy Practice," Accountant, (April 22, 1905), 495-
504. Auditor, (1905), 105, 130, 158.
"Some Special Points in Corporation Accounting," Accountant, (October 7, 1905),
402-10.
"Special Points in Accountancy Practice," Business World, (April, May, 1905),
157-61; 233-6.

DeWitt Carl Eggleston

Books:

Auditing Procedure. New York: Wiley, 1926(Wiley Accounting Series.)
Auditors' Reports and Working Papers. New York: Wiley, 1929(Wiley Accounting
Series.)
Business Costs. New York: Appleton, 1921(College of the city of New York Series
in Commerce, Civics, and Technology; In collaboration with Frederick
Bertrand Robinson.)
Cost Accounting. New York: The Ronald Press Co., 1920(Business Accounting Series,
v. 3.)
Modern Accounting Theory and Practice. New York: Wiley, 1930. 2v. (Wiley Account-
ing Series.)
Municipal Accounting. New York: Ronald, 1914(Ronald Accounting Series.)
Principles of Accounting Practice: A Series of Fifteen Coordinated Texts Covering
Advanced Accounting Theory and Practice. Chicago: LaSalle Extension Univer-
sity, c1923.
Problems in Cost Accounting. New York: Appleton, 1918(College of the City of New
York Series in Commerce, Civics, and Technology.)
Wall Street Procedure; with special reference to brokers' accounts. New York:
Greenberg Publisher, Inc., 1929.

Periodical Articles:

"Accounting System for a Municipal Hospital," Journal of Accountancy, (November, 1913), 366-70.
"Brass Foundry Cost Accounting," Foundry, (March, 1907).
"Cost Accounting in the Brass Foundry," Iron Age, (November 15, 1906).
"Department Store Accounting; Preparing and Operating the Merchandise Budget," Retailing, (October 18, 1930), 3, 14.
"Distribution of Established Charges," Business Man's Magazine, (September, 1906), 95-8.
"Doing Away With the Ledger," Business Man's Magazine, (December, 1910), 569-72.
"Evolution of the Machine Unit System at the Modern Electric Co.," Journal of Accountancy, (May, 1911), 44-57.
"For Model Cost System," Business Man's Magazine, (February, 1907), 84-8.
"Importance of New York as a Commercial Centre," New York, The author, 1929. Six typewritten pages.
"Keeping a City's Accounts," Business Man's Magazine, (August, 1911), 138-40.
"Manager Has Opinions of His Own," Business Man's Magazine, (January, 1907), 98-100.
"Motor Manufacturing Cost," Business Man's Magazine, (September, 1907), 69-71.
"Municipal Budget Accounts," Journal of Accountancy, (November, 1911), 481-92.
"Municipal Cemetery Accounts," Journal of Accountancy, (March, 1913), 174-84.
"Municipal Cost System," Journal of Accountancy, (December, 1911), 573-87.
"Municipal Returns," Journal of Accountancy, (July, 1911), 165-76.
"Municipal Revenue Accounts," Journal of Accountancy, (October, 1911), 415-21.
"Obsolescence and Depreciation," Buildings and Building Management, (April 2, 1923), 19-23.
"Recommendations for a Uniform System of School Accounts," Government Accountant, (August, 1911), 158-64.
"Schedule Order System," Business Man's Magazine, (August, 1906), 79-83.
"Series of Articles About Factory Cost Accounting," Business Man's Magazine, (December, 1907), 78-100.
"Southern Wheel Company's Cost System," Business Man's Magazine, (June, 1908), 419-21.
"System in the Inspection Department," Business Man's Magazine, (October, 1906), 114-8.
"System of Factory Cost Accounting," Journal of Accountancy, (December, 1906), 115-22.
"System of Stores Control," Business Man's Magazine, (July, 1907), 81-9.

Paul-Joseph Esquerre

Books:

Accounting. New York: Ronald Press Company, 1927.
Applied Theory of Accounts, New York: The Ronald Press Co., 1914.
Practical Accounting Problems: Theory Discussion and Solutions. New York: Ronald Press Company, c1921.
Problems Involving the Application of the Theory of Accounts. New York: The Ronald Press Co., 1915.

Periodical Articles:

"C.P.A. Problem and Its Solution," (New York, 1914). Administration, (November, 1921), 686-9.
"Goodwill, Patents, Trade-Marks, Copyrights and Franchises," Journal of Accountancy, (January, 1913), 21-34.

"New York C.P.A. Examinations of June, 1912," Journal of Accountancy, (August-
October, 1912), 77-98; 192-210; 310-21.
"New York C.P.A. Examinations of January, 1913," Journal of Accountancy, (May,
June, 1913), 377-90; 459-66.
"Philosopher-Accountant Takes Inventory of Soul of Profession," American Account-
ant, (July, 1928), 19-22.
"Resources and Their Application: Correspondence," Journal of Accountancy, (May,
1925), 424-30.
"Some Aspects of Professional Accounting," Administration, (July, 1921), 102-7.

Harry Anson Finney

Books:

Accounting Principles and Bookkeeping Methods. v. 1. New York: Henry Holt and
Company, 1924.
Consolidated Statements for Holding Companies and Subsidiaries. New York:
Prentice-Hall, Inc., 1922.
Introduction to Actuarial Science. New York: American Institute of Accountants,
c1920.
Mathematics of Accounting and Finance. New York: The Ronald Press Co., 1921.
(In collaboration with Seymour Walton.)
Modern Business Arithmetic. New York: H. Holt and Company, c1916. (In collabora-
tion with Joseph Clifton Brown.)
Principles of Accounting. 2v. New York: Prentice-Hall, Inc., 1923.
Solutions to Problems and Answers to Questions in Principles of Accounting. 2v.
New York: Prentice-Hall, Inc., c1923.

Periodical Articles:

"Accrued Dividends," Journal of Accountancy, (May, 1924), 392-3.
"Actuarial Problems," Journal of Accountancy, (June, 1926), 468-71. (In collabora-
tion with H. P. Baumann.)
"Actuarial Problem--Effective Interest Rates," Journal of Accountancy, (May, 1926),
383-5. (In collaboration with H. P. Baumann.)
"Administrative and Selling Expenses of a Factory," Journal of Accountancy,
(February, 1922), 144-46.
"Admission of a Partner," Journal of Accountancy, (May, 1923), 386-7.
"Agency Sales," Journal of Accountancy, (May, 1921), 385-7.
"American Institute Examinations, May, 1926," Journal of Accountancy, (November,
1926), 383-91. (In collaboration with H. P. Baumann.)
"Analysis of the Profit and Loss Statement," Journal of Accountancy, (June, 1922),
451-67.
"Analysis of the Revenue Statement," Journal of Accountancy, (June, 1924), 466-74.
"Analysis of Statements," Journal of Accountancy, (November, 1925), 271-83. (In
collaboration with H. P. Baumann.)
"Another Tax Problem," Journal of Accountancy, (December, 1921), 467-8.
"Bad Cheques," Journal of Accountancy, (January, 1922), 64.
"Bond Premium in Testamentary Trusts," Journal of Accountancy, (July, 1923), 62-3.
"Bonus and Tax," Journal of Accountancy, (November, 1924), 385-92.
"Bonuses and Taxes," Journal of Accountancy, (December, 1921), 463-7.
"Capitalizing Preliminary Expense," Journal of Accountancy, (December, 1920),
466-7.
"Changing from Stock with Par Value to No-Par Stock," Journal of Accountancy,
(December, 1920), 461-2.
"Common Stock Without Par Value," Journal of Accountancy, (December, 1920), 459-60.

"Consignments and Bonus," Journal of Accountancy, (August, 1924), 149-50.
"Consolidated Balance Sheet--Mutual Stock Holdings," Journal of Accountancy,
(May, 1922), 368-84.
"Consolidated Balance Sheets with Minority Interest," Journal of Accountancy,
(February, 1922), 138-9.
"Consolidated Goodwill in Relation to Minority Interest," Journal of Accountancy,
(December, 1927), 460-3. (In collaboration with H. P. Baumann.)
"Contingent Losses on Sales Commitments," Journal of Accountancy, (February, 1926),
147-8. (In collaboration with H. P. Baumann.)
"Contingent Stock Donation," Journal of Accountancy, (December, 1920), 469-70.
"Corporate Reorganization and Consolidation," Journal of Accountancy, (November,
1921), 380-2.
"Costs in a Seasonal Business," Journal of Accountancy, (March, May, 1925), 229-
33; 409-23.
"Deceptive Averages," Journal of Accountancy, (December, 1920), 456-9.
"Determining Effective Rates of Bonds," Journal of Accountancy, (December, 1925),
454-64. (In collaboration with H. P. Baumann.)
"Discounts and Price Fluctuations in Contract Costs," Journal of Accountancy,
(January, 1922), 65-6.
"Dividend Paid in No-Par-Value Stock," Journal of Accountancy, (May, 1924), 388-
90.
"Division of Partnership Goodwill," Journal of Accountancy, (December, 1922),
466-8.
"Effective Interest Rate," Journal of Accountancy, (May, 1921), 380-5.
"Expenses Confused with Dividends," Journal of Accountancy, (November, 1921), 387.
"Extinguishing Stock Discount; Common and Preferred Stock Interest in Surplus,"
Journal of Accountancy, (March, 1922), 227-8.
"Federal Taxes and Employees Bonus," Journal of Accountancy, (December, 1922),
45-63.
"Finance Interest Problem," Journal of Accountancy, (December, 1926), 458-9. (In
collaboration with H. P. Baumann.)
"Foreign Exchange," Journal of Accountancy, (June, 1921), 451-66.
"Goodwill in Consolidated Balance Sheet," Journal of Accountancy, (January, 1922),
63-4.
"Goodwill, Minority Interest and Consolidated Surplus," Journal of Accountancy,
(May, 1924), 391-2.
"Holding-Company Accounting," Journal of Accountancy, (April, 1924), 308-9.
"Income Prior to Construction," Journal of Accountancy, (May, 1922), 385.
"Incorporation of Partnership--Distribution of Stock," Journal of Accountancy,
(December, 1926), 461-9. (In collaboration with H. P. Baumann.)
"Indiana Examinations," Journal of Accountancy, (December, 1920), 456-9.
"Installment Contracts," Journal of Accountancy, (November, 1921), 382-4.
"Institute Examinations, November, 1920," Journal of Accountancy, (March-April,
1921), 214-30; 302-7.
"Institute Examinations, May, 1921," Journal of Accountancy, (July-October, 1921),
59-72; 138-53; 213-6; 300-12.
"Institute Examinations, November, 1921," Journal of Accountancy, (January-April,
1922), 51-63; 126-38; 215-31; 296-302.
"Institute Examinations, May, 1922," Journal of Accountancy, (July-September,
1922), 46-57; 132-46; 217-29.
"Institute Examinations, November, 1922," Journal of Accountancy, (January-April,
1923), 49-62; 137-50; 220-7; 295-307.
"Institute Examinations, May, 1923," Journal of Accountancy, (July-November,
1923), 47-62; 128-41; 213-24; 297-302; 371-89.
"Institute Examinations, November, 1923," Journal of Accountancy, (January-March,
1924), 51-67; 125-42; 224-9.

"Institute Examinations, May, 1924," Journal of Accountancy, (July, August, October, 1924), 52-67; 136-49; 299-309.

"Institute Examinations, November, 1924," Journal of Accountancy, (January-April, 1925), 51-68; 144-55; 217-29; 336-48.

"Institute Examinations, May, 1925," Journal of Accountancy, (July-October, 1925), 54-73; 131-44; 214-26; 301-5.

"Institute Examinations, November, 1925," Journal of Accountancy, (January, 1926), 54-69.

"Institute Examinations, November, 1925," Journal of Accountancy, (February-May, 1926), 135-47; 215-29; 296-312; 373-82. (In collaboration with H. P. Baumann.)

"Institute Examinations, May, 1926," Journal of Accountancy, (July-October,1926), 52-70; 133-41; 220-34; 300-9. (In collaboration with H. P. Baumann.)

"Institute Examinations, November, 1926," Journal of Accountancy, (January, March-May, 1927), 48-65; 212-30; 300-9, 377-90. (In collaboration with H. P. Baumann.)

"Institute Examinations, May, 1927," Journal of Accountancy, (July-November, 1927), 61-74; 135-46; 215-31, 294-307; 378-89. (In collaboration with H. P. Baumann.)

"Institute Examinations, November, 1927," Journal of Accountancy, (January-June, 1928), 51-60; 140-51; 213-26; 296-309; 379-91; 461-9. (In collaboration with H. P. Baumann.)

"Institute Examinations, May, 1928," Journal of Accountancy, (July-October,1928), 62-71; 144-9; 222-32; 299-311. (In collaboration with H. P. Baumann.)

"Interest and Construction Cost; Subsidiary Losses and Loans," Journal of Accountancy, (March, 1922), 225-7.

"Interest, Packages, and Appreciation," Journal of Accountancy, (May, 1921),388-9.

"Introduction to Actuarial Science," Journal of Accountancy, (November, December, 1919), 321-52; 435-50.

"Inventories and Supplies," Journal of Accountancy, (January, 1922), 64-5.

"Inventory Reserve," Journal of Accountancy, (December, 1920), 462-4.

"Joint Venture Profits," Journal of Accountancy, (June, 1923), 458-60.

"Joint Ventures and Partnerships," Journal of Accountancy, (December, 1922), 463-6.

"Lease and Purchase Contract," Journal of Accountancy, (November, 1921), 379-80.

"Leaseholds," Journal of Accountancy, (March, 1922), 29.

"Long-End Interest," Journal of Accountancy, (April, 1924), 309-10.

"May Institute Examination Problem 3, Part II," Journal of Accountancy, (December, 1921), 468-71.

"Mining Problem," Journal of Accountancy, (October, 1923), 303-9.

"Partnership Adjustment," Journal of Accountancy, (August, 1924), 150-1.

"Partnership Interest Adjustments," Journal of Accountancy, (March, 1922), 223-5.

"Partnership Problem," Journal of Accountancy, (May, 1924), 393-4.

"Preferred Stock Sinking Fund," Journal of Accountancy, (April, 1924), 310-1.

"Problem," Journal of Accountancy, (October, 1922), 287-305; 305-6; (November, 1922), 374-80; 380-9; (May, 1923), 376-85; (June, 1923), 450-6; (April, December, 1924), 298-307; 451-72; (June, 1927), 456-69--(In collaboration with H. P. Baumann.)

"Problem in Reserves," Journal of Accountancy, (October, 1924), 309-14.

"Problem Number Two of the Institute Examinations, November, 1925," Journal of Accountancy, (February, 1926), 149.

"Profits on Deferred Payment Sales," Journal of Accountancy, (December, 1920), 465-6.

"Receivable and Payable Offsets in Insolvency," Journal of Accountancy, (October, 1926), 309-12 (In collaboration with H. P. Baumann.)

"Relation of Cash Discount to Interest," Journal of Accountancy, (November, 1921), 380.

"Reserve for Sinking Fund," Journal of Accountancy, (March, 1922), 221.

"Reserves," Accounting, Commerce and Insurance, (January, 1923), 266-73; Journal of Accountancy, (October, 1922), 249-61; Canadian Chartered Accountant, (January, 1923), 288-98.

"Reserves and Surplus," Journal of Accountancy, (December, 1920), 464-5.

"Reserves for Contingencies," Journal of Accountancy, (August, 1924).

"Returned Purchases and Cash Discount," Journal of Accountancy, (March, 1922),221.

"Right to Offset in Partnership Settlements," Journal of Accountancy, (May, 1922), 384-5.

"Sale of Subsidiary Stock by Holding Company," Journal of Accountancy, (June, 1923), 461-2.

"Sales Cancellations and Re-Sales," Journal of Accountancy, (December, 1920),462.

"Self-Balancing Ledger," Journal of Accountancy, (December, 1920), 470.

"Short Method for Computing Interest in Installment Notes," Journal of Accountancy, (December, 1920), 467-8.

"Sinking Fund Contributions," Journal of Accountancy, (December, 1920), 460-1.

"Sinking Fund Payments," Journal of Accountancy, (December, 1927), 463-5. (In collaboration with H. P. Baumann.)

"Sinking Fund with Annual Installments and Quarterly Interest Conversions," Journal of Accountancy, (May, 1924), 390-1.

"Statement of Application of Funds; A Reply to Mr. Esquerre," Journal of Accountancy, (June, 1925), 497-511.

"Statement of Application of Funds," Journal of Accountancy, (December, 1923; October, 1925), 460-72; 305-13.

_____, Journal of Accountancy, (December, 1925), 464-9 (In collaboration with H. P. Baumann.)

"Stock Assessments," Journal of Accountancy, (November, 1921), 385.

"Stock in Treasury and in Sinking Fund," Journal of Accountancy, (February, 1922), 139-40.

"Stockholders! Gift to Corporation," Journal of Accountancy, (November, 1921), 385-6.

"Students Department," Journal of Accountancy, (September-December, 1920), 214-234; 308-15; 381-400; 456-70. (January, 1921-June, 1923), 64-79; 145-59; 214-30; 302-13; 380-91; 451-66; 59-72; 138-53; 213-27; 300-12; 372-87; 463-71; 51-66; 126-46; 215-29; 296-307; 368-86; 451-66; 46-66; 142-56; 217-31; 297-310; 374-89; 457-71; 49-62; 137-50; 229-7; 295-307; 376-87; 450-62.

"Taxes and Bonuses," Journal of Accountancy, (June, 1923), 456-8.

"This is not an Institute Examination Problem," Journal of Accountancy, (June, 1923), 460-1.

"Treasury Stock," Journal of Accountancy, (December, 1920), 468-9.

"Turnover," Journal of Accountancy, (November, 1921), 372-6.

"Unrealized Profit and Depreciation," Journal of Accountancy, (November, 1921), 386-7.

"Unrealized Profit on Appraisals," Journal of Accountancy, (May, 1921), 389-90.

"Valuation of Treasury Stock," Journal of Accountancy, (March, 1922), 228-9.

"Variation in Net Profit," Journal of Accountancy, (June, 1926), 460-8. (In collaboration with H. P. Baumann.)

"Weight Shrinkage in Process," Journal of Accountancy, (March, 1922), 221-3.

Stephen Gilman

Books:

Accounting Concepts of Profit. New York: Ronald Press Co., 1939.
Analyzing Financial Statements. New York: Ronald Press Co., 1925.

Graphic Charts for the Business Man. Chicago: LaSalle Extension University,
c1917.
Principles of Accounting. Chicago: LaSalle Extension University, 1916.

Periodical Articles:

"Fundamentals of the Business Budget," Accountants' Forum, (November, 1922), 3-5.
"Get the Range and Study the Target, You Technical Marksmen!" Certified Public
Accountant, (August, 1928), 233-4, 240.
"High-Hatting the Boss with Figures," Manufacturers News, (May, 1928), 31, 62.
"How to Use Trend Percentages in Analyzing Progress of Business," American Account-
ant, (May, 1930), 215-7.
"Method of Balance Sheet Analysis," Management and Administration, (August,1924),
147-50.
"Observations on Balance Sheet Analysis," Canadian Chartered Accountant, (March,
1926), 313. Certified Public Accountant, (February, 1926), 37-40.
"Relation of Business Statistics to Management Control," Paper, (May 11, 1921),
14-5, 42.
"Two Methods of Analyzing Statements," Certified Public Accountant, (July, 1928),
203-4, 216-7.
"When Profits Fall Off," Administration, (September, 1921), 376-80.

Harry G. Guthmann

Books

The Analysis of Financial Statements. New York: Prentice-Hall, Inc., 1925.

Periodical Article:

"Actuarial Versus Sinking Fund Type Formula for Valuation," Accounting Review,
(September, 1930), 226-30.

Henry Rand Hatfield

Books:

Accounting: Its Principles and Problems. New York: Appleton, 1927. (In reality
a revised edition of Modern Accounting.)
Modern Accounting: Its Principles and Some of Its Problems. New York: Appleton,
1909.

Periodical Articles:

"Accounting Paradox," Accounting Review, (December, 1928), 342-4.
"Earliest Use in English of the Term Capital," Quarterly Journal of Economics,
(May, 1926), 547-8.
"Historical Defense of Bookkeeping." (In American Association of University
Instructors in Accounting. Papers and Proceedings, 1923, p. 65-75.)
Journal of Accountancy, (April, 1924), 241-53.
"Some Neglected Phases of Accounting," Electric Railway Journal, (October 16,
1915), 799-802.
"What is the Matter with Accounting?" Canadian Chartered Accountant, (January,
1928), 213-25. Journal of Accountancy, (October, 1927), 267-79. Licenti-
ate in Accountancy, (January, 1938), 237-48.

David Himmelblau

Books:

Auditors' Certificates. New York: Ronald Press Co., 1927.
Complete Accounting Course. New York: Ronald Press Co., 1917-21. 3v. (In
collaboration with Arthur Andersen and Eric Louis Kohler.)
Financial Investigations. New York: Ronald Press Co., c1928. (Complete Accounting Course, Unit 6, edited by David Himmelblau.)
Fundamentals of Accounting. New York: Ronald Press Co., c1924. (Complete Accounting Course, Unit 1, edited by David Himmelblau.)
Principles of Accounting. New York: Ronald Press Co., c1924. (Complete Accounting Course, Unit 2, edited by David Himmelblau.)

Periodical Articles:

"Accounting Treatment of Securities (Retirable) Discount and Expense," Journal of
Accountancy, (August, 1928), 101-5.
"Annuity Method of Depreciation;" Paper Presented at the International Congress
on Accounting Held at Hotel Commodore, New York, September, 9-14, 1929.
16p. Accountant, (November 2, 1929), 532-7. (In International Congress on
Accounting. Proceedings, 1929. p. 335-50.)
"Depreciation and Obsolescence," Manufacturers News, (March 27, 1926), 5-6, 24.
Bulletin of the American Institute of Accountants, (June 15, 1926), 11
(resume).
"Depreciation and Obsolescence; With Special Application to Manufacturing Indus-
tries and the Computation of Taxable Income," National Income Tax Magazine,
(August, 1926), 272-4, 289. Pulp and Paper Profits, (September, 1926),
6-9, 15.
"Ideal Auditor's Certificate Conveys Precisely Right Shade of Meaning," American
Accountant, (February, 1928), 14-8.
"Income Tax on Undistributed Profits," (In American Association of University
Instructors in Accounting. Publications, December, 1925, p. 132-6.)
"Methods of Classifying Students Who Enter Advanced Courses Based on Previous
Training," (In American Association of University Instructors in Account-
ing. Papers and Proceedings, 1924, p. 84-6.)
"Refining Balance Sheet," Accounting Review, (December, 1927), 339-47. Bulletin
of the American Institute of Accountants, (January 16, 1928), 9-10(resume).
"Some Corporate Problems Created by Income Tax Laws," Accounting Review, (Septem-
ber, 1927), 263-77.
"Some Problems in Property Accounting," Accounting Review, (June, 1928), 149-60.

Roy B. Kester

Books:

Accounting Theory and Practice; a first year text. New York: The Ronald Press
Company, 1916.
Accounting Theory and Practice. New York: Ronald Press Co., 1917-21. 3v.
Depreciation. New York: Ronald Press Co., c1924.
Fundamentals of Accounting; Principles and Practice of Bookkeeping. New York:
Ronald Press Co., 1921-23. 2v. (In collaboration with Sietse Bernard Koop-
man.)
Problems and Practice Data for Elements of Accounting. New York: University
Printing Office, Columbia University, 1916.
Teacher's Manual for Fundamentals of Accounting. New York: Ronald Press Co.,
1922. (In collaboration with Sietse Bernard Koopman.)

Periodical Articles:

"Aim and Scope of Graduate and Research Work in Accounting," (In American Association of University Instructors in Accounting. Papers and Proceedings, 1920, p. 20-6.)

"Cost Accounting," Spice Mill, (May, 1921), 760-3.

"Discussion," (In American Association of University Instructors in Accounting. Papers and Proceedings, 1919, p. 64; 1921, p. 77-9; 1924, p. 86-8.)

"Importance of the Controller," Accounting Review, (September, 1928), 237-51.

"Principles of Valuation as Related to the Functions of the Balance Sheet," (In American Association of University Instructors in Accounting. Papers and Proceedings. 1923. p. 9-14.)

"Sees Accountant as Executive Understudy; Talk to Actuaries Describes Him as 'Rare Bird' Who Interprets Reports and Tactfully Suggests Action," Eastern Underwriter, (December 4, 1925).

"Standardization of the Balance Sheet;" paper presented at the International Congress on Accounting held at Hotel Commodore, New York, September 9-14, 1929, 23p. (In International Congress on Accounting. Proceedings, 1929. p. 593-615.) Accountant, (November 30, 1929), 685-92.

"Standardized Costs," Simmons Spice Mill, (December, 1920), 1982, 1984, 1986, 1988, 1990, 1992, 1994, 1996.

Joseph J. Klein

Books:

Bookkeeping and Accounting. New York: D. Appleton & Co., 1917.

Bookkeeping and Accounting: Advanced Course. New York: D. Appleton & Co., 1918.

Bookkeeping and Accounting: Introductory Course. New York: D. Appleton & Co., 1918.

Elements of Accounting Theory and Practice. New York: D. Appleton & Co., 1913.

Federal Income Taxation. New York: John Wiley and Sons, Inc., 1929.

Principles and Methods in Commercial Education. New York: The Macmillan Co.,1916.

Student's Handbook of Accounting. New York: D. Appleton & Co., 1915.

1930 Supplement to Federal Income Taxation. New York: John Wiley and Sons, Inc., 1930.

Periodical Articles:

"Accountancy and the Business Professions," New York: Students' Aid Committee of the High School Teachers' Association of New York City, 1910. (Pamphlet.)

"Accountancy, The Youngest of the Professions," New York: National Business Institute, 1912. (Pamphlet.)

"Address," Pace Student. (March, 1926), 13-4.

"Address at the Dinner in Honor of the United States Board of Tax Appeals," Bulletin of the National Tax Association, (October, 1926), 21-3.

"Address, Board of Tax Appeals," National Income Tax Magazine, (July, 1926), 238-40.

"Appreciation of the United States Board of Tax Appeals," Certified Public Accountant, (June, 1926), 165-6, 189.

"Board of Tax Appeals;" address before the Accountants' Square Club, June 4, 1925. Eight typewritten pages.

"Controller and the C.P.A.; How Can They Best Serve the Stores?" address before the Controllers' Congress of the National Retail Dry Goods Association, Chicago, Illinois, May 20, 1929. Fourteen typewritten pages. Certified Public Accountant, (June, 1929), 162-3, 165-6.

"C.P.A. and the Board of Tax Appeals," Pace Student, (August, 1926), 11-2, 24.
"Depreciation and Obsolescence from the Standpoint of Federal Income Taxation;"
     paper presented at the International Congress on Accounting held at Hotel
     Commodore, New York, September 9-14, 1929. 17p. (In International Con-
     gress on Accounting. Proceedings, 1929, p. 387-403.)
"Development of Mercantile Instruments of Credit in the United States," Journal
     of Accountancy, (September, 1911--March, 1912), 321-45; 422-49, 526-37;
     594-607; 44-50; 122-32; 207-17.
"Is the Credit Man Entitled to More Financial Facts?" American Accountant,
     (February, 1928), 5-9.
"Keeping Livestock Records," California Cultivator, (May 13, 1922), 511.
"New York Public Library--What it Offers to the Student of Economics and of Ac-
     countancy," Journal of Accountancy, (August, 1911), 287-92.
"Relation of Interest to Cost," Journal of Accountancy, (March, 1912), 236-7.
"What Shall We Look For in the Financial Statements That Come to Our Desks;"
     address before the Forum of the New York Association of Credit Men, January
     16, 1928; reprinted in the Robert Morris Associates Bulletin, (April,1928).
     Certified Public Accountant, (March, 1928), 77-81. Bulletin of the Ameri-
     can Institute of Accountants, (May 15, 1928), 10 (resume).

A. C. Littleton

Books:

Accounting Evolution to 1900. New York: American Institute Publishing Co.,c1933.
An Introduction to Elementary Accounting. Champaign, Ill.: Flannigan Pearson,
     c1919.

Periodical Articles:

"Accounting for Appreciation in Two Typical Cases Described," American Accountant,
     (July, 1930), 302-3.
"Adjusting Inventories," System, (June, 1920), 1153-5.
"Antecedents of Double Entry," Accounting Review, (June, 1927), 140.
"Appraisal of the Balance Sheet Approach," (In American Association of University
     Instructors in Accounting. Proceedings, 1922, p. 85-92.)
"Chronology of Beta Alpha Psi," Keys of Beta Alpha Psi, (September, 1930), 2-3.
"Development of Accounting Literature," (In American Association of University
     Instructors in Accounting. Publications. December, 1925, p. 7-17.)
"Discussion: Graduate and Research Work in Accounting," (In American Association
     of University Instructors in Accounting. Papers and Proceedings, 1919, p.
     83-6.
"Discussion: Principles of Valuations as Related to the Function of the Balance
     Sheet," (In American Association of University Instructors in Accounting.
     Papers and Proceedings, 1923, p. 14-5.)
"Discussion: To What Extent, If Any, Should Part-Time Outside Paid Employment of
     Full-Time University Instructors Be Encouraged?" (In American Association
     of University Instructors in Accounting. Papers and Proceedings, 1921, p.
     55-7.)
"Evolution of the Journal Entry," Accounting Review, (December, 1928), 383-96.
"Evolution of the Ledger Account," Accounting Review, (December, 1926), 12-23.
"Fifth Year in Accounting," Enterpriser, (February, 1930), 11, 20.
"Foreign Accounting Terms (German)," Accounting Review, (September, December,
     1930--March, June, 1931), 262-3; 320-2; 64-5; 147-9.
"International Congress on Accounting," Accounting Review, (December, 1929), 234-
     46. (In collaboration with Lloyd Morey, David Himmelblau, and F. E. Ross.)

"Italian Double Entry in Early England," <u>Accounting Review</u>, (June, 1926), 60-71.
"Paciolo and Modern Accounting," <u>Accounting Review</u>, (June, 1928), 131-40.
"Pioneers of Accountancy," <u>Certified Public Accountant</u>, (July, 1928), 201-2, 217.
"Relation of Accounting to the Business Cycle," (In American Association of
    University Instructors in Accounting. <u>Papers and Proceedings</u>, 1924, p.
    108-16.)
"Research Work at the University of Illinois," <u>Accounting Review</u>, (March, 1926),
    31-8.
"Thomas Jones, Pioneer," <u>Certified Public Accountant</u>, (June, 1927), 183-6.
"Two Fables of Bookkeeping," <u>Accounting Review</u>, (December, 1927), 388-96.
"Two Pioneers of Accountancy," <u>Certified Public Accountant</u>, (February, 1927), 35-
    7.
"University Education for Accountancy," <u>Certified Public Accountant</u>, (December,
    1927), 361-5.
"Value and Price in Accounting," <u>Accounting Review</u>, (September, 1929), 147-54.
"What is Profit," <u>Accounting Review</u>, (September, 1928), 278-88.
"2 to 1 Ratio Analyzed," <u>Certified Public Accountant</u>, (August, 1926), 244-6.

James Oscar McKinsey

Books:

<u>Accounting Principles</u>. Cincinnati: South-western Publishing Co., c1929.
<u>Bookkeeping and Accounting</u>. Cincinnati: South-western Publishing Co., c1920, 2v.
<u>Budgetary Control</u>. New York: Ronald Press Co., 1922.
<u>Business Administration</u>. Cincinnati: South-western Publishing Co., c1924.
<u>Financial Management: An Outline of Its Principles and Problems</u>. Chicago: Ameri-
    can Technical Society, c1922, 2v.
<u>Managerial Accounting</u>. Chicago: University of Chicago Press, 1924.
<u>Principles of Accounting</u>. Chicago: University of Chicago Press, 1920. (In
    collaboration with Albert Claire Hodge.)

Periodical Articles:

"Accounting as an Administrative Aid," <u>Journal of Political Economy</u>, (November,
    1919), 759-81.
"Accounting Courses in Preparation for Business Management," (In American Associa-
    tion of University Instructors in Accounting. <u>Papers and Proceedings</u>, 1919,
    p. 53-63.)
"Accountant's Relation to the Budgetary Program; With Discussion," (In National
    Association of Cost Accountants. <u>Year Book</u>, 1927, 237-54.)
"Approach to the Study of Municipal Accounting Problems," <u>University Journal of
    Business</u>, (February, 1923), 191-204.
"Budgetary Control and Administration," <u>Administration</u>, (January, 1921), 73-82.
"Budgetary Control for Business; by the Bureau of Commerce and Industrial Affairs,"
    Boston, Mass.: Boston Chamber of Commerce, 1921. 27 p. (Pamphlet.)
"Budgetary Control," (In <u>Management's Handbook</u>. 1924. p. 1269-1312.) (In
    collaboration with James L. Palmer.)
"Budgetary Control: Its Meaning and Advantages," <u>American Fertilizer</u>, (August 23,
    1924), 24-7. <u>Illinois Manufacturers' Costs Association Monthly Bulletin</u>,
    (December 10, 1924), 1-4.
"Budgetary Control of Plant and Equipment," <u>Administration</u>, (May, 1921), 647-58.
"Co-ordination of Sales, Production and Finance," <u>University Journal of Business</u>,
    (September, 1924), 399-405.
"Discussion: Aim and Scope of a Course in Cost Accounting," (In American Associa-
    tion of University Instructors in Accounting. <u>Papers and Proceedings</u>, 1920,
    p. 16-8.)

"Effect of Mergers on Manufacturers Problems," <u>Manufacturers News</u>, (January,
1929), 11-2, 66-71. <u>Bulletin of the American Institute of Accountants</u>,
(February 15, 1929), 13-4 (resume).
"Estimated Balance Sheet and Estimated Statement of Profit and Loss," <u>Administra-
tion</u>, (August, 1921), 227-44.
"Expense Budgets," <u>Administration</u>, (June, 1921), 812-23.
"Financial Budget," <u>Administration</u>, (July, 1921), 74-87.
"Modern Tendencies in Accounting Practice," <u>Accountants' Journal</u> (New Zealand),
(December, 1925), 171-4. <u>Journal of Accountancy</u>, (April, 1925), 299-308.
"Municipal Accounting," <u>Journal of Accountancy</u>, (February, 1921), 81-94.
"Organization and Procedure for Budgetary Control," <u>Administration</u>, (December,
1921), 793-8.
"Organization for Accounting Control," (In Kester, Roy B., <u>Accounting Theory
and Practice</u>. 1921. p. 1-17).
"President's Address: Present Trends in Public and Private Accounting Practice,"
(In American Association of University Instructors in Accounting. <u>Papers
and Proceedings</u>, 1924, p. 59-64.)
"Production Budget," <u>Administration</u>, (March, 1921), 358-67.
"Purchases Budget," <u>Administration</u>, (April, 1921), 465-76.
"Purposes Which May Be Served by Municipal Accounting: Abstract from <u>Journal of
Accountancy</u>," <u>American City</u>, (June, 1923), 555.
"Relation of Budgetary Control to Cost Accounting," <u>Cost Accountant</u>, (September,
1925), 84-90.
_____, New York: January 15, 1922, 14p. (National Association of Cost Account-
ants, Official Publications, v. 3, no. 8).
"Reorganizing Executive and Financial Management Functions," New York: American
Management Association, c1925. 30p. (Pamphlet-<u>Financial Executives'
Series</u>: no. 5.)
"Sales Budget for Business," <u>Administration</u>, (February, 1921), 195-209.
"Seasonal Problems in Financial Administration," <u>Journal of Political Economy</u>,
(December, 1920), 793-826.

Robert H. Montgomery

<u>Books</u>:

<u>American Business Manual: A Complete Guide to Modern Systems and Practice</u>. New
York: P. F. Collier & Son, 1911. 3v. (Editor).
<u>Auditing</u>. Chicago, Ill.: American Technical Society, 1929. (In collaboration
with Willard J. Graham.)
<u>Auditing Principles</u>. New York: Ronald Press Co., 1924. (In collaboration with
Walter A. Staub.)
<u>Auditing, Theory and Practice</u>. New York: Ronald Press Co., 1912.
<u>Auditing, Theory and Practice</u>. Students' edition. New York: Ronald Press Co.,
1916.
<u>Excess Profits Tax Procedure</u>. New York: Ronald Press Co., 1920.
<u>Excess Profits Tax Procedure, 1921; Including Federal Capital Stock (Excise) Tax</u>.
New York: Ronald Press Co., 1920.
<u>Excess Profits, Estate, Gift, Capital Stock, Tax Procedure, 1926</u>. New York:
Ronald Press Co., c1926.
<u>Federal Tax Practice</u>. New York: Ronald Press Co., 1929.
<u>Financial Handbook</u>. New York: Ronald Press Co., c1925. (Editor).
<u>Income Tax Procedure, 1917</u>. New York: Ronald Press Co., 1917.
<u>Income Tax Procedure</u>, 1918. New York: Ronald Press Co., 1918.
<u>Income Tax Procedure</u>, 1919. New York: Ronald Press Co., 1919.
<u>Income Tax Procedure</u>, 1920. New York: Ronald Press Co., 1920.

Income Tax Procedure, 1921. New York: Ronald Press Co., 1921.
Income Tax Procedure, 1922. New York: Ronald Press Co., 1922.
Income Tax Procedure, 1923. New York: Ronald Press Co., 1923.
Income Tax Procedure, 1925. New York: Ronald Press Co., c1925.
Income Tax Procedure, 1926. New York: Ronald Press Co., 1926.
Income Tax Procedure, 1927. New York: Ronald Press Co., 1927. 2v.
Income Tax Procedure, 1929. New York: Ronald Press Co., c1929.
New York State Income Tax Procedure, 1920. New York: Ronald Press Co., 1921.
Uniform Classification of Accounts for Anthracite Coal Operators; text, monthly
        report, prepared by R. V. Norris and R. H. Montgomery. 2v. 437 Chestnut
        Street, Anthracite Bureau of Information.

Periodical Articles:

"Accountancy Laboratory," Journal of Accountancy, (June, 1914), 405-11.
"Accountants' Limitations," address delivered at annual meeting of American
        Institute of Accountants, Del Monte, California, September 20, 1927.
        American Accountant, (October, 1927), 5-9. Canadian Chartered Accountant,
        (March, 1928), 261-84. Journal of Accountancy, (October, 1927), 245-66.
"Appraisal of Goodwill; A True Estimate of Real and Tangible Values Must Be Based
        on Business Success in Both Good and Bad Periods," Bulletin, National Re-
        tail Dry Goods Association, (March, 1926), 16-7, 34. Bulletin of the
        American Institute of Accountants, (October 15, 1926), 10 (resume).
"Auditing," (In Accountancy and Business Management. 1920. v. 4. p. 11-189).
"Auditing," (In Cyclopedia of Commerce, Accountancy, Business Administration,
        1910. v. 6. p. 11-204).
"Claims for Refund of Tax on Stock Dividends: Correspondence," Journal of Account-
        ancy, (July, 1921), 74.
"Co-operation Between Auditors and Bookkeepers," Business Man's Magazine, (Novem-
        ber, 1908), 361-5.
"Early Days," L.R.B. & M. Journal, (May, 1926), 1-3.
"Fallibility of Unverified Financial Statements," Journal of Accountancy, (July,
        1913), 1-10
"Federal Control of Corporations," American Institute of Accountants, Yearbook,
        1912, p. 193-214. Journal of Accountancy, (October, 1912). 272-90.
"Government Supervision and Its Effect on the Profession of the Public Account-
        ant," Journal of Accountancy, (May, 1910), 81-94.
"How Teachers Can Increase the Efficiency of Accounting and Bookkeeping Courses,"
        National Educational Association, Papers and Proceedings, 1916, p. 387-90.
"Importance of Uniform Practice in Determining the Profits of Public Service
        Corporations Where Municipalities Have the Power to Regulate Rates; with
        Discussion," Federation of Societies of Public Accountants in the United
        States of America. Official Record of Congress of Accountants Held at the
        World's Fair, St. Louis, September 26th, 27th, and 28th, 1904, p. 143-59.
        Abstract. Accountant, (October 22, 1904), 458-64.
"Income Tax Suggestions," Administration, (December, 1922), 641-6.
"Income Tax; Specific Cause," Incorporated Accountants' Journal, (March, 1924),
        152-6.
"Influence of the War on Balance-Sheets," Journal of Accountancy, (July, 1919),
        1-8.
"Legislation for the Accountancy Profession," Chartered Accountant, (October,
        1926), p. 5-8. Pace Student, (July, 1926), 3-5, 16-9 (In (Het) Interna-
        tional Accountants' Congress, Amsterdam 1926. p. 205-24.)
"Legislation of the Profession," (In International Accountants' Congress. Papers
        Presented At Amsterdam, 1926, 3E.) Bulletin of the American Institute of
        Accountants, (August 15, 1926), 10 (resume).

"Other Side of Questions: Correspondence," Journal of Accountancy, (January, 1906), 246-7.

"Outline of Address on the 'Income Tax Law,'" Proceedings at a Meeting Held December 6, 1913, to Discuss the"Federal Income Tax," the Pending "Currency Bill" and the National Budget, p. 5-9.

"President's Address," Journal of Accountancy, (October, 1913), 265-7.

"Professional Ethics," Journal of Accountancy, (December, 1913), 94-6.

"Professional Standards; A Plea for Co-operation Among Accountants," Journal of Accountancy, (November, 1905), 28-39.

"Reorganizations and the Closed Transaction," (In Haig, R. M. Ed. Federal Income Tax. 1921. p. 114-36).

"Report of the President," Journal of Accountancy, (October, 1914), 241-4.

"Some Recent Decisions in Income Tax Law," (In Incorporated Accountants' Students' Society of London. Lectures and Transactions for the Year 1925. p. 71-84.)

"Value and Recent Development of Theoretical Training for the Public Accountant," Business Man's Magazine, (September, 1905), 417-9.

"Why Should We Have a New Federal Tax Law?" Journal of Accountancy, (November, 1922), 334-45.

"Work of the Auditor," Auditor, (May 5, 1906), 582-6. Journal of Accountancy, (April, 1906), 492-500.

George H. Newlove

Books:

Cost Accounts. Washington: White Press Co., 1922.
Cost Accounting. Baltimore: The Author, 1927.
Consolidated Balance Sheets. New York: Ronald Press Co., c1926.
C.P.A. Accounting Theory, Auditing, and Problems. New York: D. Appleton and Co., 1920.
C.P.A. Accounting Theory, Questions, and Problems. New York: Association Press, 1921-22. 3v.
Industrial Accounting; With C.P.A. Questions and Problems. Washington: White Press Co., 1921. (In collaboration with L. A. Pratt.)
Practice Set to be Used with Cost Accounts. Washington: White Press Co., Inc., 1922. 2v.
Solutions to Cost Accounts. Washington: White Press Co., 1922.
Solutions to Problems in C.P.A. Accounting. New York: Association Press, 1921.2v.
Specialized Accounting. New York: McGraw-Hill Book Company, 1925. (In collaboration with Lester Amos Pratt.)

Periodical Articles:

"Depreciation," Australasian Accountant and Secretary, (March, 1928), 79-81.
_____, Journal of Accountancy, (December, 1927), 432-7.
"Graduate Courses in Accounting," Accounting Review, (June, 1927), 167-71.
"Graduate Schools of Business," Accounting Review, (September, 1927), 74-9.
"Manufacturing Accounts," Journal of Accountancy, (March, 1921), 176-86.
"Solution to Problem," Accounting Review, (December, 1929), 251-4.
"Step-by-Step Procedure in Preparing Consolidated Balance Sheet," American Accountant, (February, 1929), 73-6.

Jerome Lee Nicholson

Books:

Accountants' and Auditors' Manual. Scranton: International Textbook Co., 1925.

(By William M. Stone, in collaboration with Jerome Lee Nicholson, Charles
J. Nasmyth, and others.)
Cost Accounting. New York: Ronald Press Co., 1919. (In collaboration with J. F.
D. Rohrbach.)
Cost Accounting Syllabus; for use in connection with Cost Accounting Theory and
Practice (student's ed.) New York: The Author, 1916.
Cost Accounting, Theory and Practice. New York: Ronald Press Co., 1913.
Factory Organization and Costs. New York: Kohl Technical Publishing Co., 1909.
Profitable Management. New York: Ronald Press Co., 1923.

Periodical Articles:

"Interest Should Be Included as Part of the Cost," Journal of Accountancy, (May,
1913), 330-4.
"Relation of Cost Department to Other Departments," Administration, (January,
1921), 46-52.
"Fundamentals of Business Success. (In Cost Accounting Addresses. 1920. p. 1-3).
"Use of a Cost System for Reducing the Cost of Production," Administration,
(June, 1921), 803-11.

William Andrew Paton

Books:

Accountants' Handbook. 2d ed. New York: Ronald Press Co., 1932. (Editor.)
Accounting. New York: Macmillan Company, 1924.
Accounting Theory: With Special Reference to the Corporate Enterprise. New York:
Ronald Press Co., 1922.
Essentials of Accounting. New York: Macmillan Co., 1938.
Principles of Accounting. Ann Arbor, Michigan: Ann Arbor Press, 1916. (In
collaboration with Russell Alger Stevenson.)
Problems and Exercises in Accounting. Ann Arbor, Michigan: G. Wahr, 1917. (In
collaboration with Russell Alger Stevenson.)

Periodical Articles:

"Accrued Depreciation on Seasoned Properties," Certified Public Accountant,
(July, 1927), 206-10.
"Assumptions of the Accountant," Administration, (June, 1921), 786-802.
"Depreciation, Appreciation and Productive Capacity," Journal of Accountancy,
(July, 1920), 1-11.
"Discussion: Aim and Scope of Graduate and Research Work in Accounting." (In
American Association of University Instructors in Accounting. Papers and
Proceedings, 1920, p. 26-9.)
"Discussion: Invested Capital as Defined in the Federal Revenue Act and the Ef-
fect Thereof on the Accumulation of Surplus," (In American Association of
University Instructors in Accounting. Papers and Proceedings, 1919, p.
46-9.)
"Distribution Costs and Inventory Values," Accounting Review, (September, 1927),
246-53.
"Dividend Code," Accounting Review, (December, 1929), 218-20.
"Dividends in Securities," Administration, (October, 1922), 394-402.
"Drug Store's Overhead," American Druggist, (September, 1920).
"Educational Value of Training in Accounting," (In American Association of Univer-
sity Instructors in Accounting. Papers and Proceedings, 1922, p. 66-73.)
"Interest During Construction," Journal of Political Economy, (October, 1920),
680-95.

"Inventory Valuation," Administration, (March, 1922), 291-302.
"Limitations of Financial and Operating Ratios," Accounting Review, (September, 1928), 252-60.
"Methods of Measuring Business Income," Administration, (April, 1921), 509-26.
"President's Address: The Educational Value of Training in Accounting," (In American Association of University Instructors in Accounting. Papers and Proceedings, 1922, p. 66-73.)
"Proprietors' Salaries," Journal of Political Economy, (March, 1920), 240-56.
"Simplification of Federal Income Taxation," Certified Public Accountant, (June, 1923), 141-3.
"Some Current Valuation Accounts," Journal of Accountancy,(May, 1920), 335-50.
"Some Phases of Capital Stock," Journal of Accountancy, (May, December, 1919), 321-35; 474-7.
"Some Phases of Capital Stock: Correspondence," Journal of Accountancy, (August, 1919), 158-60.
"Special Applications of Discounting," Journal of Accountancy, (October, 1928), 270-82.
"Tendencies in Accounting Literature," (In American Association of University Instructors in Accounting. Papers and Proceedings, 1924, p. 64-9.)
"Theory of the Double-Entry System," Journal of Accountancy, (January, 1917), 7-26. Canadian Chartered Accountant, (April, 1919), 300-15.
"Transactions Between Partner and Firm," Journal of Accountancy, (July, 1919), 33-8.
"Two Years of Collegiate Work Required for Admission to Accounting Program--Prepares for Professional and Private Work," American Accountant, (September, 1929), 495-6.
"Valuation of Inventories," (In American Association of University Instructors in Accounting. Papers and Proceedings, 1921, p. 66-77). Accountants' Journal (New Zealand), (March-April, 1923), 322-6; 349-51. Journal of Accountancy, (December, 1922), 432-50.

Charles F. Rittenhouse

Books:

Accounting Problems; Advanced. New York: McGraw-Hill, 1924. (In collaboration with Atlee Lane Percy.)
Accounting Problems; Elementary. New York: McGraw-Hill, 1924. (In collaboration with Atlee Lane Percy.)
Accounting Problems; Intermediate. New York: McGraw-Hill, 1922. (In collaboration with Atlee Lane Percy.)
Accounting Theory and Practice. New York: McGraw-Hill, 1918. (In collaboration with Philip Francis Clapp.)
Advanced Accounting Problems; With Explanatory Notes. New York: Association Press, 1917. (In collaboration with P. F. Clapp.)
Elements of Accounts. Boston: A. D. Maclachlan, c1915.
Elements of Accounts for Individuals, Professional Men, and Institutions. New York: McGraw-Hill, 1918.
Essential Exercises in Bookkeeping. Cincinnati: South-western Publishing Co., 1923. (In collaboration with Walter E. Leidner.)
Exercises in Accounting. New York: Association Press, 1917. (In collaboration with Philip Francis Clapp.)
Illustrative Accounting Problems. New York: Ronald Press Co., 1920. (In collaboration with Harold Dudley Greeley-Business Accounting, v. 5.)
Key to New Modern Illustrative Bookkeeping, Introductory Course. New York: American Book Company, c1919.

New Modern Illustrative Bookkeeping; Advanced Course. New York: American Book
    Co., c1919.
New Modern Illustrative Bookkeeping; Elementary Course. New York: American Book
    Co., c1923.
New Modern Illustrative Bookkeeping; Introductory Course. New York: American
    Book Co., c1918.
Notes on Accounting Theory and Practice. New York: Association Press, 1917.
Practice Set. New York: McGraw-Hill, 1918. (In collaboration with Philip Francis
    Clapp for use along with Accounting Theory and Practice.)

Periodical Articles:

"Discussion: Co-operative Commerce Courses," (In American Association of Univer-
    sity Instructors in Accounting. Papers and Proceedings, 1922, p. 38-9.)
"Massachusetts Society Discusses Annual Reports to Commissioner of Corporations,"
    Certified Public Accountant, (April, 1926), 121.
"President's Address: Our Association--Its Opportunity," (In American Association
    of University Instructors in Accounting. Papers and Proceedings, 1923, p.
    59-65.)
"Scope and Content of a Course in Accounting Systems," (In American Association
    of University Instructors in Accounting. Papers and Proceedings, 1921, p.
    79-88.)
"Should Material Be Charged at Cost or Replacement Value?" (In National Associa-
    tion of Cost Accounts. Papers and Discussions, Third New England Regional
    Cost Conference, p. 6-18.)

Earl A. Saliers

Books:

Accountants' Handbook. New York: Ronald Press Co., 1923. (Editor.)
Accounts in Theory and Practice; Principles. New York: McGraw-Hill, 1920.
Depreciation in Theory and Practice. Chicago: LaSalle Extension University, 1915.
    (Pamphlet.)
Depreciation; Principles and Applications. New York: Ronald Press Co., 1922.
    (Reconstruction and broad expansion of Principles of Depreciation.)
Handbook of Corporate Management and Procedure. New York: McGraw-Hill Book Co.,
    1929.
Financial Statements Made Plain; Written for Investors. New York: Magazine of
    Wall Street, c1917.
Intermediate Accounting. New York: Ronald Press Co., c1925. (Complete Accounting
    Course, Unit 3, edited by David Himmelblau.)
Principles of Accounting. New York: LaFayette Institute, c1921.
Principles of Depreciation. New York: Ronald Press Co., 1915.

Periodical Articles:

"Accounting and Investments," Journal of Accountancy, (March, 1917), 161-66.
"Accounting Measures to Meet Business Depression," Journal of Accountancy, (Janu-
    ary, 1920), 1-9.
"Accounting Measures to Meet Business Depression in the Industry," Electric Rail-
    way Journal, (October 11, 1919), sup. 37-9.
"Bank Loans Under the New Conditions: Correspondence," Journal of Accountancy,
    (January, 1915), 80-1.
"Caring for Depreciation," Journal of Accountancy, (April, 1912), 241-50.
"Compulsory Depreciation Charge," Journal of Accountancy, (December, 1912), 431-6.

"Considerations of Consolidated Accounts," <u>Administration</u>, (June, 1921), 773-82.
"Cost, Fair Value, and Depreciation Reserves," <u>American Economic Review</u>, (June, 1920), 272-82.
"Depreciation in Valuations," <u>Journal of Accountancy</u>, (February, 1913), 106-16.
"Depreciation Reserves Vs. Depreciation Funds," <u>Journal of Accountancy</u>, (November, 1913), 358-65.
"Discussion: Problem of Standardizing University Courses in Accounting," (In American Association of University Instructors in Accounting. <u>Papers and Proceedings</u>, 1916, p. 37-41.)
"Life of Industrial Plant and Equipment," <u>Management Engineering</u>, (January, 1923), 69-72.
"Methods of Installment Sales Accounting," (In American Association of University Instructors in Accounting, <u>Publications</u>, 1925, p. 119-26.)
"Price-Making and Competition," <u>Journal of Accountancy</u>, (September, 1917),201-6.
"Production Method of Charging Depreciation," <u>Administration</u>, (May, 1922),583-6.
"Round Table on Teaching Methods: Accounting Lectures," (In American Association of University Instructors in Accounting. <u>Papers and Proceedings</u>, 1920, p. 55-60.)
"Should Obsolescence Be Capitalized?" <u>Journal of Accountancy</u>, (January, 1922), 12-21.
"Treatment of Obsolescence: Correspondence," <u>Journal of Accountancy</u>, (June, 1922), 474.

D. R. Scott

Books:

<u>The Cultural Significance of Accounts</u>. New York: Henry Holt and Co., c1931.
<u>Theory of Accounts</u>. New York: Henry Holt and Co., c1925.

Periodical Articles:

"Conservatism in Inventory Valuations," <u>Accounting Review</u>, (March, 1926), 18-30.
"Depreciation and Repair Costs," <u>Accounting Review</u>, (June, 1929), 116-20.
"Valuation for Depreciation and the Financing of Replacements," <u>Accounting Review</u>, (December, 1929), 221-6.
"Valuation of Investment Securities," <u>Accounting Review</u>, (December, 1928),375-82.

Clinton H. Scovell

Books:

<u>Cost Accounting and Burden Application</u>. New York: D. Appleton & Co., 1916.
<u>Interest as a Cost</u>. New York: Ronald Press Co., 1924.
<u>Relation of the Cost Department to the Factory Organization</u>. Boston: Clinton H. Scovell and Co., 1916. (Pamphlet.)
<u>Unearned Burden in Paper Mills; Measuring the Loss From Curtailed Production</u>. Boston: Clinton H. Scovell and Co., 1915. (Pamphlet.)

Periodical Articles:

"Accounting Group Meeting; Cost Accounting as an Aid to Industrial Control; with Discussion," (In Society of Industrial Engineers, <u>Industrial Leadership</u>, June, 1921, p. 107-25.)
"Brief in Favor of Interest as a Cost," (In National Association of Cost Accountants. <u>Yearbook 1921</u>, p. 47-64.)

"Cost Accounting Practice, with Special Reference to Machine Hour Rate," Journal of Accountancy, (January, 1914), 13-27. Iron Trade Review, (April 9, 1914), 672-6.

"Cost Accounting Practice, with Special Reference to Machine Hour Rate," New York: National Association of Cost Accountants, June 1, 1927, p. 884-906. (N.A.C.A. Bulletin, V. 8, No. 19.)

"Determination of Foundry Costs," Iron Age, (October 5, 1916), 764-5.

"Eliminating Interest as a Factor in Costs," American Industries, (November, 1917), 13-4.

"Essential Factors in Foundry Cost Accounting," Foundry, (March, 1917), 90-3.

"Ethics of Advertising for Accountants; Correspondence," Management and Administration, (March, 1924), 345-7.

"Finding Out About Factory Profits," Industrial Engineering, (June, 1914), 246-50.

"Foundry Costs," American Foundrymen's Association. Proceedings, (September, 1916).

"How Sound Accounting Increases the Efficiency of Municipal Governments," League of Cities of the Third Class in Pennsylvania. Proceedings, 1913, p.161-70.

"Importance of Sound Accounting in Credit Relations," Journal of Accountancy, (November, 1912), 365-79.

"Interest on Investment as a Factor in Manufacturing Costs; with Discussion." (In American Association of University Instructors in Accounting. Papers and Proceedings, 1919, p. 12-40.)

"Methods of Cost and Clear Accounting Essential to Efficient Mill Management," National Association of Cotton Manufacturers. Transactions, Boston, 1914, V. 95, p. 234-54.

"Necessity of Rational Cost Keeping; Abstract," Engineering Magazine, (April, 1916), 120-1.

"Neglecting Our Opportunities," Current Affairs in New England, (April 5, 1926), 5-6.

"Past Records of Accountants' Employees: Correspondence," Journal of Accountancy, (December, 1926), 470.

"Records Should Be Investigated," Journal of Accountancy, (May, 1926), 358-9.

"Searching the Record," Journal of Accountancy, (October, 1923), 284-5.

"Treating Interest as a Cost," Factory, (August, 1922), 125-7.

"Upon Searching the Record," Journal of Accountancy, (July, 1923), 31-2.

"What Does It Cost?" Nation's Business, (September, 1917), 23-5.

"Working Relations Between Public Accountants and Back Credit Men," Robert Morris Associates Monthly Bulletin, (December, 1923), 214-33.

Charles Ezra Sprague

Books:

Amortization. New York: The Author, 1908.

Extended Bond Tables. New York: Business Publishing Company, 1905.

Logarithms to 12 Places and Their Use in Interest Calculations. New York: The Author, 1910.

Problems and Studies in the Accountancy of Investment. New York: The Author, 1906.

Tables of Compound Interest. New York: The Author, 1907.

Text-book of the Accountancy of Investment. New York: The Author, 1909.

The Accountancy of Investment. New York: Business Publishing Company, 1904.

The Philosophy of Accounts. New York: The Author, 1908.

Periodical Articles:

"Algebra of Accounts." The office, May, July, August, 1889, p. 91-2, 122-3, 144-5.

"Conscription of Income a Sound Basis of War Finance." _Accountant_, May 19, 1917, p. 486-91.

"Continuity of Interest." _Accountant_, May 7, 1910, p. 655-7. _Journal of Accountancy_, March, 1910, p. 340-3.

"Detecting Errors in Accounts." _Business_, June, 1897, p. 176-9.

"Embezzlement and Accountability." _Journal of Accountancy_, June, 1909, p. 85-96.

"Fallacy in Bond Values." _Journal of Accountancy_, November, 1907, p. 1-4.

"Line-by-Line Accounts." _Business_, January, 1896, p. 29-31.

"Outlay and Income." _The Office_, November, 1889, p. 207-8.

"Philosophy of Accounts." _Journal of Accountancy_, January, 1907, p. 181-88; February, 1907, p. 261-75; March, 1907, p. 364-75; April, 1907, p. 449-61; May, 1907, p. 33-45; June, 1907, p. 122-30; July, 1907, p. 198-210; August, 1907, p. 287-97; September, 1907, p. 363-68; October, 1907, p. 432-450; November, 1907, p. 23-40; January, 1908, p. 205-10.

"Premiums and Discounts." _Journal of Accountancy_, August, 1906, p. 294-6.

"Problems and Studies in Accountancy of Investment." _Business World_, October, November, December, 1905, January, February, April, May, 1906, p. 550-5, 619-25, 691-7, 32-41, 110-6, 286-93, 386-94.

"Stock Value of a Bond," _Journal of Accountancy_, July, 1908, p. 174-6. _Accountant_, September 12, 1908, p. 314-5.

"Tabular Bookkeeping," _The Office_, September, 1890, p. 240-1.

Ross G. Walker

Books:

Classified Selection of Problems in Accounting. Ann Arbor, Michigan: George Wahr, c1922.

Problems in Accounting Principles. Chicago: A. W. Shaw Co., c1929. (Advised and editorially assisted by Paul Brown Coffman.)

Periodical Articles:

"Governmental Budget as an Instrument of Control," _Accounting Review_, (June, 1926), 20-47.

"Municipal Balance-Sheet," _Journal of Accountancy_, (March, 1923), 186-201. _Public Accountant_, (April, 1923), 318-24; 332-40.

"Principles Vs. Rules," (In American Association of University Instructors in Accounting. _Papers and Proceedings_, 1922, p. 94-9.)

John R. Wildman

Books:

Auditing Studies. New York: The William G. Hewitt Press, 1917. (Pamphlet.)

Capital Stock Without Par Value. Chicago: A. W. Shaw Co., 1928. (In collaboration with Weldon Powell.)

Cost Accounting. New York: Accountancy Publishing Co., 1911.

Cost Accounting Problems. New York City: Accountancy Publishing Company, 1910.

Cost Accounting Studies. New York City: W. Green, 1920.

Elementary Accounting Problems. New York: The William G. Hewitt Press, 1914.

Introduction to Accounting, 4th ed. New York: The William G. Hewitt Press, 1915.

Principles of Accounting. New York: The William G. Hewitt Press, 1913.

Principles of Auditing. New York: The William G. Hewitt Press, 1916.

Principles of Cost Accounting. New York: New York University Press Co., 1914. (Is in reality the Revised Edition of _Cost Accounting_.)

<u>Some Obstacles in the Path of Capital Stock Without Par Value</u>. New York: Haskins
and Sells, 1922. (Pamphlet.)

<u>Periodical Articles</u>:

"Accountants' Certificates," <u>Certified Public Accountant</u>, (June, 1928), 163-4.
"Accountant's Liability for Failure to Discover Fraud," (paper read before the
eighth annual fall conference of the New York State Society of Certified
Public Accountants, New York City, October 20, 1930.) <u>Bulletin, New York
State Society of Certified Public Accountants</u>, (October, 1930), 36-44.
<u>Robert Morris Associates Monthly Bulletin</u>, (December,1930), 224-9.
"Accounting and Modern Industry," <u>Electric Railway Journal</u>, (October 14, 1916),
793-5.
"Accounting Classification Suggested," <u>American Accountant</u>, (February, 1926),
27-9.
"Activities of American Institute," <u>American Accountant</u>, (February, 1927), 34.
"Address of the President," (In American Association of University Instructors
in Accounting. Papers and Proceedings, 1917, p. 7-10.)
"Appreciation from the Point of View of the Certified Public Accountant," <u>Ac-
counting Review</u>, (December, 1928), 396-406. <u>Haskins and Sells Bulletin</u>,
(January, 1929), 2-7.
"Certified Financial Statements as a Basis for Credit," <u>Journal of Accountancy</u>,
(September, 1920), 161-8.
"Classification of Accountancy Services," <u>Accounting Review</u>, (June, 1928),124-30.
"Consideration of the Sinking Fund Method as a Basis for Amortizing Franchises,"
<u>Haskins and Sells Bulletin</u>, (December 15, 1922).
"Correlation of Accounting Instruction in Universities with the Needs of Public
Accountants," (In American Association of University Instructors in Ac-
counting. <u>Papers and Proceedings</u>, 1921, p. 27-32).
"Correspondence Course in Accounting," (In National Electric Light Association.
<u>Proceedings</u>, 1916. Accounting Volume, p. 155-60). (In collaboration with
A. L. Holme.)
"Cost Accounting in Relation to Business Cycles," New York: National Association
of Cost Accountants, July 16, 1923. 12p. (<u>Official Publications</u>, V. 4,
No. 21.) <u>Accountant</u>, (July 19, 1924), 110-4.
"Cost Accounting," <u>Journal of Accountancy</u>, (November, 1910), 1-9, 119-126, 186-
94, 267-76, 346-57; (April, 1911), 422-38.
"Department of Practical Accounting," <u>Journal of Accountancy</u>, January, 1912, p.
58-65, February, 1912, p. 144-51, March, 1912, p. 224-35, April, 1912, p.
295-304, May, 1912, p. 370-81, June, 1912, p. 436-444, July, 1912, p. 58-
63, August, 1912, p. 133-43, September, 1912, p. 226-34, October, 1912, p.
327-333, November, 1912, p. 407-16, December, 1912, p. 494-500, January,
1913, p. 65-71, February, 1913, p. 128-33, March, 1913, p. 189-97, April,
1913, p. 264-72, May, 1913, p. 357-64, June, 1913, p. 449-58, July, 1913,
p. 54-63, August, 1913, p. 124-131, September, 1913, p. 234-44, October,
1913, p. 319-26, November, 1913, p. 375-83, December, 1913, p. 461-67.
Correspondence. Criticism of department of practical accounting. <u>Journal
of Accountancy</u>, July, 1912, p. 70-2.
"Depreciation and Obsolescence as Affected by Appraisals;" paper presented at the
International Congress on Accounting held at Hotel Commodore, New York,
September 9-14, 1929. 11p. (In International Congress on Accounting.
<u>Proceedings</u>, 1929, p. 420-30.) <u>Accountant</u>, (November 2, 1929), 538-41.
"Depreciation From a Certified Accountant's Point of View," <u>Electric Railway
Journal</u>, (April 18, 1914), 882-3.
"Discount on No-Par Shares," <u>Haskins and Sells Bulletin</u>, (May, 1928), 34.

"Diversity of No-Par-Stock Statutes Creates Problem for Accountant," American
    Accountant, (February, 1928), 19-21.
"Early Instruction in Accounting," Accounting Review, (March, 1926), 105-7.
"Educational Program of the Institute," (In American Association of University
    Instructors in Accounting. Papers and Proceedings, 1924, p. 33-6).
"Favorite Methods of Business Crookdom," (In American Association of University
    Instructors in Accounting. Publications, 1925, p. 127-9).
"Interest Owned on Capital," Journal of Accountancy, (June, 1913), 428-31.
"Interpretation of Financial Statements," Journal of Accountancy, (March, 1926),
    185-95. Canadian Chartered Accountant, (September, 1927), 80-90. New
    York Credit Men's Association Bulletin, (March, April, 1926), 112-6; 185-
    90. Pace Student, (July, 1926), 21.
"Looking at Financial Statements," Haskins and Sells Bulletin, (August, 1924),
    57-6.
"Los estades financieros visados por contadores publicos in las solicitudes de
    credito bancario;" traducida del Journal of Accountancy por Alberto,
    Arevalo. Hacienda y Administracion, (Julio-Diciembre, 1920), 217-24.
"No-Par Discount," Haskins and Sells Bulletin, (June, 1929), 46-7.
"Part Which Accounting Should Occupy in any Scheme of National Preparedness;"
    a paper read before the American Economic Association at Columbus, Ohio,
    December 29th, 1916. 8p. American Economic Review, (March, 1917), supple-
    ment, 224-8.
"Part Which Accounting Has Played in the Development of Modern Industry;" a paper
    read before the American Electric Railway Accountants' Association. 9p.
"Preferred Surplus," Haskins and Sells Bulletin, (March, 1929), 26-8.
"Profit Dividends and Appreciation," Haskins and Sells Bulletin, (March, 1928),
    21-3. Bulletin of the American Institute of Accountants, (April 18, 1928),
    14. (resume).
"Recasting Procedure," from Haskins and Sells Bulletin, (June, 1924). L.R.B.&M.
    Journal, (October, 1924), 8-9.
"Relation Between Secondary Schools and Universities with Regard to the Teaching
    of Bookkeeping and Accounting;" a paper read before the Eastern Commercial
    Teachers' Association, April 20, 1916. New York University, 1916. 21p.
"Research in Accounting," Bulletin of the American Institute of Accountants,
    (February 15, 1926), 2-5.
"Research Program," Accounting Review, (March, 1926), 43-55.
"Sensible Accounting for Social Agencies," Haskins and Sells Bulletin, (January
    15, 1922), 206.
"Service Classification," New York: Haskins and Sells (1928). Five typewritten
    pages.
"Shares of Capital Stock Without Par Value;" address before the New York State
    Society of Certified Public Accountants...January 9, 1928. News Bulletin,
    New York State Society of Certified Public Accountants, (January 26,1928).
"Significant Developments Relating to No-Par Shares," Haskins and Sells Bulletin,
    (June, 1927), 42-4.
"Sinking Fund Method for Amortizing Franchises," Journal of Accountancy,
    (January, March, 1923), 16-21; 233-5.
"Some Additional Questions: Correspondence," Journal of Accountancy, (September,
    1919), 380-1.
"Some Obstacles in the Path of Capital Stock Without Par Value," Certified Public
    Accountant, (January, 1923), 14-8, 24.
"Styles in No-Par Stock Laws," Haskins and Sells Bulletin,(December, 1927),93-5.
"Supervising the Work of the Accounting Staff," Journal of Accountancy, (October,
    1920), 245-51.
"Training Young Accountants," Journal of Accountancy, (June, 1922), 431-7.

BIBLIOGRAPHY

Books

Accountants' Index. New York: American Institute of Accountants, 1921.

_____. Supplement. New York: American Institute of Accountants, 1923.

_____. Second Supplement. New York: American Institute of Accountants, 1928.

_____. Third Supplement. New York: The American Institute Publishing Co., Inc., 1932.

_____. Fourth Supplement. New York: The American Institute Publishing Co., Inc., 1936.

_____. Fifth Supplement. New York: The American Institute Publishing Co., Inc., 1940.

_____. Sixth Supplement. New York: The American Institute Publishing Co., Inc., 1944.

_____. Seventh Supplement. New York: The American Institute Publishing Co., Inc., 1948.

_____. Eighth Supplement. New York: The American Institute Publishing Co., Inc., 1950.

_____. Ninth Supplement. New York: American Institute of Accountants, 1951.

_____. Tenth Supplement. New York: American Institute of Accountants, 1953.

_____. Eleventh Supplement. New York: American Institute of Accountants, 1955.

American Accounting Association. 1955 Membership Roster.

American Institute of Accountants. American Institute of Accountants Fiftieth Anniversary Celebration 1937. Concord, New Hampshire: The Rumford Press, 1938.

American Institute of Accountants. Officers & Committees, Trial Boards, State Boards of Accountancy, State Societies of CPA's, Minutes of Annual Meeting, Awards, 1954-1955. New York: The American Institute of Accountants, 1954.

Bentley, Harry Clark, and Leonard, Ruth S. Bibliography of Works on Accounting by American Authors. 2 vols. Boston, Mass.: H. C. Bentley, 1935.

Brown, O.S.U., Sister Isadore. "The Historical Development of the Use of Ratios in Financial Statement Analysis to 1933." Unpublished Ph.D. dissertation, The Catholic University of America, 1955.

Cattell, Jaques (ed.). Directory of American Scholars. 2d ed. Lancaster, Pa.: The Science Press, 1951.

DeMond, C. W. Price, Waterhouse & Co. In America. New York: The Comet Press, Inc., 1951.

Duerr, Alvan E. (ed.). Baird's Manual American College Fraternities. 14th ed. Menasha, Wisconsin: The Collegiate Press George Banta Publishing Company, 1940.

Fourth International Congress on Accounting, 1933. Proceedings. London: Gee & Co., Ltd., 1933.

Golenpaul, Dan (ed.). Information Please Almanac 1955. New York: The Macmillan Company, 1954.

Green, Wilmer L. History and Survey of Accountancy. Brooklyn: Standard Text Press, 1930.

Index to the Accounting Review. American Accounting Association, 1951.

International Congress on Accounting, 1929. Proceedings. New York: The Knickerbocker Press, 1930.

Marquis, Albert Nelson (ed.). Who Was Who In America. Vol. I, 1897-1942. Chicago: The A. N. Marquis Company, 1942.

_____. Who's Who In America. Vol. VII, 1912-1913. Chicago: A. N. Marquis & Company, 1912.

_____. Who's Who In America. Vol. VIII, 1914-1915. Chicago: A. N. Marquis & Company, 1914.

_____. Who's Who In America. Vol. XII, 1922-1923. Chicago: A. N. Marquis & Company, 1922.

_____. Who's Who In America. Vol. XIII, 1924-1925. Chicago: A. N. Marquis & Company, 1924.

_____. Who's Who In America. Vol. XV, 1928-1929. Chicago: A. N. Marquis & Company, 1928.

_____. Who's Who In America. Vol. XVI, 1930-1931. Chicago: A. N. Marquis & Company, 1930.

Merritt, Rita Perine (ed.). The Accountants' Directory and Who's Who-1925. New York: Prentice-Hall, Inc., 1925.

National Association of Cost Accountants. Year Book, 1920. New York: Press of J. J. Little & Ives Company, 1921.

_____. Year Book, 1924. Proceedings of the Fifth International Cost Conference (Springfield, Massachusettes, 1924). New York: J. J. Little and Ives Company, 1924.

_____. Year Book, 1925. Proceedings of the Sixth International Cost Conference (Detroit, Michigan, 1925). New York: J. J. Little and Ives Company, 1925.

_____. Year Book, 1926. Proceedings of the Seventh International Cost Conference(Atlantic City, New Jersey, 1926). New York: J. J. Little and Ives, 1926.

_____. Year Book, 1927. Proceedings of the Eighth International Cost Conference. (Chicago, Illinois, 1927). New York: J. J. Little and Ives Company, 1927.

_____. Year Book, 1936. Proceedings of the Seventeenth International Cost Conference(Cincinnati, Ohio, 1936). New York: Press of J. J. Little and Ives Company, 1936.

_____. 1951 Conference Proceedings(Chicago, Illinois, 1951). New York:National Association of Cost Accountants, 1951.

Perine, Rita (ed.). The Accountants' Directory and Who's Who-1920. New York: The Forty-Fifth Street Press, 1920.

Sprague, Charles Ezra. The Philosophy of Accounts. 5th ed. New York: The Ronald Press Company, 1923.

The Journal of Accountancy Index. Vols. XXXV-LXX inclusive. New York: American Institute Publishing Co., Inc., 1941.

Who Was Who In America. Vol. II, 1943-1950. Chicago: The A. N. Marquis Company, 1950.

Who's Who-1923. London: A.& C Black, Limited, 1923.

Who's Who-1935. London: A & C Black, Limited, 1935.

Who's Who In America. Vol. XXVI, 1950-1951. Chicago: A. N. Marquis & Company, 1950.

Who's Who In America. Vol. XXVIII, 1954-1955. Chicago: A. N. Marquis & Company, 1954.

Periodical Articles

"Accountant Aids Study of Reduction of War Profits," The American Accountant, XVI, No. 4(April, 1931), 110.

"Accountants Club Members Guests of President," The American Accountant, XII, No. 6(July, 1927), 25.

"Accountant Criticises Alternative Plan for Railroad Depreciation Accounting," The American Accountant, XIII, No. 10(October, 1928), 18ff.

"Accounting Hall of Fame Names Andrews; W. A. Paton Presents Citation," The Journal of Accountancy, XCVI, No. 1(July, 1953), 16.

"Accounting Hall of Fame," (News Report) The Journal of Accountancy, CI, No. 6 (June, 1956), 6.

"Accounting Hall of Fame," The Canadian Chartered Accountant, LXV, No. 4(October, 1954), 182-3.

"Advertisement," The American Accountant, XII, No. 5(June, 1927), 49.

"American Institute of Accountants-Annual Meeting Held in St. Louis on September 15, 16, 17, and 18," The Pace Student, IX, No. 11(October, 1924), 166-7.

American Institute of Accountants, "Committee on Annual Awards. Annual Institute Awards--Report to Council of the Institute--Excerpt," (Official Decisions and Releases). The Journal of Accountancy, LXXX, No. 6(December, 1945), 492.

Austin, E. Burl. "Association Notes," The Accounting Review, XXIII, No. 2(April, 1948), 216; XXIV, No. 2(April, 1949), 219-20; XXV, No. 1(January, 1950), 113-4; XXV, No. 4(October, 1950), 461; XXVI, No. 3(July, 1951), 430-2; XXVI, No. 4(October, 1951), 593; XXVII, No. 3(July, 1952), 397; XXVIII, No. 1(January, 1953), 142; XXVIII, No. 2(April, 1953), 293; XXVIII, No. 4 (October, 1953), 592-4; XXIX, No. 1(January, 1954), 154; XXIX, No. 3 (July, 1954), 522-3; XXX, No. 2(April, 1955), 326.

"Award of Merit for Hatfield Book Should Stimulate Authors," The American Accountant, XIV, No. 1(January, 1929), 28-30.

"Book on Economics of Accountancy Chosen as Best of Year," The American Accountant, XVI, No. 1(January, 1931), 22-3.

Brundage, Percival F. "Milestones on the Path of Accounting," Harvard Business Review, XXIX, No. 4(July, 1951), 71-81.

Cannon, Arthur M. "Check List For an Accounting Library," The Accounting Review, XXV, No. 4(October, 1950), 425-40.

Carey, John L. (ed.), "Col. Robert H. Montgomery," The Journal of Accountancy, XCV, No. 6(June, 1953), 677-8.

Chaffee, Allen. "Colonel Robert H. Montgomery," The Pace Student, XI, No. 8(July, 1926), 8-9.

Chaffee, Allen. "Dr. Joseph J. Klein, C.P.A.," The Pace Student, XI, No. 7(June, 1926), 3-4.

"Clinton Homer Scovell," The American Accountant, XII, No. 1(February, 1927), 31.

"Colonel Carter New President of Accountants Club," The American Accountant, XV, No. 2(February, 1930), 83.

"Colonel Montgomery Defines Professional Responsibilities," The American Accountant, XII, No. 9(October, 1927), 5-10, 58-61.

"Colonel Robert H. Montgomery, . . . ," The Pace Student, VIII, No. 6(May, 1923), 82.

"Convention Report," American Accounting Association, Proceedings of the Twenty-Second Annual Convention, (Atlantic City, New Jersey, December 27-29, 1937), The Accounting Review, XIII, No. 1(March, 1938), 97.

"Dickinson, Hatfield Chosen for 1951 Awards at Ohio State's Hall of Fame," The Journal of Accountancy, XCII, No. 2(August, 1951), 135.

Dixon, R. L. "Association Notes," The Accounting Review, XVII, No. 3(July, 1942), 333-4; XXII, No. 3(July, 1947), 326-7.

"Elected Chairman of Board," The American Accountant, XVII, No. 4(April, 1932), 127.

"Extensive Public Service Marks Record of Illinois Accountants," The American Accountant, XII, No. 4(May, 1927), 27-30.

"First Award of John F. Forbes Medal Made in California," The American Accountant, XIV, No. 2(February, 1929), 113-4.

"Fortieth Anniversary Celebrated by American Institute," The American Accountant, XII, No. 10(November, 1927), 13.

Gilman, Stephen. "How to Use Trend Percentages in Analyzing Progress of Business," The American Accountant, XV, No. 5(May, 1930), 215-7.

Gluick, L. "What's Wrong With Our Textbooks?" The Accounting Review, XXII, No. 1 (January, 1947), 36-8.

Gore, Edward E. (Editorial), The Journal of Accountancy, XXXVIII, No. 3(September, 1924), 207.

Greer, Howard C. "Discussion," The American Association of University Instructors in Accounting, Papers and Proceedings of the Ninth Annual Meeting(Chicago, Illinois, 1924), 89-91.

Hassler, Russell H. "Report of the 1953 President," The Accounting Review, XXIX, No. 2(April, 1954), 297-301.

Heckert, J. Brooks. "Accounting Hall of Fame," The Accounting Review, XXV, No. 3 (July, 1950), 260-1.

"Historical Dates in Accounting," The Accounting Review, XXIX, No. 3(July, 1954), 486-93.

"Historical Sketch of National Association of Cost Accountants," The American Accountant, XIII, No. 6(June, 1928), 6-8.

"Honor Conferred on R. H. Montgomery by Roumanian Minister," The American Accountant, XV, No. 8(August, 1930), 382.

Husband, George R. "Report of the 1952 President," The Accounting Review, XXVIII, No. 2(April, 1953), 267-74.

"International Congress Indicates Advanced Status of Profession," The American
    Accountant, XIV, No. 3(September, 1929), 467-8.

"International Congress of Accountants," The American Accountant, XIII, No. 6
    (June, 1928), 27.

Kerrigan, Harry D. "University Notes," The Accounting Review, XV, No. 2(June,
    1940), 299; XV, No. 4(December, 1940), 541; XVI, No. 2(June, 1941), 230;
    XVI, No. 3(September, 1941), 319; XVI, No. 4(December, 1941), 445.

Kester, Roy B. "Discussion," The American Association of University Instructors
    in Accounting, Papers and Proceedings of the Ninth Annual Meeting(Chicago,
    Illinois, 1924), 86-8.

Klein, Dr. Joseph J. "Is the Credit Man Entitled to More Financial Facts?" The
    American Accountant, XIII, No. 2(February, 1928), 5.

Littleton, A. C. "The Development of Accounting Literature," Publications of
    the American Association of University Instructors in Accounting, IX, No. 2
    (December, 1925), 7-17.

"Major Jerome Lee Nicholson," The Pace Student, X, No. 2(January, 1925), 27-8.

Mann, Helen Jo Scott. "Charles Ezra Sprague," Dictionary of American Biography.
    Edited by Dumas Malone. New York: Charles Scribners' Sons, 1935. Vol.
    XVII, 471-2.

Mayors, W. "Four-Year Struggle Made Accounting Law Possible in Missouri," The
    American Accountant, XII, No. 6(July, 1927), 26-30.

"Montgomery Heads Joint Committee of Congress of Accountants," The American Ac-
    countant, XIII, No. 2(February, 1928), 52.

Murphy, Mary E. "Arthur Lowes Dickinson: Pioneer in American Professional Ac-
    countancy," Bulletin of the Business Historical Society, XXI, No. 2(April,
    1947), 27-38.

"Libraries for Students of Accounting," The Accounting Review, XXIV, No. 4(Octo-
    ber, 1948), 420-1.

"New York Society to Have Anniversary Dinner," The American Accountant, XII, No.
    3(April, 1927), 48.

"New York State C.P.A. Society Holds Special Conference," The Pace Student, VIII,
    No. 12(November, 1923), 191.

"New York State Society of C.P.A.'s Elects Officers," The Pace Student, IX, No. 8
    (July, 1924), 123.

"Officers Reelected in Massachusetts," The American Accountant, XII, No. 7
    (August, 1927), 50.

"Ohio Society of C.P.A.'s," The Pace Student, IX, No. 11(October, 1924), 169.

Pace, Homer S. (ed.). "Editorial Comment," The American Accountant, XVIII, No. 9
    (September, 1933), 261-2.

_____. "International Convention of Accountants," The Pace Student, XI, No. 6 (May, 1926), 2.

_____. "The Editor's Page," The American Accountant, XII, No. 9(October, 1927), inside front cover.

_____. "The Editor's Page," The American Accountant, XV, No. 7(July, 1930), 290.

Paton, Professor William A. "How Michigan Trains Her Young Men for Accountancy Careers," The American Accountant, XIV, No. 9(September, 1929), 495-6.

_____. "Recent and Prospective Developments in Accounting Theory," (Harvard Business School, Bureau of Business Research, Business Research Studies, No. 25). Boston, Mass.: Harvard University Press, 1940.

_____. "Tendencies in Accounting Literature," The American Association of University Instructors in Accounting. Papers and Proceedings of the Ninth Annual Meeting(Chicago, Illinois, 1924), 64-9.

"Philosopher-Accountant Takes Inventory of Soul of Profession," The American Accountant, XIII, No. 7(July, 1928), 19-22.

"Popular Vote Being Taken to Choose Best Accounting Book of Year," The American Accountant, XV, No. 7(July, 1930), 323.

"Prizes for Cost Essays," The Pace Student, XI, No. 5(April, 1926), 11.

Richardson, A. P. (ed.). "An International Accountant Passes," The Journal of Accountancy, LIX, No. 4(April, 1935), 248-9.

_____. "Sir Arthur Lowes Dickinson," The Journal of Accountancy, XXXVI, No. 3 (September, 1923), 202.

"Roumania to Confer Decoration on Colonel Robert H. Montgomery," The American Accountant, XV, No. 3(March, 1930), 118.

Sanders, Thomas H. "Significant Recent Accounting Literature," Harvard Business Review, XV, No. 3(Spring, 1937), 266-88.

Scovill, H. T. "Reflections of Twenty-Five Years in the American Accounting Association," The Accounting Review, XVI, No. 2(June, 1941), 167-75.

Smith, Frank P. "Association Notes," The Accounting Review, XXIII, No. 1(January, 1948), 104.

_____. "Report of the President," The Accounting Review, XXX, No. 2(April, 1955), 323-9.

Stacey, Nicholas A. H. "The Accounting Hall of Fame," The Accountant, CXXXI (July 31st, 1954), 108.

The Committee on History. "Charles Ezra Sprague--Public Accountant," The New York Certified Public Accountant, XXII, No. 7(July, 1952), 430-2.

"The New York State Society of Certified Public Accountants," The Pace Student, XI, No. 11(October, 1926), 6-9.

"To Choose Best Book," The American Accountant, XVI, No. 6(June, 1931), 184-5.

Tucker, Arthur R. "Great Progress Made by Accountancy During Past Year," The American Accountant, XIV, No. 5(May, 1929), 251-6.

"University Instructors in Accounting Hold Annual Meeting," The Pace Student, IX, No. 4(March, 1924), 58.

"University Notes," The Accounting Review, I No. 2(June, 1926), 101-2; I, No. 3 (September, 1926), 100; I, No. 4(December, 1926), 101-3; II, No. 1(March, 1927), 72; II, No. 2(June, 1927), 209; II, No. 3(September, 1927), 300; II, No. 4(December, 1927), 425; III, No. 1(March, 1928), 81-2; III, No. 2 (June, 1928), 229-33; III, No. 3(September, 1928), 330; IV, No. 2(June, 1929), 145; IV, No. 3(September, 1929), 209-11; V, No. 3(September, 1930), 275; V, No. 4(December, 1930), 339; VI, No. 2(June, 1931), 158-9; VI, No. 3(September, 1931), 247; VI, No. 4(December, 1931), 328; VII, No. 2 (June, 1932), 151; VIII, No. 2(June, 1933), 183; VIII, No. 4(December, 1933), 373; IX, No. 2(June, 1934), 200; X, No. 1(March, 1935), 130; XI, No. 3(September, 1936), 315; XII, No. 2(June, 1937), 207; XII, No. 3 (September, 1937), 335; XII, No. 4(December, 1937), 454; XIII, No. 3 (September, 1938), 332; XIII, No. 4(December, 1938), 438; XIV, No. 1 (March, 1939), 91; XIV, No. 2(June, 1939), 201; XIV, No. 3(September, 1939), 330; XIV, No. 4(December, 1939), 464.

"Varying View-Points on Principles of Valuation Presented," The American Accountant, XIV, No. 10(October, 1929), 544-55.

"Views of Profession with Respect to Depreciation Clearly Stated," The American Accountant, XIV, No. 10(October, 1929), 537-44.

Walker, Ross Graham. "Explorations in Accounting," Harvard Business Review, XVIII, No. 3(Spring, 1940), 384-96.

"What National and State Societies Have Accomplished in Year," The American Accountant, XIV, No. 5(May, 1929), 261-5.

"What Was Best Book on Accounting Published During Year?" The American Accountant, XIV, No. 7(July, 1929), 383-4.

White, John Arch. "Abstracts of Dissertations for 1953 and 1954," The Accounting Review, XXX, No. 4(October, 1955), 673-93.

"Wildman-Powell Book Designated as Most Notable of Year," The American Accountant, XV, No. 1(January, 1930), 18-9.

Yntema, Theodore O. "Discussion," The American Association of University Instructors in Accounting, Papers and Proceedings of the Ninth Annual Meeting (Chicago, Illinois, 1924), 88-9.

Book Reviews

Adams, James P. Review of Management Through Accounts, by James H. Bliss, The American Economic Review, XVI, No. 2(June, 1926), 309-11.

_____. Review of Principles of Accounting, by H. A. Finney, Publications of the American Association of University Instructors in Accounting, IX, No. 2 (December, 1925), 157-8.

Arnett, Trevor. Review of Accounts, Their Construction and Interpretation, by William Morse Cole, A.M., The Journal of Political Economy, XVII, No. 2 (February, 1909), 165-6.

Bauer, John. Review of Principles of Depreciation, by Earl A. Saliers, The American Economic Review, VI, No. 1(March, 1916), 129-31.

Beights, D. M. Review of Principles of Accounting, Intermediate, 3d ed., by H. A. Finney, The Accounting Review, XXII, No. 1(January, 1947), 95.

Bennett, George B. Review of Fundamentals of Accounting, by E. A. Saliers, The Accounting Review, X, No. 4(December, 1935), 428.

Blough, Carman G. Review of Accounting Concepts of Profit, by Stephen Gilman, The Journal of Accountancy, LXIX, No. 6(June, 1940), 505.

"Book Notices," Review of Accountants' Handbook, edited by Earl A. Saliers, Harvard Business Review, II, No. 3(April, 1924), 383-4.

_____. Review of Accounting, by W. A. Paton, Harvard Business Review, IV, No. 2 (January, 1926), 254.

_____. Review of Accounting Problems: Advanced, by Charles F. Rittenhouse and Atlee L. Percy, Harvard Business Review, II, No. 3(April, 1924), 383.

_____. Review of Analyzing Financial Statements, by Stephen Gilman, Harvard Business Review, IV, No. 4(July, 1926), 509.

_____. Review of Consolidated Balance Sheets, by George Hillis Newlove, Harvard Business Review, V, No. 3(April, 1927), 380-1.

_____. Review of Financial and Operating Ratios in Management, by James H. Bliss, Harvard Business Review, III, No. 1(October, 1924), 124.

_____. Review of Interest as a Cost, by Clinton H. Scovell, Harvard Business Review, III, No. 2(January, 1925), 255-6.

_____. Review of Management Through Accounts, by James H. Bliss, Harvard Business Review, III, No. 2(January, 1925), 252.

_____. Review of The Analysis of Financial Statements, by Harry G. Guthmann, Harvard Business Review, IV, No. 3(April, 1926), 380-1.

Bryant, R. A. Review of Accounting Evolution to 1900, by A. C. Littleton, The Accounting Review, X, No. 4(December, 1935), 411-2.

Carey, John L. Review of C.P.A. Accounting, 2nd ed., by George Hillis Newlove, The Journal of Accountancy, XLI, No. 4(April, 1926), 314.

_____. Review of C.P.A. Accounting, 3rd ed., by George H. Newlove, The Journal of Accountancy, XLVI, No. 6(December, 1928), 475.

Chase, Harvey S. Review of Municipal Accounting, by DeWitt Carl Eggleston, The American Economic Review, V, No. 2(June, 1915), 339-40.

Clowes, Francis J. Review of Income Tax Procedure, 1925, by R. H. Montgomery, The Journal of Accountancy, XXXIX, No. 3(March, 1925), 235-6.

Coffman, Paul B. Review of Auditors' Reports and Working Papers, by D. C. Eggleston, The Accounting Review, IV, No. 1(April, 1929), 60-1.

Cole, William Morse. Review of Auditing Theory and Practice, 2nd ed., by Robert H. Montgomery, The American Economic Review, VII, No. 1(March, 1917),130-2.

_____. Review of Modern Accounting, by Henry Rand Hatfield, The Journal of Political Economy, XVII, No. 9(November, 1909), 647-8.

_____. Review of Principles of Auditing, by John Raymond Wildman, The American Economic Review, VI, No. 3(September, 1916), 644-7.

Couchmann, Charles B. Review of The Analysis of Financial Statements, by Harry G. Guthmann, The Accounting Review, I, No. 4(December, 1926), 93-5.

D'Alessandro, Alfred. Review of Depreciation, Principles and Applications, 3rd ed., by E. A. Saliers, The Accounting Review, XIV, No. 2(June, 1939), 194-5.

Elwell, F. H. Review of Auditing Procedure, by DeWitt C. Eggleston, The Accounting Review, II, No. 1(March, 1927), 67-8.

_____. Review of Introduction to Principles of Accounting, by H. A. Finney, The Accounting Review, VII, No. 4(December, 1932), 309-10.

Fairchild, Fred Rogers. Review of Federal Income Taxation, by Joseph J. Klein, The American Economic Review, XIX, No. 3(September, 1929), 508-9.

F., H. C. Review of Income Tax Procedure 1917, by Robert H. Montgomery, The Journal of Accountancy, XXIII, No. 2(February, 1917), 157-60.

Filbey, Edward J. Review of Consolidated Balance Sheets, by George H. Newlove, The Accounting Review, II, No. 2(June, 1927), 195-6.

Finney, H. A. Review of Accounting Problems: Advanced, by Charles F. Rittenhouse and Atlee L. Percy, The Journal of Accountancy, XXXVIII, No. 2(August, 1924), 153-4.

Fisher, Allan J. Review of Basic Financial Statement Analysis, by Alexander Wall; Financial Statement Analysis, by John N. Myer; Analysis of Financial Statements, Third Edition, by Harry G. Guthmann, The Accounting Review, XVIII, No. 3(July, 1943), 281-3.

Fiske, W. P. Review of Accounting Concepts of Profit, by Stephen Gilman, The American Economic Review, XXX, No. 2(June, 1940), 400-1.

_____. Review of An Introduction to Corporate Accounting Standards, by W. A. Paton and A. C. Littleton, The American Economic Review, XXX, No. 3 (September, 1940), 623.

_____. Review of Introduction to Principles of Accounting, Rev. ed., by H. A. Finney, The American Economic Review, XXVII, No. 1(March, 1937), 158.

_____. Review of Introduction to Principles of Accounting, by H. A. Finney, The American Economic Review, XXIII, No. 4(December, 1933), 730.

FitzHugh, M. M. Review of Cost Accounting and Burden Application, by Clinton H. Scovell, The American Economic Review, VII, No. 1(March, 1917), 137-9.

Freeman, Herbert C. Review of Accounting Evolution to 1900, by A. C. Littleton, The Journal of Accountancy, LVI, No. 5(November, 1933), 389-91.

_____. Review of Auditing-Theory and Practice, by Robert H. Montgomery, The Journal of Accountancy, XIV, No. 4(October, 1912), 341-5.

Friday, David. Reviews of Principles of Cost Accounting, Elementary Accounting Problems, and Principles of Accounting, by John Raymond Wildman, The American Economic Review, VI, No. 1(March, 1916), 125-7.

Gibbs, Wayne F. Review of Modern Accounting Theory and Practice, by DeWitt C. Eggleston, The Accounting Review, V, No. 4(December, 1930), 325-6.

Glover, Charles A. Review of Principles of Accounting, Rev. ed., Vols. I and II, by H. A. Finney, The Accounting Review, III, No. 4(December, 1928), 407-8.

G., L. Review of Factory Organization and Costs, by J. Lee Nicholson, C.P.A., The Journal of Accountancy, VIII, No. 1(July, 1909), 222.

Gray, W. R. Review of Accounting Practice and Procedure, by Arthur Lowes Dickinson, The American Economic Review, IV, No. 4(December, 1914), 909-11.

_____. Review of The Applied Theory of Accounts, by Paul-Joseph Esquerre, The American Economic Review, V, No. 2(June, 1915), 337-8.

Greeley, Harold Dudley. Review of Cost Accounting and Burden Application, by Clinton H. Scovell, The Journal of Accountancy, XXXIII, No. 5(May, 1917), 399-400.

_____. Review of New Modern Illustrative Bookkeeping, by Charles F. Rittenhouse, C.P.A., The Journal of Accountancy, XXVIII, No. 4(October, 1919), 315-6.

Hanson, A. W. Review of Accounting, by W. A. Paton, The American Economic Review, XV, No. 1(March, 1925), 120.

_____. Review of Principles of Accounting, Volume I. Intermediate, by H. A. Finney, The Accounting Review, IX, No. 3(September, 1934), 273.

_____. Review of Principles of Accounting, Volume II, Advanced, by H. A. Finney, The Accounting Review, X, No. 1(March, 1935), 128-9.

_____. Review of Accounting: Its Principles and Problems, by Henry Rand Hatfield, Ph.D., The American Economic Review, XVII, No. 4(December, 1927), 714-5.

_____. Review of The Analysis of Financial Statements, by H. G. Guthmann, The American Economic Review, XVI, No. 2(June, 1926), 314-5.

_____. Review of The Analysis of Financial Statements, Rev. ed., by H. G. Guthmann, The American Economic Review, XXV, No. 3(September, 1935), 551; The Accounting Review, XI, No. 1(March, 1936), 97.

Hatfield, Henry Rand. Review of Accounting, by W. A. Paton, The Journal of Accountancy, XL, No. 5(November, 1925), 389-90.

_____. Review of Accounting Practice and Procedure, by Arthur Lowes Dickinson, The Journal of Accountancy, XVIII, No. 6(December, 1914), 480-2.

_____. Review of Auditing Theory and Practice, by Robert H. Montgomery, The Journal of Political Economy, XXI, No. 8(October, 1913), 781.

_____. Review of Introduction to Principles of Accounting, by H. A. Finney, The Journal of Accountancy, LIV, No. 6(December, 1932), 474-5.

_____. Review of Managerial Accounting, by James Oscar McKinsey, The Journal of Accountancy, XXXIX, No. 5(May, 1925), 432-3.

_____. Review of The Cultural Significance of Accounts, by D. R. Scott, The Journal of Accountancy, LIV, No. 3(September, 1932), 230.

Hensel, Philip H. Review of Accounting Theory and Practice, Vol. II, by Roy B. Kester, The Accounting Review, V, No. 4(December, 1930), 335-6.

H., H. R. Review of The Philosophy of Accounts, by Charles E. Sprague, The Journal of Accountancy, VII, No. 5(November, 1908), 67-9.

Hosmer, W. A. Review of Accounting Concepts of Profit, by Stephen Gilman, Harvard Business Review, XVIII, No. 3(Spring, 1940), 387-8.

Howard, Stanley E. Review of Cost Accounting, Rev. ed., by J. Lee Nicholson and John F. D. Rohrbach, The American Economic Review, IX, No. 3(September, 1919), 566-8.

Jackman, W. T. Review of Elements of Accounting, by Joseph J. Klein, The American Economic Review, III, No. 4(December, 1913), 924-6.

Jackson, J. Hugh. Review of Accounting, Its Principles and Problems, by Henry Rand Hatfield, The Journal of Accountancy, XLIV, No. 4(October, 1927), 308-9.

_____. Review of Accounting Principles, Their Use in Business Management, by Spurgeon Bell, The American Economic Review, XII, No. 2(June, 1922), 296-7.

_____. Review of Auditors' Certificates, by David Himmelblau, The Accounting Review, II, No. 4(December, 1927), 413-4.

_____. Review of Budgetary Control, by J. O. McKinsey, The American Economic Review, XIII, No. 2(June, 1923), 315.

_____. Review of Capital Stock Without Par Value, by John R. Wildman and Weldon Powell, The Accounting Review, IV, No. 4(December, 1929), 262-4.

_____. Review of <u>Depreciation Principles and Applications</u>, by E. A. Saliers, <u>The American Economic Review</u>, XIV, No. 3(September, 1924), 550; <u>The Journal of Accountancy</u>, XXXVIII, No. 2(August, 1924), 152-3.

_____. Review of <u>Depreciation Principles and Applications</u>, 3rd ed., by E. A. Saliers, <u>The Journal of Accountancy</u>, LXVIII, No. 2(August, 1939), 142-3; <u>The American Economic Review</u>, XXIX, No. 3(September, 1939), 605-6.

Kapp, Edgar B. (ed.). Article digest of "The Construction, Use, and Abuse of Cost Accounts," by Sir Arthur Lowes Dickinson, <u>The American Accountant</u>, XIII, No. 12(December, 1928), 40.

_____. Review of <u>Auditors' Reports and Working Papers</u>, by DeWitt Carl Eggleston, <u>The American Accountant</u>, XIV, No. 6(June, 1929), 350.

_____. Review of <u>Capital Stock Without Par Value</u>, by John R. Wildman and Weldon Powell, <u>The American Accountant</u>, XIV, No. 3(March, 1929), 158.

_____. Review of <u>C.P.A. Accounting</u>, 3rd ed., by George H. Newlove, <u>The American Accountant</u>, XIII, No. 12(December, 1928), 42.

_____. Review of <u>Federal Income Taxation</u>, by Joseph J. Klein, <u>The American Accountant</u>, XIV, No. 4(April, 1929), 222-3.

_____. Review of <u>Modern Accounting Theory and Practice</u>, by DeWitt C. Eggleston, <u>The American Accountant</u>, XV, No. 8(August, 1930), 376-7.

_____. Review of <u>Problems in Accounting Principles</u>, by Ross G. Walker, <u>The American Accountant</u>, XIV, No. 9(September, 1939), 491-2.

Knight, Frank H. Review of <u>Interest as a Cost</u>, by Clinton H. Scovell, <u>The Journal of Political Economy</u>, XXXIII, No. 4(August, 1925), 468-70.

Kohler, E. L. Review of <u>Federal Income Taxation</u>, by Joseph J. Klein, <u>The Accounting Review</u>, VI, No. 3(September, 1931), 245-6.

Krebs, William S. Review of <u>Accounting Problems: Intermediate</u>, by Charles F. Rittenhouse and Atlee L. Percy, <u>The Accounting Review</u>, VII, No. 1(March, 1932), 87-8.

Lawton, W. H. Review of <u>Accounting</u>, by Paul-Joseph Esquerre, <u>The Journal of Accountancy</u>, XLV, No. 3(March, 1928), 227-8.

_____. Review of <u>Accounting Principles</u>, by Spurgeon Bell, <u>The Journal of Accountancy</u>, XXXV, No. 1(January, 1923), 66.

_____. Review of <u>Accounting Problems: Elementary</u>, by Charles F. Rittenhouse and Atlee L. Percy, <u>The Journal of Accountancy</u>, XXXIX, No. 3(March, 1925), 236.

_____. Review of <u>Accounting Problems: Intermediate</u>, by Charles F. Rittenhouse and Atlee L. Percy, <u>The Journal of Accountancy</u>, XXXV, No. 4(April, 1923), 313.

_____. Review of <u>Accounting Problems: Intermediate</u>, by Charles F. Rittenhouse and Atlee L. Percy, <u>The Journal of Accountancy</u>, LIII, No. 2(February, 1932), 148-9.

_____. Review of <u>Accounting Theory and Practice</u>, Vol. I(first year), 3rd ed. revised and enlarged, by Roy B. Kester, <u>The Journal of Accountancy</u>, L, No. 2(August, 1930), 149-50.

_____. Review of <u>Accounting Theory and Practice</u>, Second edition revised, by Roy B. Kester, <u>The Journal of Accountancy</u>, XLI, No. 5(May, 1926), 390-2.

_____. Review of <u>Accounting Theory and Practice--Advanced Accounting</u>, Third revised edition, by Roy.B. Kester, <u>The Journal of Accountancy</u>, LVI, No. 6 (December, 1933), 473-4.

_____. Review of <u>Accounting Theory with Special Reference to the Corporate Enterprise</u>, by William Andrew Paton, <u>The Journal of Accountancy</u>, XXXV, No. 4(April, 1923), 313-4.

_____. Review of <u>Accounts in Theory and Practice</u>, by Earl A. Saliers, <u>The Journal of Accountancy</u>, XXX, No. 6(December, 1920), 471-2.

_____. Review of <u>Analyzing Financial Statements</u>, by Stephen Gilman, <u>The Journal of Accountancy</u>, XLI, No. 6(June, 1926), 473-4.

_____. Review of <u>Auditors' Reports and Working Papers</u>, by DeWitt Carl Eggleston, <u>The Journal of Accountancy</u>, XLVII, No. 5(May, 1929), 392-3.

_____. Review of <u>Fundamentals of Accounting</u>, by Earl A. Saliers, <u>The Journal of Accountancy</u>, LX, No. 2(August, 1935), 151.

_____. Review of <u>Management Through Accounts</u>, by James H. Bliss, <u>The Journal of Accountancy</u>, XXXVIII, No. 6(December, 1924), 474-5.

_____. Review of <u>Problems in Accounting Principles</u>, by Ross Graham Walker, <u>The Journal of Accountancy</u>, XLVIII, No. 5(November, 1929), 394-5.

_____. Review of <u>The Philosophy of Accounts</u>, by Charles E. Sprague, <u>The Journal of Accountancy</u>, XXXV, No. 1(January, 1923), 67-8.

Lukas, G. E. Review of <u>The Cultural Significance of Accounts</u>, by D. R. Scott, <u>The Accounting Review</u>, VII, No. 1(March, 1932), 80-1.

L., W. H. Review of <u>Accounting Theory and Practice</u>, by Roy B. Kester, <u>The Journal of Accountancy</u>, XXIV, No. 6(December, 1917), 488-90.

_____. Review of <u>Applied Theory of Accounts</u>, by Paul-Joseph Esquerre, <u>The Journal of Accountancy</u>, XXI, No. 4(April, 1916), 317.

_____. Review of <u>Auditing, Theory and Practice</u>, 2d ed., by Robert H. Montgomery, <u>The Journal of Accountancy</u>, XXI, No. 6(June, 1916), 478-80.

_____. Review of <u>Principles of Auditing</u>, by John Raymond Wildman, M.C.S., C.P.A., <u>The Journal of Accountancy</u>, XXII, No. 1(July, 1916), 70-1.

Madden, J. T. Review of <u>Accounting</u>, by W. A. Paton, <u>Publications of the American Association of University Instructors in Accounting</u>, IX, No. 2(December, 1925), 158-60.

May, George O. Review of <u>Interest as a Cost</u>, by Clinton H. Scovell, <u>The Journal of Accountancy</u>, XXXVII, No. 6(June, 1924), 475-6.

McDonough, J. E. Review of Analyzing Financial Statements, by Stephen Gilman, The American Economic Review, XVI, No. 6(December, 1926), 689-90.

McKinsey, J. O. Review of The Fundamentals of Accounting, by William Morse Cole, A.M., with the collaboration of Anne Elizabeth Geddes, A.B., The Journal of Political Economy, XXX, No. 6(December, 1922), 856-8.

Mitchell, Thomas Warner. Review of Auditing, Theory and Practice, by Robert H. Montgomery, The American Economic Review, III, No. 2(June, 1913), 382-4.

Montgomery, R. H. Review of Accounting: Its Principles and Problems, by Henry Rand Hatfield, The Accounting Review, II, No. 2(June, 1927), 189-93.

_____. Review of Accounts, Their Construction and Interpretation, by William Morse Cole, The American Economic Review, V, No. 3(September, 1915), 606-8.

Mucklow, Walter. Review of Financial and Operating Ratios in Management, by James H. Bliss, The Journal of Accountancy, XXXVII, No. 2(February, 1924), 152-4.

_____. Review of Principles of Accounting, Vol. I, Intermediate, by H. A. Finney, The Journal of Accountancy, LVIII, No. 6(December, 1934), 473-6.

Oakey, Francis. Review of Budgetary Control, by J. O. McKinsey, The Journal of Accountancy, XXXV, No. 1(January, 1923), 65.

Parks, Walter E. Review of C.P.A. Accounting, 3rd ed., by George Hillis Newlove, The Accounting Review, IV, No. 4(December, 1929), 266.

Paton, W. A. Review of Depreciation: Principles and Applications, 3rd ed., by Earl A. Saliers, The Journal of Political Economy, XLVII, No. 5(October, 1939), 735-8.

_____. Review of Interest as a Cost, by Clinton H. Scovell, The American Economic Review, XV, No. 2(June, 1925), 321-6.

_____. Review of Managerial Accounting, Vol. I, by J. O. McKinsey, The Journal of Political Economy, XXXIII, No. 4(August, 1925), 470-2.

Peisch, Archie M. Review of Accounting Theory and Practice, Volume II, Second Edition-Revised, by Roy B. Kester, The Accounting Review, I, No. 2(June, 1926), 90.

Peloubet, Maurice E. Review of Analysis of Financial Statements, by Harry G. Guthmann, The Journal of Accountancy, LXI, No. 2(February, 1936), 151-2.

_____. Review of Analyzing Financial Statements, by Stephen Gilman, The Journal of Accountancy, LXI, No. 3(March, 1936), 236.

Phillips, H. G. Review of Accounts, Their Construction and Interpretation, by William Morse Cole, A.M., The Journal of Accountancy, VII, No. 1(January, 1909), 244-5.

Plehn, Carl C. Review of Income Tax Procedure, 1918, by Robert H. Montgomery, The American Economic Review, VIII, No. 2(June, 1918), 380-5.

_____. Review of Income Tax Procedure, 1919, by Robert H. Montgomery, The American Economic Review, IX, No. 2(June, 1919), 354-7.

_____. Review of Income Tax Procedure, 1920, by Robert H. Montgomery, The American Economic Review, X, No. 2(June, 1920), 372-6.

Prickett, A. L. Review of Analyzing Financial Statements, by Stephen Gilman, The Accounting Review, I, No. 4(December, 1926), 95-6.

Reighard, John J. Review of Managerial Accounting, Vol. I, by James O. McKinsey, The Accounting Review, I, No. 2(June, 1926), 94-6.

Review of Accounting, by Paul-Joseph Esquerre, The American Accountant, XII, No. 7 (August, 1927), 49-50.

Review of Accounting Evolution to 1900, by A. C. Littleton, Ph.D., The American Accountant, XVIII, No. 10(October, 1933), 316-7.

Review of Accounting: Its Principles and Problems, by Henry Rand Hatfield, Ph.D., The American Accountant, XII, No. 4(May, 1927), 50.

Review of Auditing Theory and Practice, 2d ed., by Robert H. Montgomery, The Journal of Political Economy, XXIV, No. 7(July, 1916), 734.

Review of Auditors' Certificates, by David Himmelblau, The American Accountant, XII, No. 5(June, 1927), 48.

Review of Consolidated Balance Sheets, by G. H. Newlove, Ph.D., C.P.A., The American Accountant, XII, No. 2(March, 1927), 43.

Review of Cost Accounting and Burden Application, by Clinton H. Scovell, The Journal of Political Economy, XXV, No. 6(June, 1917), 639-40.

Review of C.P.A. Accounting, 2d ed., by George H. Newlove, Ph.D., The American Accountant, XII, No. 5(June, 1927), 47-8.

Review of Elements of Accounting, by Joseph J. Klein, The Journal of Political Economy, XXI, No. 9(November, 1913), 877-8.

Review of Interest as a Cost, by Clinton H. Scovell, A.M., The Pace Student, IX, No. 11(October, 1924), 176.

Rittenhouse, Charles F. Review of Accountants' Handbook, edited by Earl A. Saliers, Publications of the American Association of University Instructors in Accounting, IX, No. 2(December, 1925), 168-70.

Rusk, Stephen G. Review of Federal Income Taxation, by Joseph J. Klein, The Journal of Accountancy, XLVII, No. 5(May, 1929), 391-2.

_____. Review of Income Tax Procedure, 1927, by Robert H. Montgomery, The Journal of Accountancy, XLIII, No. 3(March, 1927), 232-3.

Saliers, Earl A. Review of Elements of Accounting, by Joseph J. Klein, The Journal of Accountancy, XVI, No. 2(August, 1913), 167.

_____. Review of Theory of Accounts, by D. R. Scott, The Accounting Review, I, No. 2(June, 1926), 90-1.

Scovell, Clinton H. Review of Accounting Theory and Practice, by R. B. Kester, The American Economic Review, IX, No. 4(December, 1919), 830-1.

Shugrue, Martin J. Review of Accounts in Theory and Practice, by Earl A. Saliers, The American Economic Review, XI, No. 1(March, 1921), 117-8.

_____. Review of Accounting Principles and Bookkeeping Methods, Vol. I, by H. A. Finney, The American Economic Review, XV, No. 1(March, 1925), 115-6.

_____. Review of Accounting Problems: Elementary, by C. F. Rittenhouse and A. L. Percy, The American Economic Review, XV, No. 2(June, 1925), 336.

Steele, F. R. Carnegie. Review of Accounts, Their Construction and Interpretation, 1915 ed., by William Morse Cole, M.A., The Journal of Accountancy, XX, No. 3(September, 1915), 242-3.

Stevenson, R. A. Review of Management Through Accounts, by James H. Bliss, Publications of the American Association of University Instructors in Accounting, IX, No. 2(December, 1925), 160-1.

_____. Review of The Cultural Significance of Accounts, by D. R. Scott, The American Economic Review, XXIII, No. 2(June, 1933), 286-9.

Taggart, H. F. Review of Problems in Accounting Principles, by R. G. Walker and P. B. Coffman, The American Economic Review, XX, No. 1(March, 1930), 120-1.

Taylor, Jacob B. Review of Introduction to Principles of Accounting, Rev. ed., by H. A. Finney, The Accounting Review, XI, No. 4(December, 1936), 403-4.

Thornton, F. W. Review of Consolidated Balance-Sheets, by G. H. Newlove, The Journal of Accountancy, XLIII, No. 1(January, 1927), 66-7.

_____. Review of Modern Accounting Theory and Practice, by DeWitt C. Eggleston, The Journal of Accountancy, XLIX, No. 5(May, 1930), 384-5.

_____. Review of Theory of Accounts, by D. R. Scott, The Journal of Accountancy, XLI, No. 4(April, 1926), 313.

Wade, Harry H. Review of Principles of Accounting, Advanced, 3rd ed., by H. A. Finney, The Accounting Review, XXII, No. 1(January, 1947), 96-7.

Walton, Seymour. Review of Modern Accounting, by Henry Rand Hatfield, Ph.D., The Journal of Accountancy, X, No. 3(September, 1910), 387.

Weidenhammer, Robert. Review of Analyzing Financial Statements, Revised Edition, by Stephen Gilman, The Accounting Review, IX, No. 4(December, 1934), 347-8.

Wildman, John Raymond. Review of Cost Accounting, by J. Lee Nicholson, C.P.A., and John F. D. Rohrbach, C.P.A., The Journal of Accountancy, XXVII, No. 4 (April, 1919), 318.

_____. Review of New Modern Illustrative Bookkeeping, by Charles F. Rittenhouse, C.P.A., The Journal of Accountancy, XXVII, No. 5(May, 1919), 397.

Yntema, Theodore, O. Review of Accounting, by W. A. Paton, The Journal of Political Economy, XXXIII, No. 4(August, 1925), 478-9.

_____. Review of <u>Accounting Theory</u>, by William Andrew Paton, <u>The Journal of Political Economy</u>, XXXIII, No. 3(June, 1925), 366.